Australia

THE WORLD'S LANDSCAPES

edited by Dr J. M. Houston

Australia
China
France
Ireland
New Zealand
Soviet Union
Terrain Evaluation
Urban Japan
Wales

Australia

R. L. Heathcote
Reader in Geography, Flinders University of South Australia

with a Foreword by

Dr J. M. Houston
Principal of Regent College, Vancouver

Longman
London and New York

Longman Group Limited London and New York

Associated companies, branches and representatives throughout the world

Published in the United States of America by Longman Inc., New York

First published 1975

Library of Congress Cataloging in Publication Data

Heathcote, R. L.
Australia.

(The Worlds landscapes)
Bibliography: p.
Includes index.
1. Man–Influence on nature–Australia. 2. Australia–Description and travel–1951– I. Title. II. Series.
GF801.H38 919.4.02 75–22092
ISBN 0 582 48166 X cased
ISBN 0 582 48179 1 paper

Set in IBM Baskerville 9 on 11pt
and printed in Great Britain by
Whitstable Litho Ltd, Kent

To Elizabeth

Contents

List of illustrations

Foreword

by Dr J. M. Houston, Principal of Regent College, Vancouver

Despite the multitude of geographical books that deal with differing areas of the world, no series has before attempted to explain man's role in moulding and changing its diverse landscapes. At the most there are books that study individual areas in detail, but usually in language too technical for the general reader. It is the purpose of this series to take regional geographical studies to the frontiers of contemporary research on the making of the world's landscapes. This is being done by specialists, each in his own area, yet in non-technical language that should appeal to both the general reader and to the discerning student.

We are leaving behind us an age that has viewed Nature as an objective reality. Today we are living in a more pragmatic, less idealistic age. The nouns of previous thought forms are the verbs of a new outlook. Pure thought is being replaced by the use of knowledge for a technological society, busily engaged in changing the face of the earth. It is an age of operational thinking. The very functions of Nature are being threatened by scientific takeovers, and it is not too fanciful to predict that the daily weather, the biological cycles of life processes, as well as the energy of the atom will become harnessed to human corporations. Thus it becomes imperative that all thoughtful citizens of our world today should know something of the changes man has already wrought in his physical habitat, and which he is now modifying with accelerating power.

Studies of man's impact on the landscapes of the earth are expanding rapidly. They involve diverse disciplines such as Quaternary sciences, archaeology, history and anthropology, with subjects that range from pollen analysis, to plant domestication, field systems, settlement patterns and industrial land-use. But with his sense of place, and his sympathy for synthesis, the geographer is well placed to handle this diversity of data in a meaningful manner. The appraisal of landscape changes, how and when man has altered and remoulded the surface of the earth, is both pragmatic and interesting to a wide range of readers.

The concept of 'landscape' is of course both concrete and elusive. In its Anglo–Saxon origin, *landskift* referred to some unit of area that was a natural entity, such as the lands of a tribe or of a feudal lord. It was only at the end of the sixteenth century that, through the influence of Dutch landscape painters, the word also acquired the idea of a unit of visual perceptions, of a view. In the German *landschaft*, both definitions have been maintained, a source of confusion and uncertainty in the use of the term. However, despite scholarly analysis of its ambiguity, the concept of landscape has increasing currency precisely because of its ambiguity. It refers to the total man–land complex in place and time, suggesting spatial interactions, and indicative of visual features that we can select, such as field and settlement patterns, set in the mosaics of relief, soils and vegetation. Thus the 'landscape' is the point of reference in the selection of widely ranging data. It is the tangible context of man's association with the earth. It is the documentary evidence of the power of human perception to mould the resources of nature into human usage, a perception as varied as his cultures. Today, the ideological attitudes of man are being more dramatically imprinted on the earth than ever before, owing to technological capabilities.

Australia has unique interest in the light of these developments. Its long period of geological isolation has endowed it with special forms of life. Its late discovery and settlement by Europeans has meant that changes of landscape have occurred only within the last two centuries. Relict landscapes and indigenous ecosystems still comprise a third of the continent. In a world of land hunger, 20 per cent of the land is still vacant. Skilfully, Dr Heathcote shows in this book the essential characteristics and changes of the major ecosystems and landscapes of this unique continent, effected in such a relatively brief span of time. He also analyses the types of perception that man has selected to see the meaningful traits of the Australian scene. This is an original study, well documented with new maps and other illustrations. By it, Dr Heathcote will help thoughtful Australians to anticipate the impact of current trends upon their future scenic heritage. It is also a book worthy of serious consideration by all who are concerned with man's increasing ability to create irrevocably environmental changes on planet earth.

J. M. Houston

Preface

Like King Alfred's cakes, this book has been overlong in the making. It was begun amid a bleak Braunschweig winter and continued more recently in the occasional 'century heat' of Adelaide's summers. While the end-product may well resemble the cakes, the length of the period of composition has had compensations.

Writing began in the heady optimism of the late 1960s, when the Australian mining boom was well under way and when, if anything could have been said to symbolise the nation at that time, it would have been a bulldozer or perhaps one of the 200 ton earth-movers designed for the new iron ore fields. Foreign capital and workers were flooding into the continent to develop the resources of 'the slumbering giant'.

Writing was completed in the last days of 1973, when the more sobering influence of the world's eco-crisis and energy crisis loomed over the continent and when the fledgling Commonwealth Labour Government was finding it not as easy as it thought when first elected in December 1972, to socialise a society which had had twenty-three years of a Liberal (conservative) Government.

The last decade in fact has brought significant changes in both world-wide and Australian appreciation of the landscapes in which we live, and these changes are likely to be imprinted upon any future landscapes. In part these changes have reflected an increase in knowledge of the environment, but essentially they have been changes in attitudes to that environment. In the case of Australia those changes can be found in attitudes of governments to resource development by 'foreigners', the attitudes of Aborigines to Anglo–Australians and, in particular, to themselves, and the attitudes of the man-in-the-street to 'conservation', 'pollution', and the 'environment' itself. As a result, had this book been completed by the due date of 1969, it would have 'dated' even more rapidly than might be reasonably expected. As it is, the book is an attempt not only to provide a guide to the evolution and present character of the continental landscapes before they are modified, possibly beyond recognition, by the new ideas, but also to suggest some of the implications of these new ideas for the future landscapes. If it goes some way to achieving these aims, a few years of procrastination may have been worthwhile after all.

R. L. Heathcote

Acknowledgements

Grateful acknowledgement is made for help in the production of this book, first to the individuals and institutions who provided the illustrative materials, the source of which is indicated in each caption; to Messrs G. Willoughby and A. Little, cartographers, for the maps; to the ladies of the School of Social Sciences Office, Flinders University, especially Mrs M. Marshall and Mrs L. Lovell, for their conscientious and cheerful typing of the manuscripts; to my colleagues at Flinders University for their helpful ideas and discussions; to the Australians, old and new, whose tolerance of their fellows is one of the major attractions of the Australian scene; and finally to my wife, whose support in times of need, critical eye and hard labour in checking and correcting the text, have been a vital contribution to the finished product.

A note on the references

In the text, except where a specific quotation or documentation is given, all reference to sources has been omitted. A brief overview of the basic sources for the three parts of the book will be found in 'A note on the sources' at the end of the book, immediately before the 'Bibliography', wherein will be found the full citation of authors referred to in the text by this method – author's name, date of publication and page number, if necessary, e.g. (Smith, 1957, p. 304).

Introduction

The air traveller to the Commonwealth of Australia in the 1970s, should he travel by the national airline QANTAS, will be intrigued by the decorative motifs of the menu cards for his dinner inflight. Often they will show two scenes of Australia, the first a copper engraving or more likely a lithograph of some town or country scene in the nineteenth century, and the second a colour photograph of the same site in the 1970s. Apart from their aesthetic appeal, the illustrations will bring home to the traveller three features of the Australian scene which are worth emphasising at the outset of this book.

The first and most obvious feature is the short history of European settlement of the continent: less than 200 years for the first base at Sydney, for much of the continent less than 100 years and locally often less than 50 years. Despite the shortness of this period, however, the second impressive feature is the rapidity with which European forms of culture and the trappings of settlement have been established. In the centres of population virtually the whole visible scene is obviously European in design, and of the landscape prior to European settlement, virtually nothing remains. Even the form of the land is buried beneath the layers of asphalt, brick and cement. The third and final feature is in one sense a confirmation of the other two: the rapid but effective transformation of the past scenery into present and future landscapes is still, very obviously, going on apace (Fig. 0.1). In the cities, the demolition gangs are at work and new structures rise beneath the crane jibs: in the country bulldozers are still clearing new land for farms and mines.

The mutability of the Australian landscape itself poses questions of understanding and problems of interpretation of the sequence, direction, and pace of change. These have been long standing problems facing all writers on Australia. In 1886 in his book *Oceana or England and her colonies* (1886, p. 189), the English historian Froude acknowledged that his attempt to describe the condition of Australia, as one of the 'colonies', was compromised from the outset because of the rapidly changing conditions:

> The growth of colonies is so rapid, and the change of circumstances so frequent, that a man who might be trusted [as a representative in London] wholly one year would be half-trusted the next, and the third would not be trusted at all.

The same problems face this writer in that all the evidence available suggests

Fig. 0.1 The changing face of Canberra
Three views from Red Hill northeast to site of present airport across the valley of Molonglo River. Slopes of Mt Pleasant left centre. 1927: 1, Construction workers' camp; 2, Railway station; 3, Power station; 4, Collins Park tree plantation. 1952: 5, Airport. 1970: 6, East Basin, Lake Burley Griffin.

(*Source:* Department of Human Geography, Australian National University)

Fig. 0.1 – continued

that the decade of the 1970s will be one of the most significant periods of resource development in the history of the Australian Commonwealth. It is likely, therefore, that many of the economic details here described will be significantly altered within the next decade. It is hoped, however, that this will not detract from the main function of the book, which is to describe the nature of the changes wrought on the continent by European settlement and to try to account for the past and present patterns of that settlement.

To try to cope with these points, the method which I have adopted is first, in Part one, to reconstruct the landscape of the continent before European settlement, to establish as it were a base line for change; second, in Part two, to describe the continent as it is in the early 1970s, emphasising the contrasts with the original condition and analysing in some detail aspects of the European settlement from 1788 to the 1970s which have produced the significant modifications of the original scenes. Here, I shall be concerned with what might be termed various 'systems' for the use of the resources of the continent, the ways in which these systems were conceived and elaborated through time, the areas in which they were developed, and the landscapes associated with them. Finally, in Part three, I shall try to summarise the changes which have taken place over the 200-year period, by analysing the changes in the attitudes to, and knowledge of, the resources of Australia. In effect I shall try to reconstruct the views which the settlers themselves, and the officials who guided them, had of the continent and its possibilities, for it will become obvious that their views would rarely be still held today. In fact, I believe that here, in the changing settlers' perception

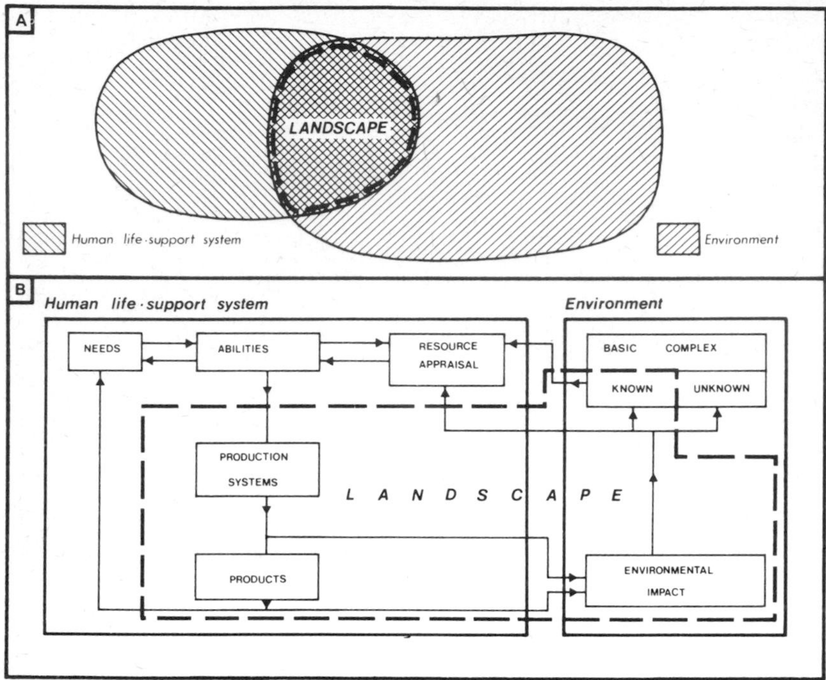

Fig. 0.2 The concept of landscape
A. Landscape as the product of the interaction of human life-support systems and the global environment.
B. A model of the components of landscape
Basic human needs are translated through abilities and the appraisal of the resource potentials into systems of production and actual products, which satisfy those needs and have an impact upon the environment, both the known and the as yet unknown components of the basic complex of matter.

of the resources which they *thought* were available to them, we may find the clues to many of the landscape modifications which are otherwise inexplicable from hindsight. From this brief analysis it may then be possible to forecast some of the modifications of the continent which may take place as the result of the present and future reassessments of the continental resources.

The term landscape is used here to describe the product of the interplay between what might be identified as the 'Human Life-Support System' and the 'Environment' (Fig. 0.2). From the interaction of human needs, abilities, and appraisal of resources – these latter being those components of the basic complex of the environment thought to be useful to man – stems a system of production which processes resources to meet human needs. These latter achievements, however, also result in modification of the environmental complex through environmental impact, which in turn also seems to affect the resource appraisal process. The landscape then combines the production system, its achievements (in terms of outputs, human population involved in and supported by it, and the man-made structures and communication networks associated with it), plus a large proportion of the environment, whether modified by environmental impact or not. I say 'a large proportion' only, because there is no doubt that there are components of the environment which are as yet unknown to man but which may be discovered at some future date, and there is also no doubt that the usefulness of many *known* components will be modified by new human abilities in the future.

For practical purposes I shall be concerned with the visible scene, visible that is to the traveller by land, sea or air. In parts of the continent the lack of spatial variety enables a broad 'aerial' view but elsewhere, particularly in the cities, the traveller needs to pick his way 'on foot' to sample the complex detail, whether of house styles, street furniture or patterns of commuting.

To avoid some of the confusion which already exists, not least in Australia, over the nomenclature of both the original and contemporary inhabitants of the continent, for this book I have adopted the following definitions. The *Indigenes* are the original inhabitants of the continent in occupation in 1770, i.e. immediately preceding effective European contact and settlement. The term applies to the total population in 1770, which seems to have included at least two separate cultural groups who will be described in Chapter 5.

The *Aborigines* are those people who, subsequent to 1770, were and are now recognised to be (and think of themselves as), the descendants of the Indigenes, by either direct (full-blood) or indirect (mixed-blood) descent. The *Europeans* are those people from Europe who, from 1788 onwards, came and are still in the 1970s coming to Australia as immigrants to make their home on the continent. The *Anglo–Australians* are the descendants of those Europeans who think of Australia as their home because they were born or live there. The *Australians* I have used as a general term for the composite population of Australia since the first effective European settlement in 1788.

Finally, this book is concerned essentially with continental Australia and will not attempt to survey the landscape of the Australian territories in Papua–New Guinea or Antarctica except in so far as events there may have affected the character of the landscape of the continent itself.

Part one

Australia 1770

1
The quiet continent: Australia 1770

Few records exist of what the continent was like in 1770. Some clues are available from study of growth rings of trees long since buried in preserving swamps, some from analysis of lake muds and salts and the sequences of gravels and silt in valley-floors, and some from relics of indigenous occupance. To them may be added inferences from seventeenth century European descriptions of the north and west coasts, those of Cook and his contemporaries in the eighteenth and early nineteenth centuries for the south and east, the inland explorers of the nineteenth century and the guesses from hindsight in the twentieth century. What follows therefore must be an amalgam of all these, factual whenever possible, but often an impressionistic account of things as they might have been.

To an imaginary observer in a satellite stationed over the continent the first impression would probably have been one of a calm unchanging land, apparently empty of animal life – a great compact mass, red-brown at the core and fringed by a mantle of dull green vegetation. The surface of the continent appeared remarkably even. Only at the extremities of the southeast and northwest did the land appear to stand in any marked highlands. Even here, although cut deeply by narrow river valleys and clothed in an endless sea of woods, the summits had an evenness and symmetry which suggested not earth-shattering cataclysmic change, but slow imperceptible movements broken only rarely by sudden fractures and sharp folds.

On closer inspection, however, the continent showed some irregularities of relief. Across the core lay two complexes of parallel ranges, coiling in jagged red-brown curves amid the dull red and yellow sand plains. In the west, isolated ranges broke the seeming endless horizontal surfaces and in the south a narrow range of highlands stretched inland to the edge of the sand seas. Even from a satellite, certain patterns would be visible: the slender flutings of the sand ridges of the great deserts of the interior curving anticlockwise around the central ranges; the sinuous lines of river bed and gallery woodland passing out from the green girdle of the eastern highlands into the interior plains and losing themselves in the harsh white glare of the great salt lakes.

Onto these broad patterns the seasonal climatic changes were subtley grafted. In the winters (June to September) two major air movements covered the continent. Across the centre and north passed a succession of cells of the subtropical high pressure system, bringing crystal clear mornings, and warm cloudless days after cold to freezing starbright nights. South of the continent, but often impinging onto the southern coasts, lay the path of the sub-Antarctic depressions, swinging out from the Antarctic low-pressure cells and bringing banks of grey clouds, squalls of wind and rain or hail (with snow on the highest peaks of the southeast) and low to freezing temperatures. By day the clouds would break, the sun dry off the dripping foliage until another depression would approach, the clouds reform, the rains begin and the temperatures drop once more. From west to east across the Great Australian Bight, the depressions would bring rain to soak the south-eastern corner of the continent, gales to pound its coasts, erode the dunes and collapse the cliffs. Creeks, dry since summer, would begin to run, carrying old leaves, branches and trees, silt and gravel in their floods. Between the trees, grasses and herbs would begin to sprout. On the southern fringes of the great deserts the occasional downpour brought, within days, a thin carpet of minute flowering plants, to be followed within weeks by a sea of grasses and herbs.

In their winter quarters on the islands of the south-eastern coast and along the cliffs overlooking them, the muttonbirds were roosting after their daily foraging in the surrounding ocean prior to beginning their 13 000 km migrations north along the east coast to Japan and eastern Siberia to breed again. Around Tasmania and the south-eastern coasts of the continent, Black whales were feeding on the crustaceans in the shallow waters and rearing their young in the shelter of the bays.

From September onwards, with the increasing height of the sun and the approach of the equatorial low-pressure cells, days and nights would become warmer, frosts become less frequent and finally disappear in all but the highest areas. The belt of storms moved off the continent over the empty ocean to the south, and clear cloudless days saw temperatures climb to 100°F (38°C) or more and stay over 80°F (27°C) overnight. In the north violent tropical storms from the equatorial cells would sweep from west to east, then to swing south along the north-eastern coast. Winds of hurricane force might level trees, blast the dunes and ranges of the northwest coast, lash the tropical forests in the valleys of the northeast and whip up high seas on the shallow coastal waters over the coral reefs. Far over the plains draining to the northern gulfs, swollen creeks and rivers spread their floodwaters, leaving a flotsam of dead and dying plants and animals on their margins and around the few higher points of refuge. From coastal mangrove swamps and inland lagoons clouds of mosquitoes would rise each evening, to be replaced by myriads of sand and bush flies at break of day. In what had been a parched wilderness, life would rapidly reappear. Behind the retreating flood-waters spread a green sea of grasses. Insects, especially ants and termites, began their harvests; mobs of kangaroos and emus moved through the open woodland; the harsh cries of flocks of parakeets and cockatoos filled the air.

In the south and centre, the sun blazed day-long out of empty skies. The sea of green grass and flowers turned rapidly brown and gold, then withered and blew away, leaving a bare scorched earth. Along the creeks, the waters shrank from sun-cracked banks; in the ringed water holes the mud-hopper's buried themselves deep in the cool mud to await the next winter, and other fish – their eggs safe in the mud – began to die; birds began to migrate away to the coastal waters, and the numbers of kangaroos thinned as the mobs broke up into smaller groups to forage. Whirling spirals of dust and broken plants crossed the plains and sand moved along the bare crests of the long inland dunes.

On the islands of Bass Strait, black fur seals had established their summer breeding colonies, while in the open seas to the west and east of the continent schools of Sperm whales moved south to cooler and richer grazing grounds. Along the east coasts, flotillas of 'Portuguese men-o'-war', or 'blue-bottles' as they became known later, drifted south before the breezes – not man-made ships but the blue 'sails' of countless jelly-fish (*Physalia utriculus*).

After December, with the sun past its peak, the northward shifts of tropical airmasses began. With the slow withdrawal of their high temperatures and matching humidities, the cooling of the southern portion of the continent began once more, while to the far south the depressions began to deepen and curve further north each month. The seasonal cycle had begun once more.

Of human occupation on the continent there was scant evidence. From a satellite, plumes of occasional large bush fires might suggest a human presence, but only a closer inspection would notice the thin spirals of pungent smoke from many campfires breaking the canopy of the woods, or the larger blazes on the grasslands which, tended by the Indigenes, drove game into the arms of waiting hunters. In the interior, small family groups wandered from waterhole to waterhole, purposefully searching, hunting, fishing, collecting, digging up roots. Off the northern and north-eastern coasts and on the larger inland waterways, frail bark canoes carried fishermen out to reefs and deeper waters with net and spear, and sea divers brought up abalone and smaller shellfish. Along inland lakes and water holes, and in coastal surf it was the women who collected shellfish while the men hunted and fished.

There were, however, no great villages nor cities; no centres where man had made an indelible mark on the land. Here a clearing in the scrub was surprisingly bare of all plants or stones; there the stones were grouped in unnatural symmetries. Here a dark cave held bright-painted figures of stick-men, gods and animals which danced and gestured through the midday gloom; there a smooth outcrop of rock was pitted with small cavities, some recognisably human shapes, other mythical creatures. Here a bundle of decaying bark and twigs high in the branches of a tree gave off the sickly-sweet odour of a decaying corpse; there mounds of earth or small brush shelters marked human burial sites.

Of contact between Indigenes and the islanders to the north and east before 1770, evidence is scanty. Across the shallow northern seas small canoes may have carried some trade in pearl shells, which seems to have brought adaptation of some New Guinea cultural traits in the Cape York peoples. On the western coasts the few shipwrecks of European vessels appear to have gone generally unnoticed by the bulk of the Indigenes. In contrast, the more regular visits of the Malay trepang fishing fleets to the northern coast left their mark on the land. On the sites where the *bêche-de-mer* (*Holothuria eddis*) was smoked for trepang were the charcoal and blackened stones of old hearths and the occasional Tamarisk tree, growing as seed from fruit brought ashore during the brief camps. Often also the brief visit seems to have been marked by conflict with the indigenous people.

The overall view then *was* of a calm, relatively unchanging, continent. For two recent writers (Harris and Forbes, 1967) it was 'The Land that Waited' – waited that is for the European invasion; to a recent historian (Pike, 1962) it was, even after the invasion, 'The Quiet Continent'. Certainly, by 1770, there seems to have been no evidence of any massive disruption to the major patterns of life and landscape, certainly none to equal the impact of the events which were to follow from HMS *Endeavour*'s voyage of discovery along the eastern coast. The results of that voyage however, not only modified those patterns but were in turn affected by them, and we need to sketch-in the framework of the environment which was to so influence and to be itself influenced by the next 200 years of human occupation.

2
The land

To understand the form of the continent in 1770, the nature of its rocks and soils, and their potentials, we must examine the basic structure and geology of the land mass. On the basis of the type and age of the rocks their formation and alignment, it is possible to divide the land mass above sea level into three components. These are, first, a *Shield Zone*, which forms the ancient western core around which the later components were accumulated; second, a north–south *Highland Zone* forming the eastern rim of the continent; and third, an intervening *Lowland Zone* separating this from the Shield (Fig. 2.1).

If the boundaries of the continent are extended to the 100 fathom line to include the offshore *Continental Shelf*, which most nations now claim as territorial rights, a fourth component forming a link with the island of New Guinea could be distinguished. However, as noted in the introduction, attention here will be limited to the main continental area and the Continental Shelf will only be considered as far as it is relevant to the main land mass and human activities upon it.

Fig. 2.1 The structure of the land

A. Patterns of terrain

I. *Shield zone:* **a**, Swan Coastal Lowlands; **b**, Carnarvon Basin; **c**, West Australian Shield; **d**, Euela Basin; **e**, Canning Basin; **f**, Kimberley Plateau; **g**, Hamersley Plateau; **h**, Macdonnell Ranges; **i**, Musgrave Ranges; **j**, Arnhem Land Plateau; **k**, Barkly Tableland; **l**, Flinders Ranges.

II. *Highland zone:* **a**, Great Dividing Range; **b**, Cobar Plain; **c**, Victorian Plain; **d**, Toowoomba Plateau; **e**, Atherton Tableland; **f**, Maryborough Basin; **g**, Clarence Basin; **h**, Sydney Basin; **i**, Tasmanian Plateau; **j**, Tasmanian Lowland; **l**, Ben Lomond Plateau.

III. *Lowland zone:* **a**, Great Artesian Basin; **b**, Murray Basin.

B. Cross-sections of relief and geology: **1**, Pre-Cambrian rocks (over 600 million years old?); **2**, Paleozoic rocks (270–600 million years old?); **3**, Mesozoic rocks (135–225 million years old?); **4**, Cainozoic rocks (10–70 million years old?); **5**, 'Recent' rocks (less 1 million years old?). Note that the vertical scale of the sections has been exaggerated and the horizontal scale varies between the sections.

(*Source:* Gentilli and Fairbridge, 1951)

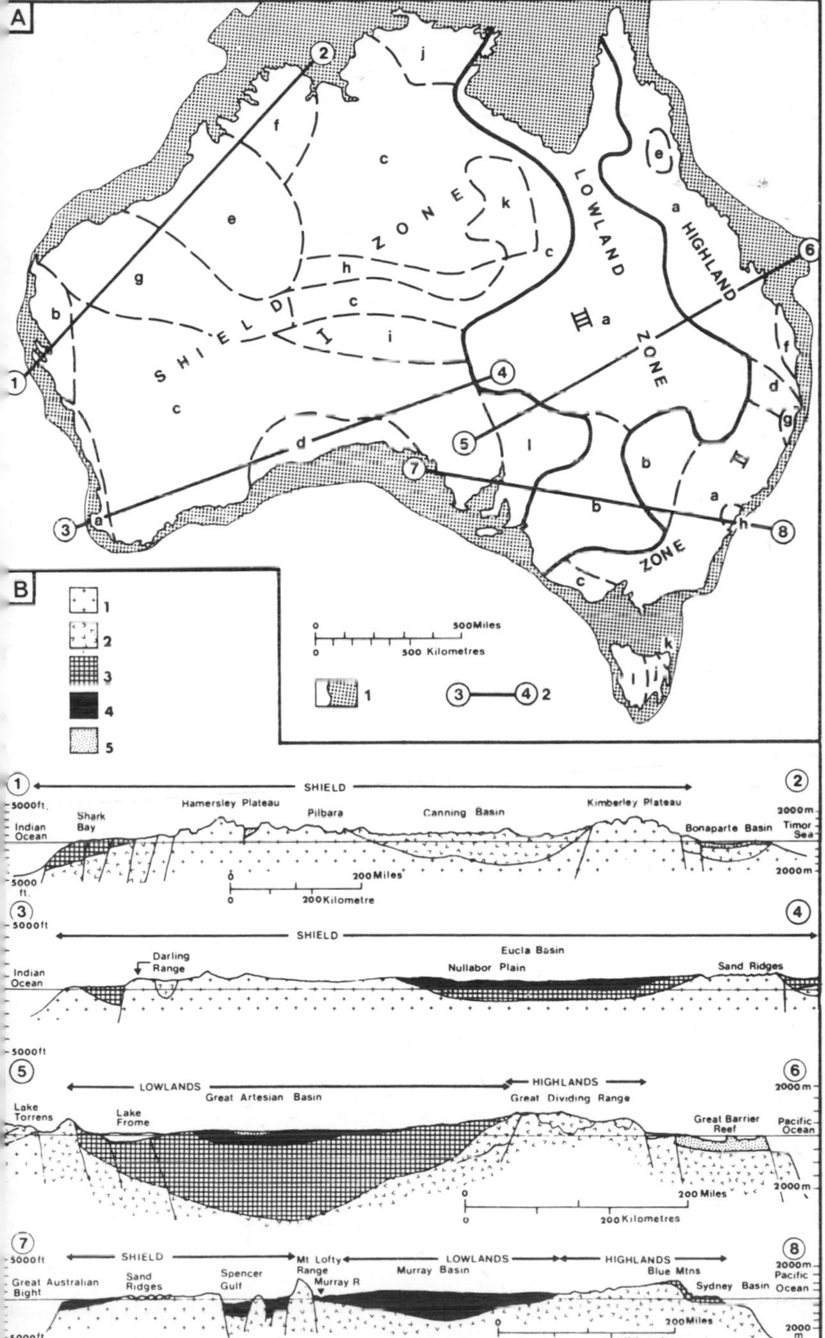
A
SHIELD ZONE
LOWLAND ZONE
HIGHLAND ZONE
I
II
III
B
1
2
3
4
5
500 Miles
500 Kilometres
SHIELD
5000 ft.
Indian Ocean
Shark Bay
Hamersley Plateau
Pilbara
Canning Basin
Kimberley Plateau
Bonaparte Basin
Timor Sea
2000 m
200 Miles
200 Kilometre
Darling Range
Eucla Basin
Nullabor Plain
Sand Ridges
LOWLANDS
HIGHLANDS
Great Artesian Basin
Great Dividing Range
Lake Torrens
Lake Frome
Great Barrier Reef
Pacific Ocean
Great Australian Bight
Sand Ridges
Spencer Gulf
Mt Lofty Range
Murray R
Murray Basin
Blue Mtns
Sydney Basin
200 Kilometres

The Shield Zone

This enormous area (some 1800 miles (2880 km) northeast southwest) one of the world's basic geological 'plates', consists of some of the earth's oldest surface rocks, many over 600 million years old. Since their formation they have been relatively little disturbed by earth movements (plate tectonics) which elsewhere created the Alps, the Rocky Mountains, and the Himalayas. The granites, gneisses and schists, which form most of the surface rocks have, it is true, been considerably contorted and intruded by deep-seated molten rocks, and the subsequent cooling and impact of heat and pressure has chemically re-sorted and physically re-hardened and re-shaped rocks to produce quartz veins bearing gold, silver, lead and zinc, and vast plateaus and ranges of iron ores within the Shield.

Yet the local relief of the Shield is relatively low, partly because of the lack of deep folding or faulting from earth movements (destructive earthquakes are relatively rare in Australia), but partly also because of the great age of many of the exposed surfaces (some have been tentatively dated at more than 70 million years old – having been eroded and then buried by deposition, before being exposed and eroded again). The highest points rarely exceed 4000 ft (1200 m) and the bulk of the land surface varies from 1500–2000 ft (450–600 m). Isolated mountains such as Ayers Rock may rise 600 ft (180 m) with almost vertical slopes, but over the Shield as a whole, slopes are gentle to flat, and where steep they tend to be short, separating large areas of flat to rolling plains at different levels (Fig. 2.2). Over almost half the surface of the Shield lie layers of sand, varying in thickness from 1 ft (0.3 m) to over 100 ft (30 m). Derived mainly from the rocks on which they lie, these sands form both flat unmarked plains and long narrow dune systems locally up to 100 ft (30 m) high and up to 1 mile (1.6 km) apart, apparently oriented to prehistoric wind circulations. The bulk now are fixed and no longer active except under severe drought conditions (Fig. 2.3).

In detail the Shield has been significantly modified and several areas are worth separating out. The western edge was broken and faulted down to form the *Swan coastal lowlands* where younger (Mesozoic) rocks form a coastal plain crossed by rivers draining the western rim (the Darling Ranges) of the Shield proper. A similar larger lowland forms the *Carnarvon Basin* to the north, where extensive sand dunes have mantled a small basin of artesian but saline water. The *West Australian Shield* itself has extensive plains broken only by low ranges of intruding igneous rocks, richly mineralised, the broad sweep of the low sand ridges of the Great Victorian Desert, and in the north the sand plains of the Tanami Desert. To the south younger limestones form the *Eucla Basin*, beneath the featureless, waterless and treeless Nullarbor plain abruptly terminating in cliffs 200 ft (60 m) above the surf at the head of the Great Australian Bight. A similar but sandstone structure forms the *Canning Basin* in the north, but here the surface is mantled by extensive dune systems and the coastline is of low sand dunes. In both basins artesian water is found, but again of generally brackish quality.

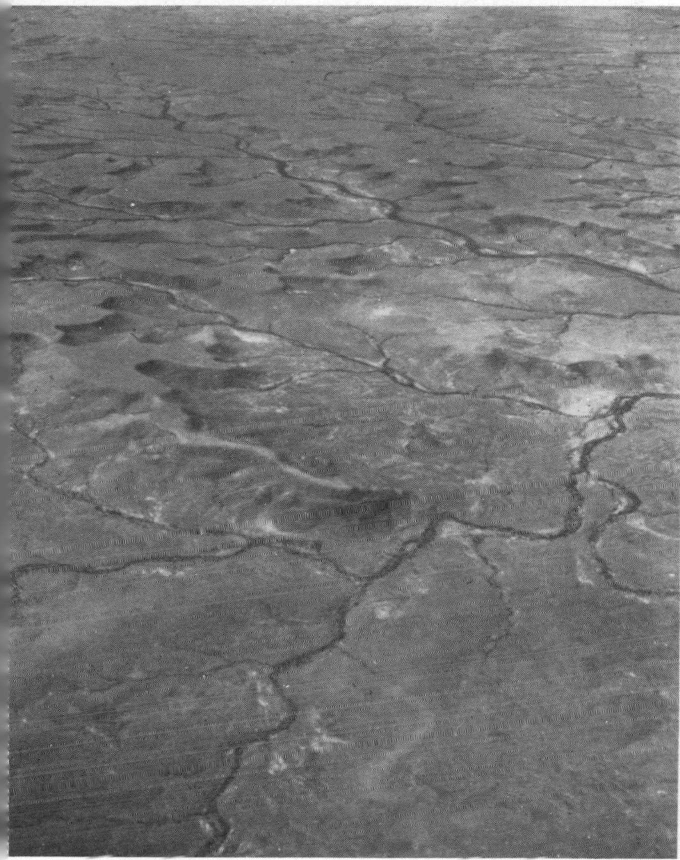

Fig. 2.2 Shield surface
Dissected plateau between Dalhousie and Mt Dare homestead, northern S.A. Watercourses are picked out by trees, gibber-strewn surfaces in foreground. Occasional pastoral land use. Desert ecosystem.

Standing out from the general level of the Shield plains are a series of folded domes or faulted block structures which provide more rugged terrain, offer local catchments for more permanent surface waters and ecological niches for less drought tolerant plant and animal life forms. The *Kimberley Plateau* is a highly dissected rugged mass of sandstones and quartzitic mountains having generally even summits at 2200–2800 ft (670–850 m). Many watercourses have been deeply carved into the strata, and in the summer rains valleys are rapidly filled by raging floodwaters. On the other side of the Canning Basin lie the *Hamersley* and *Pilbara plateaus*, less dissected but otherwise similar to the Kimberley area. The Hamersley plateau is higher with plateau summits to just over 4000 ft (1200 m) but the faulted Pilbara block is lower, averaging 1200 ft (360 m) over much of the area. In both, seasonally dry watercourses have been cut deeply into massive

Fig. 2.3 Pillar Range on edge of Simpson Desert, S.A.
Parallel sand dunes of background show distortion around edge of ranges in foreground, where micro-relief variations provide contrasting ecological niches. Bare dune summits show as lighter colour, dark spots are clumps or individual mulga and myall trees, dark grey patches are clay flats between spinifex covered sides of dunes. Desert ecosystem.

sandstones, ironstones and quartzites before they emerge onto the narrow coastal plain.

In the centre of the Shield lie two parallel east–west tending groups of sharply tilted folded ranges, the northerly being the *Macdonnell Ranges*, the southerly being the *Musgrave Ranges*. In both, the narrow steepsided ranges, less than half a mile (0.8 km) wide for the most part, rise to 3500 ft (1000 m) and are divided by narrow valleys through which wind dry sandy watercourses before plunging suddenly through deep, but often incredibly narrow, gorges into the next parallel valley. As an example, Serpentine Gorge in the Macdonnell Range is over 100 ft (30 m) deep and is *c.* 4 ft (1.2 m) wide at its narrowest.

The *Arnhem Land Plateau* in the north of the Shield is a remarkably even but dissected coarse sandstone mass averaging *c.* 900 ft (275 m) in height, interlaced by a trellis-work of narrow valleys cut along joints in the massive rock, averaging *c.* 300 ft (90 m) deep and less than half a mile (0.8 km) wide. The *Barkly Tableland* is a flat treeless limestone area only sparsely dissected at approximately 800 ft (240 m) above sea level and with little surface water. In the south of the continent, the *Flinders Ranges* complex is a zone of rock fractures at the edge of the Shield proper where younger (Paleozoic) rocks have been faulted into blocks of high and lowland, the latter either occupied by arms of the sea (as in Spencer Gulf) or by salt lakes (as Lake Torrens and Lake Frome). The highest peaks form highlands – the Mt Lofty and Flinders ranges proper – up to 3900 ft (1100 m) but in the northeast an extension of the highlands forms only a low range some 1000 ft (300 m) high bordering the sand deserts.

The Highland Zone

The *Highland Zone* is basically a series of younger Paleozoic rocks, many only slightly less than 300 million years old and which may be the deposited remains of the eroded surfaces of the Shield. These deposits have been slightly folded, but mainly faulted into highland and lowland blocks, so that, as in the Shield Zone, the overall impression is of even or rounded summits, with the steepest slopes, often vertical, separating large areas of relatively flat or even surfaces. Most of the zone has been, and is still being, eroded by permanent streams flowing down the steep short valleys to the eastern coast. The dominant rocks are sedimentary limestones, sandstones and locally metamorphosed dolomites, quartzites, and schists. Mineralised zones are frequent and local basins, preserve younger (Mesozoic) coal and iron ores.

The *Great Dividing Range* is misnamed, since in fact for most of its length it forms a series of high plateaus with the divide between east- and west-flowing drainage barely perceptible on the summit plateau surfaces. To the human intruder from the east however, the vertical cliffs fringing the plateaus must have seemed as effective a barrier as a mountain range. The highest summits are in the southeast, where the Snowy Mountains reach 7316 ft (2273 m) in Mt Kosciusko and where rock scratches and a semi-permanent snow drift are sole remnants of the last Ice Age. The summit levels decrease rapidly to 3200 ft (975 m) in western Victoria, while to the north the range loses height less rapidly, at the Queensland border it is still 5000 ft (1500 m) and 2000 ft (600 m) in the Cape York Peninsula. Inland from the range, the highlands merge gradually into the plains of the *Lowland Zone*. Rainfall run-off flows away eastwards through smooth open valleys, then narrow rocky clefts, to burst over the plateau edges in magnificent waterfalls before meandering briefly across the alluvial plains of the narrow coastal valleys. Westwards, the waters flow first through open valleys then gradually out onto the plains, where the meandering waters slacken, loss from seepage and evaporation increase and the watercourse and its contents may finally disappear.

Set within the range are several areas of special interest mainly from their particular rock composition. The *Cobar Plain* is geologically a part of the Highlands but by erosion has been reduced to a low rolling platform of mineralised rocks, barely distinguishable at the surface from the lowland to north and northwest. Elsewhere a series of volcanic eruptions, beginning in later (Cainozoic) time but extending until approximately some 5000 years ago in Victoria, have left large areas of lava deposits as plateaus and plains, occasionally dotted by the remnants of cinder cones and lava plugs as significant landmarks (Fig. 2.4). The soils derived from these basalt rocks

Fig. 2.4 Mt Ngungun, Qld.
This 775 ft (233 m) peak, seen from Mt Beerwah, forms part of the Glasshouse Mountains, a series of volcanic 'plugs' – the remnant cores of Cainozoic volcanoes long since eroded away – and offers a striking and unusual vertical theme in the Highland Zone. Mixed sclerophyll and rain forest ecosystem.

are generally richer in plant nutrients than surrounding non-volcanic soils and supported a richer stand of vegetation as a result. The *Victorian Plain*, a rolling area dotted by old cones rising *c.* 300 ft (90 m) above the general 1200 ft (360 m) surface, is a southern example of such volcanic country, while the *Toowoomba Plateau* at 4000 ft (1200 m) and the *Atherton Tableland* at 5000 ft (1500 m) form northern examples.

Off the eastern rim of the Highland Zone are a series of down-folded basins containing younger (Mesozoic) strata, often coal-bearing. These form the most extensive plains along a coast otherwise noteworthy for the absence of any large coastal plains or continental shelves. The *Maryborough* and *Clarence basins* both have extensive alluvial floodplains near the coast, the *Sydney Basin* has by contrast a low plateau some 200 ft (60 m) high of coarse sandstones, and the alluvial area of the main drainage system (Hawkesbury River) is much less extensive. In *Tasmania* the *plateau* rises to 4000 ft (1200 m) and shows evidence of past glacial action in ice-gouged valleys and moraine-dammed lakes, while the down-faulted *lowland* forms now the main south–north routeway through the island, followed by the two main rivers and covered by the best agricultural soils on the island. The *Ben Lomond* section of the plateau is a faulted block rising to 5160 ft (173 m).

The Lowland Zone

Between the two geologically older areas lies the trough of the *Lowland Zone*. Level, apparently limitless plains of Cainozoic sedimentary rocks sandstones, limestones, silts and clays – stretch over 1200 miles (1900 km) from the Gulf of Carpentaria to the mouth of the River Murray (Fig. 2.5). Beneath this great saucer-shaped depression, at depths of up to 3000 ft (900 m) lie strata saturated with fresh and saline waters, natural gas and oil. On the western margins close to Lake Eyre some of these strata outcrop and mound springs of hot brackish water flow incessantly.

On the surface of the lowland, ancient as well as present rivers from the eastern highlands have lain thick deposits of sands, brown loams and black clays. Occasionally the plains are broken by flat-topped mesas – remnants of a higher land surface long since eroded away. In the west, the parallel dunes of the central deserts loop out to form the Simpson Desert (Fig. 2.3) either side of the Channel Country – a region of grey clay flood plains and dotted rock-dammed water holes where floods bring tropical run-off from eastern Queensland down a vast braided watercourse network perhaps one year in seven (Fig. 2.6).

The subterranean 'saucer' of the *Great Artesian Basin* stretches from the mangrove mud-flats of the coast of the Gulf of Carpentaria beneath the Channel Country to the meandering tributaries of the Darling River. In the *Murray Basin*, pockets of water-bearing strata are broken by the Cobar plain bedrock, but the Murray and Murrumbidgee rivers carry permanent streams across almost flat flood plains broken only by the sinuous pine-clad

Fig. 2.5 Lake Frome clay plains, S.A., Lowland Zone
Vehicle bogged after half an inch of rain fell overnight. Saltbushes showing effects of grazing in foreground. Curnamona pastoral homestead on right horizon (2 miles away). Average rainfall *c*. 6 inches (150 mm). Mixed desert–grassland ecosystem.

sand ridges of the ancient watercourses, or 'prior streams'. Inside the great bend of the river and to the south, bands of east–west trending dunes (possibly related to the central dune systems) occasionally reach 300 ft (90 m) but are more usually 20–30 ft (6–9 m) high and marked by monotonous stands of mallee woodland.

The Continental Shelf and Coastline

The largest area of the shallowest off-shore waters lies to the north, linking, as far as geologists can guess, the structure of the continental land-mass with the mountain ranges of New Guinea. For Australia's 'Alps' or 'Rocky Mountains' one must look across the Torres Strait to the Cainozoic fold mountains of New Guinea and their possible extension to the southeast in New Zealand. The shallowness of this northern shelf, at its shallowest only *c*. 40 ft (*c*. 12 m) deep at low tide has encouraged the growth of coral reefs which virtually choke the Torres Strait. The corals extend along the north-west and south along the north-eastern coast where they form the Great Barrier Reef. Both in the northwest and northeast, equatorial ocean currents bring minute plankton and vertebrate life-forms on which the coral feed and survive down to depths of 180 ft (54 m). South of latitude 25° S the waters become too cool to support coral organisms and the reefs disappear. The coastal waters fringed by the reefs, however, contain a great variety of fish,

Fig. 2.6 The Channel Country, Qld., in flood
Tropical rainfall run-off flowing south-westward towards the Lake Eyre basin spills across the flat alluvial plains of the Lowland Zone. The main watercourses are lined by coolabahs and red gums, the intervening bare plains show by their varying tones the extent of soil moistening from the flood, which will produce a mass of annual and perennial grasses and herbs once the waters recede.

(*Source:* State Public Relations Bureau, Qld.)

crabs and shell-fish, for in terms of its productivity of life-supporting chemicals, the reefs are some of the richest ecosystems in the world.

Elsewhere around the continent, the shelf is narrow and offshore waters deepen rapidly. The major exception is the Bass Strait, where shallow waters cover the shelf linking the island to the mainland structure, and westerly winds make for rough seas all year. The geology of the shelf here as in the north shows evidence of subterranean oil and natural gas supplies.

The continental coast offers a wide variety of forms but few natural harbours – the first *Australian Encyclopaedia* (Jose and Carter, 1925) for example listed only seventeen in the whole 12 000 miles (20 000 km) of coastline. The low desert and dune-backed coasts of the northwest contrast with the cliffs of the Bight and the eastern coasts, and the few but large estuaries of the north. Estuaries in the south were even less attractive to navigators. The Murray, the largest river, flows to sea over a shallow and shifting bar formed by sand brought north along the 60 miles (96 km) of the Younghusband Peninsula – a dune ridge complex paralleling inland older and fossilised dune ridges. Port Phillip Bay and Western Port offer ports of refuge with only narrow entrances and shallow waters beyond. They punctuate a bleak cliffed coast broken elsewhere by only shallow indentations – hardly bays – and often barred by sand spits across the small estuaries. Cook, cruising northwards along the south-eastern coast found his first useful harbour at Botany Bay after some 250 miles (400 km) of sailing. The high cliffs and narrow entrance of the better harbours of Port Jackson (where Sydney – the first settlement – was established) (Fig. 2.7) and Pittwater to the north escaped his scrutiny. Further north, entrances opened up amid the high mountain-backed coast, but many had dangerous sand bars and the rivers shoaled rapidly upstream. North from 25° S latitude the coral reefs hindered the approach to a coast whose hilly hinterland was covered

Fig. 2.7 Sydney, N.S.W.
View south over harbour bridge, central business district to: 1, Botany Bay and airport; 2, Sydney Cove – Circular Quay – Ferry terminals with liner docked at ocean passenger terminal; 3, Domain. Public parklands and Governor's residence; 4, Opera House.

(*Source:* Department of Tourism, N.S.W.)

Fig. 2.8 Hobart, Tas.
One of the few points of entry for original settlement, the state capital is also the main port and industrial employer. View is over the central business district, adjacent Parliament House, government offices and wharves, across the Derwent estuary to the fastest-growing area of the state (in terms of population) – the eastern suburbs of Clarence Municipality. Off the photograph to the left is the concrete curve of the Tasman Bridge over the estuary, which allows commuters to build their new homes in the eastern suburbs, and off the photograph to the right is the latest addition to the city's skyline and so far unique in Australia – the Wrest Point Casino.

(*Source:* Don Stephens Pty. Ltd)

by subtropical forest and the river flats covered by thick brush and mangroves. The lowest coasts, around the Gulf of Carpentaria, were mud flats – mainly mangrove covered, and even the rugged cliffs of Arnhem Land and the great estuaries of the northern rivers had a fringe of mangroves and occasional reefs offshore. Tasmania by contrast had several large inlets and the two major rivers of Derwent and Tamar both had estuaries useful for ocean shipping (Fig. 2.8).

The soil mantle

Early knowledge and opinions on Australian soils were handicapped by the assumptions that experience from other parts of the world could be indiscriminately applied to Australia. This assumption overlooked the fact that much of the surface of the continent is among some of the oldest land surfaces on the earth and as a result soils were more often relics of the past rather than products of contemporary conditions.

In general, the present-day soil mantle of the continent shows a great variety of characteristics, with textures varying from soft silts and muds of the coastal swamps, through the loams of the most fertile volcanic plains, the coarse sands of the inland dunes, the peats of the Snowy Mountains and Tasmanian mountain summits, to those developed on the rock-hard (and possibly 13–14 million years old) duricrust caps of the inland and eastern plateaus. If any one colour may be said to dominate, it is the reddish-brown range – the basis for the 'wide brown land' of the poets – but there is a full range from the jet black of sodden clays to white and yellow ochres of the arid inland.

If we examine the soils by their texture, colour, and stratification, and then attempt to first explain their origin as a partial explanation of their resource potential three major processes seem to have been at work. Since the mineral and chemical components of all soils have their ultimate origin in the rocks from which they are weathered, we might expect that most soils in the continent would show some relationship in texture and chemistry to the rocks over which they lie. In fact in Australia it would appear that only approximately 20 per cent of the soils have such a relationship. These represent the thin stony soils on the inland ranges and plateaus, the stony plains of the 'gibber' deserts and red basaltic soils from the lava flows of the Highland Zone.

If the relationship with the underlying rock is slight, the other major formative influence usually suggested is the climate, that is the amount and effectiveness of rainfall will determine the movement of water and dissolved chemicals down through the soil and the temperatures will assist or delay the breakdown of chemicals and plant debris in the soil. In Australia, however, only approximately 32 per cent of the soils seem to show a relationship to climatic influences.

The high rainfall and cool temperatures of the eastern highlands seems to have helped produce the podsols and high moor (alpine) leached soils and the humus-rich black earths of Queensland, while inland the drier climates seem to have produced the relatively unleached red-brown earths. But these represent only 17 per cent of the area and for the other 15 per cent we must look to *past* (prehistoric) climates for an explanation. Here we have to acknowledge the age of some of the continental surfaces, for the existing soils cannot be explained by the present climatic influences. Often their present condition reflects rather the moister climatic influences, which may be as old as the Cainozoic and certainly at least as old as the glacial periods of 9000–600 000 years ago. Only in these terms can the pedologists explain the extensive red laterites of the inland and northern half of the continent, the salt-impregnated soils of the Mallee country, and the light textured highly leached (trace element deficient) brown soils of the plains.

For the remaining areas, the most important formative influence seems to have been weathering and soil modification by physical erosion or deposition. Here, the contemporary climate is obviously important, but the physical modifications have continuously affected the character of the soils and prevented any vertical zonation of chemicals within them. Thus, the soils of the desert sand dunes (19% of the total) owe much of their character to wind action. The alluvial soils of the inland flood plains, especially the Channel Country, and coastal estuaries (some 28% of the total) owe their character to water movements as do the tidal mud flats (1% of the total). In sum, the soils which show dominant influences of past and present direct weathering processes occupy some 48 per cent of the continent. While zonation of chemicals and textures may be absent, the youth and alluvial origin of about two-thirds of these soils meant that they contained reasonable amounts of plant nutrients in contrast with the leached soils.

Bearing in mind the origins and the processes which seem to have produced the array of different soils, these soils might be grouped according to their potential usefulness for agriculture. The best, most useful, soils would be those which were easiest to cultivate, had sufficient inherent plant nutrients to sustain plant growth for several years without fertilisers, contained sufficient soil moisture for most types of useful domesticated plant growth, and were located in areas where the temperature was sufficiently high but not too great to encourage plant growth for at least one crop per year. Given these prerequisites how did the soils in 1770 measure up?

The best soils comprised the red loams on the basalt lavas, the black earths of the north-eastern Highland Zone and the red-brown earths of the south-eastern Lowland Zone – altogether some 8 per cent of the continent. Here inherent fertility was high, whether from the breakdown of the bedrock, as with the red-browns and black earths, or from wind derived (loess-type) clays of the red-brown earths, and the growing-season and moisture were adequate for most bread grain crops.

This small area of good soils (see Fig. 9.1A, p. 108) is bounded on the seaward edge by generally higher rainfalls and by the main area of podsolised soils on the continent. These are soils where the growing season is generally adequate but which are deficient in fertility, having lost many of the original nutrients by excessive leaching from the higher rainfall on coarse-textured rocks. Approximately 12 per cent of the continents' soils might be thus described.

For the remaining 80 per cent of the continent the soils were in various ways unsuitable for agriculture. For 16 per cent of the continent, the tidal marshes and stony tablelands, there was no soil to be cultivated; the high altitude frost hazard affected a very small area (less than 2%), while for almost two-thirds (63%) of the continent the soils were too arid. If agriculture was to be successfully established the initial locations would have to be very carefully chosen.

The land in summary

The relatively undisturbed geological structure of the continent, together with the great age of many of the present-day surfaces has produced a land of plains and plateaus rather than peaks and high mountain chains. The observer travelling through the western two-thirds of the continent would be impressed by the monotony of the level horizon, broken only rarely by vertical features; in the eastern third he would be impressed by the steepness of the deep valleys cut down into the high but, for the most part, still horizontal surfaces.

The observer would equally be impressed by the relative scarcity of good soils and the constraints upon the possibilities of agricultural production from the lack of soil moisture, but also the surprising lack of soil fertility even in areas of effective rainfall. The latter is a function of the age of the land surfaces and their long exposure to climatic weathering, the former is a function of the patterns of the contemporary climate.

3
The seasons

Some forty years before the first permanent European settlement, the climate of *Terra Australis Incognita* had been rationalised by analogy with climates in equivalent latitudes of the northern hemisphere. While great, and generally erroneous, hopes resulted (see Chapters 14 and 15), the method has some value in explaining the seasonal patterns of what has come to be recognised as a 'sunburnt country'.

Patterns of temperature and precipitation

In its global location Australia has the same relationship to the Equator as the Sahara Desert of North Africa. It is dominated by the seasonal shift of the 'heat equator' following the passage of the overhead sun. Astride the Tropic of Capricorn, the sun is overhead in northern Australia for over three months of the year and never less than 45° above the midday horizon anywhere on the continent.

Given this and the global pattern of descending air over the continent from equatorial and sub-polar high pressure systems, it is not surprising that Australia is one of the warmest continents with only a small portion of the south-eastern highlands having winter temperatures sufficiently low to inhibit plant growth. Average winter temperatures range from 50°F (10°C) in the southeast to 75°F (24°C) in the northwest while the absolute minimum of –8°F (–22°C) has been recorded only at over 4000 ft (1200 m) on the high plains of the Snowy Mountains. Of more concern because of the physiological stress involved, have been the summer temperatures, when averages range from 65°F (18°C) to 85°F (29°C) from south to north across the continent, but averages which hide extremely high shade temperatures. Maxima have reached 111°F (44°C) at Melbourne, 116°F (47°C) at Adelaide and 121°F (49°C) at Bourke. The longest spells of high temperatures occur in the northwest interior where Marble Bar has a record of over 150 consecutive days with temperatures over 90°F (32°C). One saving grace of such extreme heat, however, is its dryness, as relative humidities are low (usually less than 30%) so that evaporative cooling of sweat from the skin is very efficient. High relative humidities on the north-eastern and northern coasts, resulting from the summer monsoonal rainfalls, promotes an oppressive 'prickly heat', when evaporative skin cooling is difficult in air which is close to saturation point anyhow.

Associated with the north–south shift of the heat equator is the realignment of the belts of air pressures and paths of pressure cells and associated wind patterns across the continent. In January, at the height of summer low pressure cells from equatorial systems oscillate off the northwest coast and occasionally cross west–east across northern coasts to swing south along the Queensland coast. Some of these have the characteristics of cyclones with hurricane-force winds gusting over 100 miles (160 km) per hour with torrential rain storms delivering up to 20 inches (500 mm) in twenty-four hours. By contrast the southern half of the continent has clear hot days with afternoon convectional thunderstorms the main source of the occasional rainfall. By July the winter pattern has become established, high pressure cells dominate the northern half of the continent and a succession of low pressure cells ('depressions') pass west–east across the southern coasts covering on average about 300 miles (480 km) per day. They bring a fairly regular sequence of rainstorms followed by clear days along their path, bringing snow 3 to 10 ft (1–3 m) deep to the highest plains and gales off the coasts. In effect the southern coasts in winter occasionally feel the edge of the 'Roaring Forties' wind systems circulating around the Antarctic continent.

The result of these oscillations is a pattern of precipitation (Fig. 3.1) which is basic to an understanding not only of the condition of the continent in 1770, but of the sequence of European and Anglo–Australian resource use which has followed since 1770. Immediately apparent from the map is the large area of the continent with low annual precipitation and peripheral nature of the maxima.

A 'sunburnt country' implies aridity and Australia has been labelled one of the most arid continents. Certainly by comparison with continental USA almost equivalent in area, Australia has only a quarter of the area having over 40 inches (1016 mm) of precipitation. Of the annual average continental precipitation of 16.5 inches (420 mm) only some 1.8 inches (45 mm) remains as run-off in Australia compared with the rest of the world averages of 9.8 inches (248 mm) from rainfall of 26 inches (660 mm). The flow of Australia's longest river, the Murray, is infinitesimal (0.05 m^3 per second) compared with the Mississippi River's 18.4 m^3 per second. Not only is Australia's rainfall generally low, but its effectiveness as a moisture source is considerably reduced by high rates of evaporation. In central Australia with all seasons dominated by high pressure cells of clear cloudless skies and moderate to high daily temperatures, evaporation has been estimated at between 70 and 100 inches (1780 to 2540 mm). In such areas between $\frac{1}{2}$ and 1 inch (13–25 mm) of rainfall in one continuous fall is needed to achieve any vegetational response.

The peripheral rainfall maxima are the result in part of the major oceanic sources of moisture and the low interior of the continent bordered by highlands on the northwest and east. Thus the highest rainfalls in the northeast result from on-shore moist air masses passing over the northern Highland Zone and providing both frontal and orographic precipitation. Northern

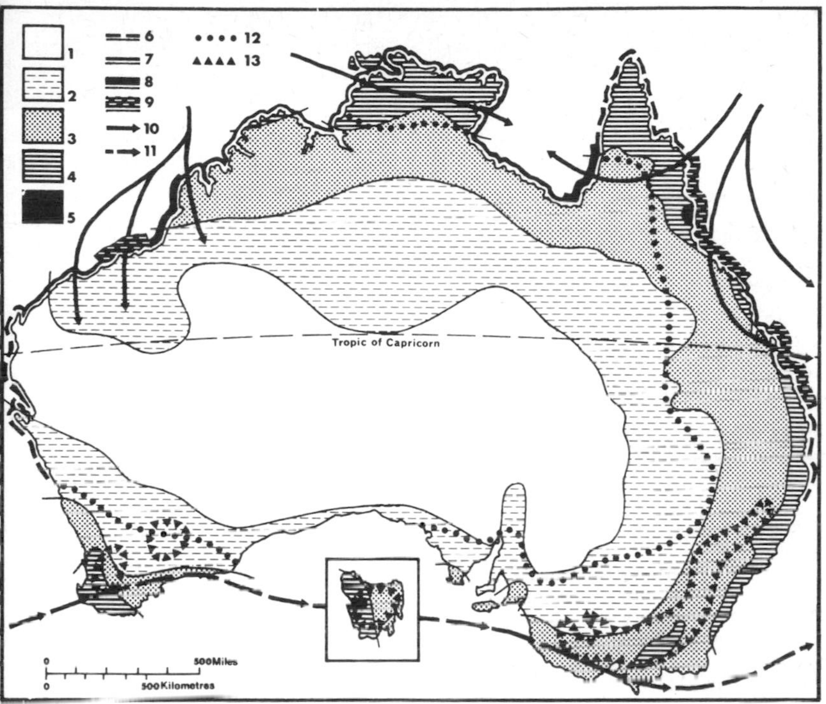

Fig. 3.1 The patterns of climate
Annual precipitation: 1, Less than 250 mm; 2, 250 to 499 mm; 3, 500 to 999 mm; 4, 1000 to 3500 mm; 5, Over 3500 mm.
Cyclones (occurrences since 1909): 6, Recorded but not frequent; 7, At least one per year (over 60); 8, Between one and two per year (over 90); 9, Over two per year (over 120); 10, Usual tracks of cyclones.
Temperate storms: 11, Usual track of winter depressions.
Plant-growing season: 12, Inner area unsuitable for grain crops; 13, Frost likely on up to 200 days of year.

(*Sources:* Coleman, 1972; Gentilli, 1971)

coasts benefit from frontal rainfalls associated with the summer 'monsoons' and cyclones, but the influence of these rapidly decreases inland, where remoteness from maritime moisture sources, generally descending air in local 'rain-shadows' (south of the Kimberleys and west of the Queensland Highland Zone) and global air movements restricts precipitation to isolated occurrences. At Alice Springs, with an average rainfall of 9.9 inches (252 mm), observations by the CSIRO over three-and-a-half years at six-minute intervals for twenty-four hours each day showed only thirteen occasions when rainfall was sufficient to give some run-off! Effective precipitation in the interior is a rare event.

Given this pattern, it is not surprising that the areas of continuous temperature and precipitation availability for plant growth should be restricted to the periphery of the continent. Estimates of average soil moisture retention and evaporation losses have suggested that the interior 78 per cent of the continent has either no useful growing season at all or one up to five months long but liable to frequent interruptions by droughts. Only the peripheral 22 per cent has a growing period of over five months, i.e. sufficient to support grain cultivation. These are figures based upon average rainfalls but actual figures show considerable variations and there have been sequences of above and below average conditions which have had significant effects on the history of Anglo–Australian land settlement, as we shall see.

The variability of precipitation is difficult to comprehend except at first hand (Fig. 2.5). Unless one has seen for oneself a photo of the same landscape in 'good years' after high rainfalls and in 'bad years' after droughts, figures tend to be meaningless. However, for what they are worth, the meterologists claim that over three-quarters of the continent has rainfalls which vary, up or down, by more than 20 per cent, and for over half the continent (the interior in particular) the variation is more than 30 per cent. The reliability of the rainfall generally increases with the size of the annual averages and in areas of low average rainfalls the risk of complete failure appears to be highest, although no part of Australia has completely reliable rainfall.

The climatic hazards – drought

One consequence of the variability of the continental precipitation is the occurrence of drought. To define it, however, is less easy than might at first appear. The usual definition is of a deficiency of moisture which has an observable detrimental effect on plant and animal life. Such definitions tend to imply that the detrimental effects are not merely in the direct effects on the plants and animals, but also include the indirect effects through them on man and his activities. Thus a recent official definition has suggested that drought is 'a period of rainfall deficiency, extending over months or years, of such a nature that crops and pasturage for stock are seriously affected, if not completely burnt up and destroyed, water supplies are seriously depleted or dried up, and sheep and cattle perish' (Foley, 1957, p. 4). A further official definition (Gibbs and Maher, 1967) suggested that a drought existed when the annual rainfall for a locality was among the lowest 10 per cent on record. The reason for the 10 per cent was that this coincided usually with complaints of drought occurrences from resource users. These definitions illustrate that drought, as most 'natural hazards', is defined on two standards, one an absolute statistical limit based for example on plant wilting thresholds and the other a relative assessment based upon man's experience of the moisture required for the particular resource use attempted.

Whichever definition is used, however, there is no doubt that droughts were a common occurrence in the continent before European settlement began, for the explorers noted dead trees and dried-up water holes in some of the watercourses, while reconstructed aboriginal legends mentioned periods of water shortages prior to European arrival. Records since 1788 have shown a continuation of drought occurrences throughout the continent and there is no reason to believe that conditions were much different in 1770. Plant and animal life on the continent, therefore, must have been periodically exposed to drought stress, although the contemporary evidence suggests that the incidence of such stresses would have been least in the higher rainfall areas.

The climatic hazards – cyclones

In contrast with drought – which may have no observable beginning, the moisture deficits gradually accumulating over the rainless months until plants begin to wilt and surface waters finally disappear – cyclones are of much shorter and more easily defined duration. The high winds and torrential rains may last only hours and the most destructive events may take only a matter of minutes and be very limited in area (Fig. 3.1).

Of the effects of cyclones in the eighteenth century we have scant record, but from records thereafter we can obtain some idea of the destruction involved to reefs, river catchments and natural vegetation. Thus on the northeast coast records from 1867 to 1939 showed cyclones occurring in fifty-eight of the seventy-two years of record. During this period the following towns were battered and many buildings destroyed or damaged beyond repair: Bowen in 1884, Townsville in 1903 (and again 1971), Port Douglas in 1911, Innisfail in 1918 and Mulloy in 1920. Despite the material damage, loss of life was relatively slight, but in 1899 the whole fleet of pearling craft operating out of Broome (Western Australia) were sunk with the loss of over 300 lives. From such evidence it is not difficult to imagine the situation before 1770, when whole stands of vegetation and generations of wildlife must have been periodically destroyed and swept out to sea, where reefs must have been pounded by the massive waves associated with the cyclone. The quiet continent was not always so.

Water on the land

With such a low average rainfall, the concentrations of surface water were vitally important to all life forms, not least man. The low average run-off figures mentioned above have to be considered with the availability of rainfall, the high evaporation rates of the inland areas, and the lack of any permanent snowfields to slow down the transfer of moisture from the land to the oceans. The overall results were to ensure that such water as was on the land did not remain there long. 'Permanently' flowing rivers in Australia are confined to eastern and south-eastern catchments, but even they may have variations in flows of from 1 : 6 to the Darling River's 1 : 11 000 and locally floods may be a greater hazard than droughts. For the most of the continent, however, watercourses are empty for most of the year and for approximately one-third of the continent there is no coordinated surface drainage at all, and if we include the areas of inland drainage, for 51 per cent of the land area there is no surface water drainage to the sea.

Most of the continental run-off occurs in summer and from the northern half of the continent where the summer rains produce almost twice the volume of run-off of the southern winter rains. Much of this northern run-off takes place in drainage systems which are dry for part of the year but raging torrents in the summer, when river banks cannot hold the flood crests which spill out over the surrounding countryside (Fig. 2.6). Thus in terms of potential, the northern flows are more valuable than the southern, but until adequate storages are built, this advantage was and still is nebulous, for it was the eastern coast where a combination of higher and more regular rainfall produced permanently flowing streams and the few permanent lakes, of more immediate attraction to the first Europeans.

The seasons in summary

For Australia as a whole, water on the land was a scarce commodity in 1770. The uneven pattern of occurrence in space and over time produced stresses both of over and undersupply which had marked effects on contemporary plant, animal and human life and the ecosystems of which they were a part. The surface resources were complemented by the presence of underground reserves of artesian and subartesian water, for the most part located in the lower rainfall areas (Fig. 8.1, p. 87). Although not all of them were potable, even for animals with higher salt tolerances than man, they were a major resource to be exploited in later years. In 1770, however, their existence was only hinted at by the low mounds on the edge of Lake Eyre, from which hot brackish water bubbled away across the shimmering salt flats.

4 The ecosystems

Onto the basic structure and climates of the continent had been grafted an array of plant and animal life whose most impressive feature, at least to the Europeans who first experienced it, was its uniqueness in comparison both with anything else they had seen and even in comparison with the life-forms of the neighbouring islands and mainland of Asia. This latter contrast so impressed the zoologist A. R. Wallace that in 1876 he drew a line dividing Australia and New Guinea from the islands and Asia, claiming that this marked a major global division between two very different zoological and botanical realms. In detail his line has been modified subsequently, but the basic division is still recognised.

A second impressive feature is the number of plant and animal species which can tolerate extremely dry conditions for long periods. While the first feature appears to be related to the history of plant and animal colonisation, the second seems more obviously related to the climate patterns of this continent and the evolution of species able to tolerate them.

The details of these plant and animal patterns can best be described by the identification of a series of separate but often mutually interdependent ecosystems; that, is areas of the continent where plant and animal life appeared to be in some kind of dependent relationship with each other and the local climate and terrain. Since the plants were the main prop of the other life forms the ecosystem will be mainly identified in terms of dominant vegetation forms, although the influence of the terrain and climate will become obvious.

The ecosystems in 1770

The range and variety of such ecosystems, as can be reconstructed for 1770, is impressive. From the coastal reefs, marshes and rain forests where life in all forms was prolific and ever active, they ranged to the alpine meadows where life-cycles were generally dormant in the freezing temperatures and snowfalls of winter, to the bare stony plains of the arid interiors where excessive heat and insufficient moisture limited many life-forms to nocturnal or highly irregular periods of activity.

The continental patterns of these ecosystems are indicated on Fig. 4.1A and their basic characteristics outlined on Fig. 4.1B. As illustrated, the basic

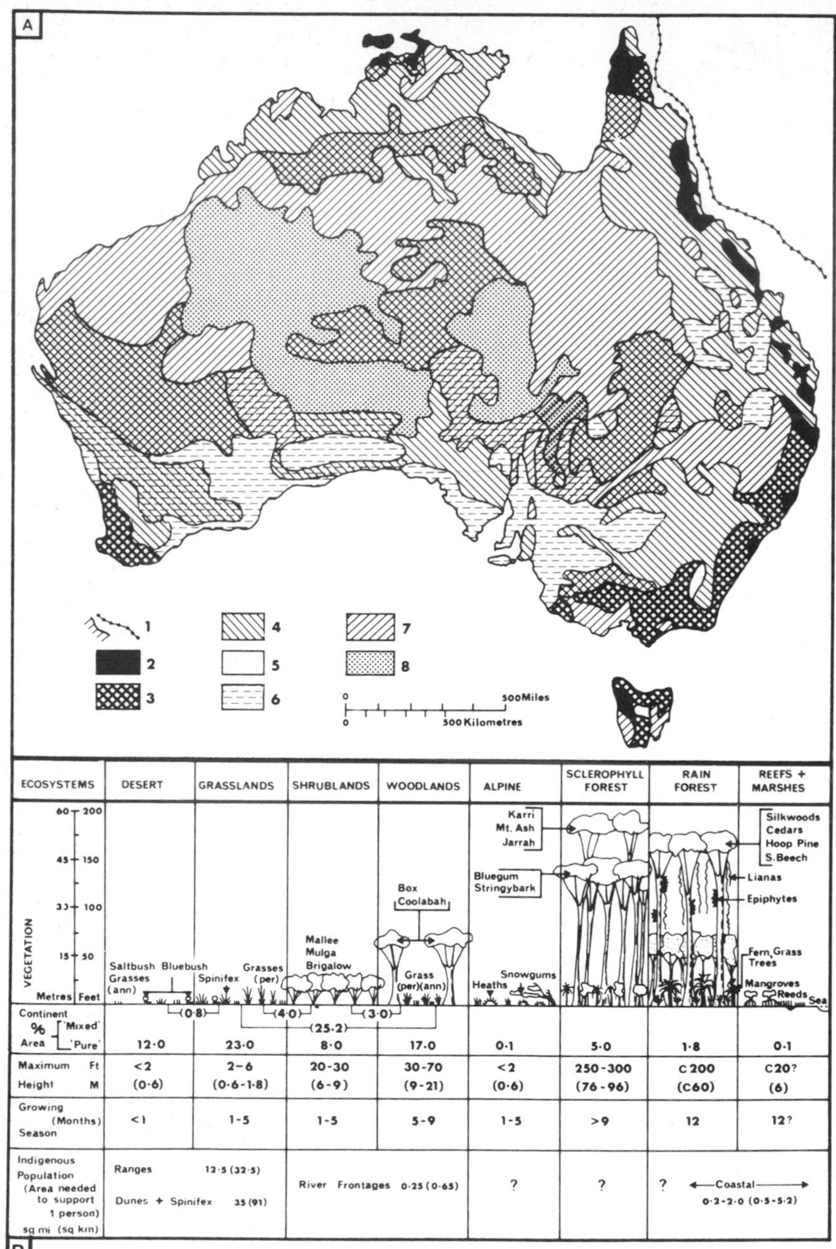

ECOSYSTEMS	DESERT	GRASSLANDS	SHRUBLANDS	WOODLANDS	ALPINE	SCLEROPHYLL FOREST	RAIN FOREST	REEFS + MARSHES
Continent % Area 'Mixed' / 'Pure'	12·0	23·0	8·0	17·0	0·1	5·0	1·8	0·1
Maximum Height Ft (M)	<2 (0·6)	2–6 (0·6–1·8)	20–30 (6–9)	30–70 (9–21)	<2 (0·6)	250–300 (76–96)	c 200 (c60)	c20? (6)
Growing Season (Months)	<1	1–5	1–5	5–9	1–5	>9	12	12?
Indigenous Population (Area needed to support 1 person) sq mi (sq km)	Ranges 12·5 (32·5); Dunes + Spinifex 35 (91)		River Frontages 0·25 (0·65)		?	?	? ←Coastal→ 0·2–2·0 (0·5–5·2)	

Fig. 4.1 The ecosystems of 1770

A. Pattern of ecosystems: **1**, Great Barrier Reef; **2**, Rain forest; **3**, Sclerophyll forest; **4**, Woodland; **5**, Alpine; **6**, Shrublands; **7**, Grasslands; **8**, Desert.

zonation is from peripheral ecosystems relatively 'rich' in life-forms to interior ecosystems with a relatively 'poorer' range of life-forms. The details, however, need elaboration.

The coastal reefs and marshes

Fringing the great land-mass of the continent was a narrow, often broken, zone of off-shore reefs and coastal marsh lands, inundated by high tides or periodic freshwater floods. The greatest extent of the reefs was in the north-eastern tropical waters where sea temperatures generally above 68°F (20°C) favoured the growth of coral-forming polyps whose minute skeletons compacted together formed the limestone reefs laid bare at low tide. The greatest of these reefs, the Great Barrier Reef, is not one but a complex of many reefs, stretched for some 1260 miles (1900 km) along the north-eastern coast. Its seaward fringe, a jagged knife-edged mass of broken coral rocks pounded by Pacific breakers fell away rapidly to deep waters, while the land-ward side formed sand-smoothed beaches fringing quieter lagoons unaffected by the destructive surf. Occasionally the surface of the reef was punctuated by islands of older sand-cemented coral (Fig. 4.2) or bed-rock formations, the latter being summits of the drowned mountain chains on which the reefs supposedly have been built. Most of these higher islands carried a rich tropical vegetation on their leeward slopes but the exposed seaward slopes carried a thinner, more salt-spray tolerant vegetation.

On and in the reefs could be found an amazing number and variety of living things. Some 340 different types of coral-forming polyp provided the living rock of the surface of the reef, while molluscs and fish of all sizes and varieties of startling colours moved over and through its honeycombed interior. Over the dry sand banks of the low coral islands in early summer crawled turtles coming ashore to lay their eggs; among the casuarina trees fringing the lagoons nested birds migrating along this western coast of the Pacific in spring and autumn; within the lagoons swarmed more fish, dugong grazing the seaweed beds, and over its floor myriads of shellfish moved in search of food.

On parts of the reef especially well sheltered from surf and spray small colonies of mangroves were established, but their greatest extent was in the shallow waters of the Gulf of Carpentaria and the indented northern coast, where river alluvium formed extensive marshy floodplains and the relatively freshwater inhibited coral growth. Along the southern coasts mangroves formed isolated pockets on sheltered inlets such as Spencer Gulf and the estuary of the Hawkesbury River. Here, between high- and low-tide levels on the exposed mudflats were to be found the minute forests of breathing-

---

Caption to Fig. 4.1 – continued

Combined symbols showed mixed ecosystems. Not shown because of the map scale are the coastal marshes along the Gulf of Carpentaria.

B. Generalised cross-section from East coast inland

(*Sources:* Ross Cochrane, 1963; and CSIRO, 1960)

Fig. 4.2 Green Island, Barrier Reef, Qld.
A vegetated low coral island amid the coral platform of the main reef. Clumps of underwater coral show as dark clusters in foreground with sand floor of lagoon showing as light grey. Tourist accommodation and jetty, from where glass-bottomed boats traverse the sheltered lagoon. Open sea and edge of reef in background.

(*Source:* State Public Relations Bureau, Qld.)

tubes and the tangled mass of stilt-like roots which supported the trunks and branches of the mangroves. In tropical waters these could rise to over 20–30 ft (6–9 m) but they were usually smaller and less luxuriant in growth in the cooler southern waters.

These reefs and coastal marshes provided one of the richest environments in the continent if we consider the natural processing of chemicals and the production of living matter per unit area, but because of their unstable surface conditions, high insect populations and constant threat of flooding they were not attractive as *living sites* to man, although they did offer him a wide variety of edible fish and molluscs throughout the year, as they did also for larger birds such as pelicans (*Pelecanus* spp.) and black swans (*Cygnus atratus*) as well as many species of wading birds.

The rain forests

Of the land ecosystems the rain forests were the richest in variety of plant and animal life although their extent was probably limited to less than 2 per cent of the continent. Two types seem to have existed, a temperate rain forest found only in Tasmania, which was dominated by the southern beech (*Nothofagus* spp.), and a subtropical rain forest in pockets along the northern and eastern coast of the mainland. Distinguished in terms of the temperature tolerances of their species, both rain forests, as their names suggest, occupied areas of the highest continental rainfalls.

In appearance these forests formed a mass of vegetation, grouped by height into three fairly distinct layers. The tallest trees, southern beech and red cedar (*Cedrus Australis*), soared over 170 ft (50 m), towering above a second layer of trees averaging 60 ft (18 m) in height, which itself dominated a third layer of tree ferns, grass trees (*Xanthorrhoea* spp.) and 'brush' undergrowth some 30 ft (9 m) high. Intermingled with these three layers were the festoons of epiphytes and tree-orchids draped high on branches and tree-trunks, through which only a pale grey light filtered through to the damp floor of the forest, on which micro-organisms and small insects decomposed the litter of dead plant materials (Fig. 4.3). Wherever richer soils were found, as on the alluvial river flats or volcanic soils of the Atherton Tableland of Queensland, the richest variety of species and the largest individual specimens thrived.

Amid this wealth of vegetation lived an abundance of animal and insect life, many in larger forms than might be found in other less endowed ecosystems. Large bird-eating spiders lurked among the foliage, bright-coloured butterflies and myriads of flies and wasps sampled the blooms of orchids and flowering trees, while overhead raucous gaudy parrots and rosellas hunted seeds and nectar and small brown tree-creeping birds poked the bark for insects and grubs. Through the undergrowth, usually by night, moved honey-eating wallabies (*Macropodinae* spp.), insect and nut-eating musk rat-kangaroos (*Hypsiprymnodon moschatus*). While among the branches grazed tree-kangaroos (*Dendrolagus* spp.), giant fruit-bats ('flying foxes' *Pteropus* spp.) and gliding squirrels (*Petaurus* spp.).

For man this offered perhaps the richest store of edible plant and animal life, especially if found close to the major rivers of the northeast coast where freshwater fish and molluscs could supplement the diet.

The sclerophyll forests

Where local climates appear to have been cooler and drier than those favoured by the subtropical rain forest, or soils less fertile, the forest lands changed to sclerophyllous, or hard scaly-leaved drought-resistant, types (Fig. 2.4). Some 5 per cent of the continent was thought to carry this type of forest land, mainly in the south and south-eastern humid fringes (Fig. 4.4). Here, despite the slightly lower average rainfalls, were found the tallest trees in the continent, giants of 200 to 300 ft (60–90 m) in the Mountain Ash (*Eucalyptus regnans*) forests of the southeast, and the Karri

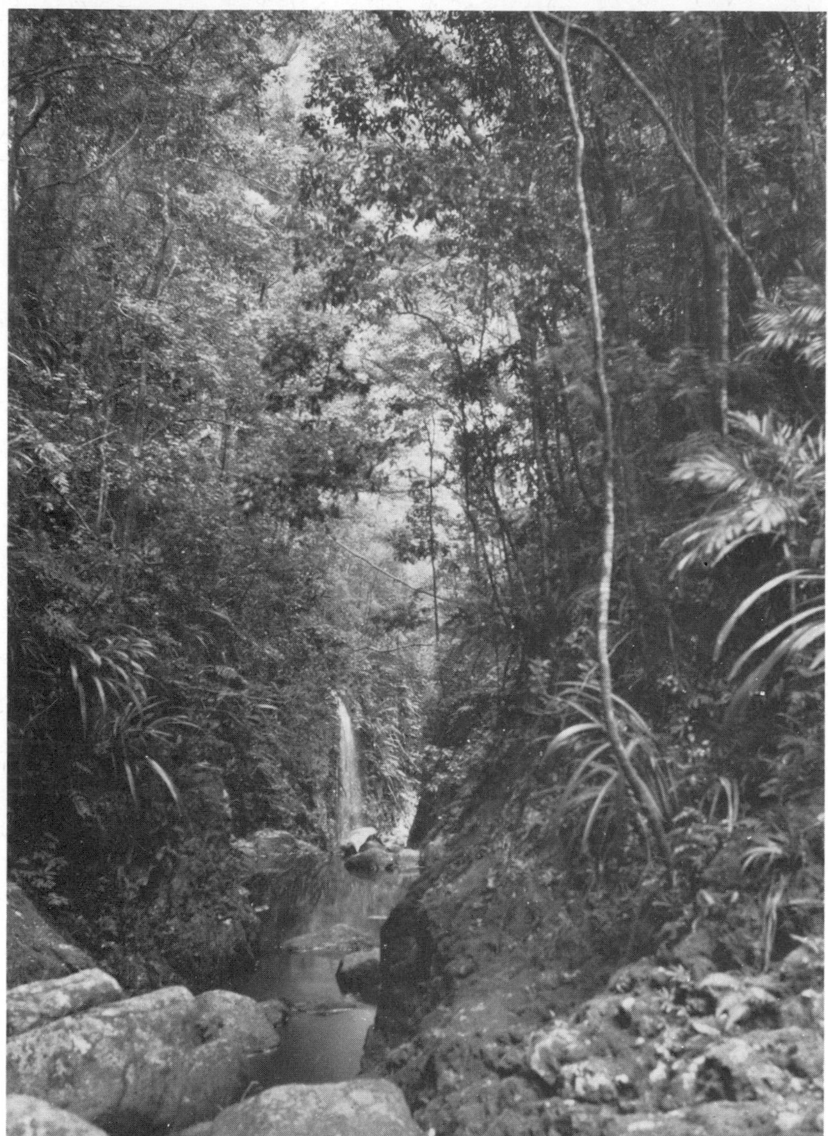

Fig. 4.3 Coomera Crevice, Lamington National Park, Qld.
Tropical rain forest ecosystem. Average rainfall over 60 inches (1500 mm).

(*Source:* Government Tourist Bureau, Qld.)

(*E. diversicolor*) and Jarrah (*E. marginata*) forests of the southwest. Below these giants was a substrata of shrubs such as bottle brushes (*Banksia* spp., *Grevillea* spp.), and, if the humidity remained high enough during the year,

Fig. 4.4 Clearing the forest, Gippsland, Vic.
The original woodland in the background is being gradually felled, dragged into windrows to be burnt (right and left centre) before seeding to exotic pastures (foreground). The stack of timber provides rapid cash income for the pioneer settlers.

some tree ferns also. Grass trees (*Xanthorrhoea* spp.) marked the poorest soils.

Through these relatively open forests moved a slightly less varied range of marsupials and insect life, although bird species may have been more varied here than in the rain forests according to some recent studies in Tasmania. Grey kangaroos (*Macropus major*) and wombats (*Vombatus* spp.) moved over the forest floor, while koalas (*Phascolarctos cinereus*) and opposums (*Phalangeridae* spp.) grazed the branches and young shoots of the peppermint gums (*E. odorata*). Large spiders were still to be found, and between the sparser orchids and herbs of the forest floor ants scavenged incessantly. In the permanent creeks swam the platypus (*Orithorhynchus paradoxus* as originally described by biologists perplexed by its webbed feet, duck bill, fur and egg-laying abilities, now *O. anatinus*), grazing on the shells and fresh-water prawns and retiring to a beaver-like tunnel in the stream bank. Over the waters swooped bright coloured kingfishers (*Alcyone* spp.) and the forests echoed to the 'hysterics' of the Kookaburra (*Dacelo* spp.).

The woodlands

On its drier fringes the sclerophyll forest merged into the more extensive if less prolific woodland ecosystem. Here, covering some 17 per cent of the continent as relatively 'pure' stands and a further 28 per cent as mixed stands with other ecosystems (grasslands and shrublands) was a 'sea' of trees, not as tall or as dense as the forest species, but from a treetop – as the first European explorers found – stretching off into the infinite distance in monotonous grey-green waves. Beneath and between the scattered trees were grasses and herbs, here quite thick where the tree canopies were thin and widely spaced, there relatively sparse where the trees stood closer and threw more shade.

The ring of woodlands grading into the drier interior ecosystems was broken mainly in the south and west where the increased aridity seems to have produced the mixed pattern of grassland and woodland, and shrub and woodland. In each case the patches of woodland became thinner and less frequent inland.

Overall, the height of trees in the woodlands was less than half that of the forests, and because the bole of the trees tended to be shorter than the crown, most trees had an open-branched, or at the extreme in the mallee of the shrublands, a bushy appearance. The tallest trees, white box (*E. albens*), iron barks (*E. melanophloia*), peppermint (*E. odorata*), had understories of she-oak (*Casuarina luehmauni*). In the open glades of the northern summer rainfall areas would be found perennials such as Flinders Grass (*Iseilima* spp.) and Mitchell Grass (*Astrebla* spp.), while in the southern winter rainfall areas Wallaby Grass (*Danthonia* spp.) seems to have dominated. For several months after heavy rains the open ground between the perennial grass tussocks would be carpeted with succulent herbs and annual grasses (*Trifolium* spp., *Bromus* spp.).

Animal, insect and bird life in the woodlands, although perhaps not as prolific as in the forests, was still abundant and varied. The large Grey Forest Kangaroo (*Macropus major*) was common along with smaller scrub wallabies (*Setonix* spp. and *Thylogale* spp.) and rat-kangaroos (*Potoroinae* spp.) in the more grassy areas, with many varieties of parrots and large crows (*Corvus* spp.) nesting in the trees, wood moths burrowing in the bark, brown and black snakes, small lizards and biting ants (in the south) and wood-eating termites (in the north) amid the leaf litter on the woodland floor. In the permanent rivers and water holes was a range of freshwater, edible fish, including the Murray River cod (*Maccullochella macquariensis*), which could be up to 180 lb (80 kg) in weight, and eels, with freshwater crayfish (*Cherax* spp.) and molluscs.

The shrublands

The drier southern fringe of the continent was occupied by the shrubland ecosystem, although these were also found as outliers in some basins in the north-eastern highlands where lower rainfall and heavy clay soils seem to have prevented colonisation by forest species. This northern outlier was characterised by Brigalow (*Acacia harpophylla*) whereas the southern core areas were dominated by Mallee (*E. oleosa*) and Mulga (*Acacia aneura*).

As suggested in the description of the woodlands, the tree forms in drier areas tended to have a bushy character with multiple branching trunks. The extreme example in the shrublands is found in the mallee species which have not one trunk, but many, branching successively to merging canopies 25–30 ft (8–9 m) high. Often these stands were dense thickets of intertwined trunks, impassable to man or large animals, with canopies so mixed as to give dense shade and prevent all but the hardiest of grasses and heaths from surviving in competition (Fig. 4.5). In such impenetrable 'scrubs' large animals were rare. Only rodents such as jerboa-rats (*Notomys* spp.), small hare-wallabies (*Lagorchestes* spp.) and rat-kangaroos, reptiles such as small harmless whip snakes and venomous tiger snakes, geckoes and small lizards, small birds such as honey eaters and ground running Mallee Fowl (*Leipoa ocellata*) along with the ubiquitous ants and bush flies were abundant.

The Mulga and Brigalow forms were taller and generally more open, but

Fig. 4.5 Peebinga silo, Murray Mallee, S.A.
Peebinga is the terminus of a spur wheat railway line built into the South Australian mallee in 1914. Poorer than average soils have discouraged clearance of this mallee despite the presence of both railway and the silo, serving scattered farms closeby, but rarely filled. The township has a post office and run-down store.

still difficult to traverse and, where surface water was scarce, relatively inhospitable to man or beast.

The grasslands

Approximately one-quarter of this continent had an original cover of grass species while another quarter had either a mixture of grasses and woodland or grasses and shrubs. In effect, grasses covered the largest area of any of the major species of vegetation – a fact which probably was the result of the relatively large area of arid or semi-arid climate but also possibly the result of some human action as we shall see in the next chapter.

Most of the grasslands lay in the northern half of the continent and had a seasonal dry period during which the grasses matured and set seed for the next growing season. The higher rainfall areas of the eastern grassland carried the perennial Flinders and Mitchell grasses, while the drier western and interior areas carried more saltbushes (*Atriplex* spp.) and spinifex (*Troidia* spp.) (Fig. 2.5). After heavy seasonal rains the plains of the grasslands were a dense carpet of multicoloured annual flowers and succulent herbs, such as white and yellow daisies (*Helipterum* spp.) and purple bindy-i (*Calotis* spp.) interspersed with, or occasionally dominated by, tussocks of the perennial grasses up to 5–6 ft (1.5 m) in height. In droughts the plains might appear to be completely devoid of vegetation – the annuals having dried up and blown away and the perennials reduced to scattered black tufts of last season's growth.

Animal life tended to be seasonally varied with marsupials and birds extending their feeding from the wood and shrublands in the wet season but gradually reducing in numbers as the dry season progressed. Large wallabies (*Wallabia* spp.) and emus (*Dromaius novae-hollandiae*), cockatoos and galahs (*Kakatoë* spp.) and Zebra finches (*Poëphila guttata*) would move through the grasslands, rarely remaining all year in any one location.

The only permanent inhabitants of specific localities appear to have been the termites (*Armitermes, Drepanotermes, Nasutitermes* and *Tumulitermes*), whose role – along with that of their remote relatives the ants – is only now being fully documented. The grazing activity of termites in the grassland seems to have been an important factor not only in affecting the availability of grasses but the nature and composition of the local soils. Thus it has been claimed recently that in good (wet) seasons over 150 nests (of *Drepanotermes* spp.) per acre (*c*. 380 per hectare) have been recorded and several hundred pounds of forage per acre removed each year. The scavenging effects of the termites, the bare mounds of excavated earth over their nests and the compacted bare area around them have been claimed to be significant influences on micro-patterns of soil erosion in the grasslands, reducing the capacity of the soil to receive, hold, and germinate seeds in the next wet season.

Periodically, after heavy rains and mild winters locust (*Chorotoicetes terminifera*) hatchings would reach plague proportions and clouds of 'hoppers' would move downwind stripping bare all vegetation in their path until themselves destroyed or decimated by birds or larger insects in their turn.

The deserts

The core of the continent, some 12 per cent of its area, may be classed as a desert ecosystem where plant and animal life is dominated by general drought conditions only occasionally broken by effective rainfalls. The higher central ranges of the Shield Zone, with the less arid micro-climates and ecological niches which they offered, separated the western from the eastern deserts.

The sand deserts formed parallel linear ridges of coarse red to yellow brown dune sands some 20 to 30 ft (6–9 m) high separated by vales of loamier greyer sandy soils up to 1 mile (1.6 km) wide. Bare mobile sand might be found on the crests of the dunes but elsewhere vegetation held the surface relatively firmly. Spinifex, cane grass (*Zygochloa* spp.) and salt-bushes and bluebushes (*Kochia* spp.) covered the higher slopes while isolated mulga or mallee trees might be found on the vales (Fig. 2.3), except where as in the Channel Country surface drainage brought sufficient moisture for coolabah (*E. coolabah*) trees (Fig. 2.6).

Where sands gave way to bedrock, gibber plains of wind-polished pebbles stretched to the horizon, broken by remnant buttes of higher plains or dry beds of intermittent creeks lined by mulga or myalls (*Acacia sowdenii* or *A. pendula*) (Fig. 2.2). After rains the succulent purple flowering herb Parakeelya (*Calandrinia* spp.) would dot the gibbers, and daisies cluster in low places where water had been trapped long enough to percolate into the pockets of soil.

Occasionally, among the sand dunes or on lower-lying bedrock, clay pans and salt flats would break the thin scatter of vegetation. Here were to be found only the hardiest of plants – small salt-tolerant herbs – but most of the time, over most of their alternately rock-hard or salt-encrusted surfaces plants were absent.

Among the stones, in and around the dunes and sheltered by the sparse bushes and shrubs, a sparse but highly specialised and adapted animal and insect life managed to survive. The extremes of midday heat and dessication were usually avoided by nocturnal activities or limited daytime exposure and the general lack of surface moisture was countered by low metabolic rates, highly efficient water use and periods of estivation during the summer. Thus scorpions, spiders and termites provided food for lizards, goannas and snakes, and the native bush flies feasted on the remains and excrement. Birds were occasional visitors, most following the surface waters as they dried out after rains – their presence indeed being used later by European explorers as sure signs of water nearby.

The alpine ecosystem

At the opposite end of the temperature spectrum, above *c.* 6000 ft (1800 m) in a small area of Mt Kosciusko Plateau and above 3600 ft

(1200 m) on the central plateau of Tasmania (a total of less than 0.1% of the continent) was an ecosystem limited by a short growing season for plants and the possibility of snow cover for one or two months in the winter.

The transition to this Alpine Ecosystem from the Sclerophyll Forest was through a zone of open stands of subalpine woodland, mainly of the snow gum (*E. niphophila*) with a ground cover of herbs and summer 'snow grass' (*Danthonia nudiflora*). This formed an altitudinal zone approximately 1000 ft (300 m) in height before the true alpine heath was encountered at its higher limit.

In conditions which varied from the winter extremes of abundant moisture and low, often freezing, temperatures to the summer high temperatures and droughts from frequent wind exposure, plants tended to be small, compact and hardy. Thus the alpine heath was dominantly of snow grasses and herbs with patches of badly drained fen vegetation (*Carex* spp. and *Sphagnum* spp.) in the valleys, and on more exposed slopes, low growing heaths (*Oxylobium* and *Podocarpus* spp.) showing the effects of wind-blasting in the 'die-back' of windward branches.

Summer brought a rapid flowering of the herbs and seeding of the grasses with the invasion of the Bogong Moths (*Agrotis infusa*) into the subalpine woodland to feed on the flower nectar and to breed. Butterflies and bees moved onto the flowering slopes and birds followed. The cooler temperatures of autumn saw an exodus down slope and winter snows blanketed the bare landscape before the spring thaw set the creeks in motion again and the green shoots broke through the semidecayed ground litter once more.

The origins of the ecosystems

The patterns of the ecosystems of *c.* 1770 present certain anomalies which while themselves interesting from a scientific viewpoint, illustrate some of the problems inherent in any attempt to explain the origins of those ecosystems.

Anomalies in the patterns of ecosystems

So far our description has tended to suggest a system of concentric zones of differing ecosystems from outer richer to inner poorer zones – the main distinctions between which appeared to be the result of the increasing importance of aridity toward the centre of the continent. This generalisation falls down in detail however, and the apparent link between climate and vegetation is not as straightforward as might at first appear. Shrublands, for example, occurred in the southern half of the continent where rainfall would in theory have supported woodlands; heaths and grasslands occurred where shrubs might have been expected, and in the north, grasslands occupied lands where woodlands might have been expected from the available rainfalls. All these anomalies in fact were negative in the sense that vegetation was found to be 'poorer' than that which might have been expected.

There were, however, positive anomalies also, that is vegetation 'richer' than the contemporary climate would, in theory, support. Thus in the core of the desert areas of the centre were islands of subtropical flora and fauna in the more humid ecological riches of Palm Valley and the valleys between the Olgas, Northern Territory. Palm Valley is the best known, containing *Livistona manae* palms whose nearest relatives are on the northern and Queensland coasts. A zoologist (Laseron, 1953, p. 75) described the valleys of the Mt Olga group as late as 1953:

> The variety of plants is astonishing, and it is from here that most of the 600 species recorded from the area were taken. The bottoms of the gorges are filled with a dense semitropical scrub, matted together with lianas and vines, and containing a wealth of animal life, rock wallabies, lizards, spiders, insects and land shells.

Within a few hundred metres of these valleys lay the sands of the central desert areas.

Specific adaptations to the environment

Such anomalies existed alongside remarkable evidence of species adaptation to environmental conditions – particularly adaptions to the increasing stress of aridity in the continental interior. At times of drought many life-forms were drastically modified – herbs and annual grasses disappeared, perennial grasses became dormant and old leaves were broken up and blown away by the wind, while trees and shrubs became generally dormant. At such times the animal and insect life, its food supply seriously depleted, was itself significantly reduced, either by starvation or emigration to more favoured locations. Yet given drought-breaking rains, prolific plant, animal and insect life reappeared as if by magic – their ability to survive the stresses giving evidence of complex adaptive mechanisms to ensure their survival.

For the plants, many survived the drought stress as seeds within tough pods able to survive high temperatures and often requiring mechanical abrasion, or fire-cracking, or solution by rainfall of chemical inhibitors in the cover before the seed could germinate. There is some evidence to suggest that mulga stands of relatively even age may reflect a past fire and flood combination which caused rapid germination of many seeds, and there is evidence of the Oldman Saltbush (*Atriplex nummularia*) setting two types of seeds which germinate under different moisture conditions – hence effectively providing a 'fail-safe' survival mechanism.

For the animals and insects survival derived either from endurance of the drought in egg or larvae forms which were triggered to life after favourable rains (as with the grasshoppers, locusts and flies), or creation of micro-environments in burrows or treeholes where aridity was much reduced (as with most of the reptiles and small rodents), or ability to travel widely and swiftly, to escape the droughts and return to take advantage of the post-drought conditions. Recent evidence has claimed that the Red or Plains kangaroo can travel at least 120 miles (190 km) in search of food in droughts, and the Zebra Finch not only migrates to favoured areas but may have larger than normal egg clutches and breed continuously in particularly good seasons, with no breeding at all during severe drought periods.

This evidence of a fine adjustment to environmental stress is not universal however. Thus the drought-resistant protective seed pods are found in *Banksia, Grevillea* and *Hakea* species in locations where restrictions on germination seem hardly necessary since general conditions are much more humid than the continental interior. Further, some of the *Banksia* and *Eucalyptus* species have maximum growth in the summer even though they are growing in a summer–dry winter–rain part of the continent. This latter lack of coincidence of the plant growth cycle with environmentally *optimal* conditions suggests some further anomalies in the patterns of Australian flora and fauna.

Evolution of Australian ecosystems

The basic individuality of Australian ecosystem had been defined spatially by Wallace although it had been recognised ever since the botanists with Captain Cook attempted to classify their specimens. This individuality seems to have been derived from a long period of relative isolation dating from prehistoric time (possibly over 50 million years) – a period during which the migration of animals and insects and the spread of plants into the continent was interrupted and those already there had time to evolve peculiar adaptions to their particular environment. Perhaps the best example is the marsupial order whose ancestry is claimed to be American and species of which are thought to have entered Australia from the north before the severance of the 'land bridge' with Asia. By 1770, however, these initial invaders had evolved into a wide range of forms from rat and mouse-like creatures, through ant-eaters, bandicoots, possums and koalas to the kangaroos. Along the way, larger forms had flourished on the inland plains in times of more humid climates, only to be exterminated when the subsequently drier climates reduced the carrying-capacity of the country and the attacks of prehistoric indigenous man-made inroads in their numbers. The bones of these ancestors of the surviving kangaroos were to be found in the clay pans of the Lake Eyre Basin by European explorers.

The individuality of Australian ecosystems does not of itself explain the anomalies and we need to turn to the paleo-botanical records for clues to the past environmental conditions in which much of the plant and animal life evolved.

Most authorities suggest that the plants found in Australia *c.* 1770 could be grouped into three major genera. First, Eremaean or Australian, that is found only on this continent, New Zealand and some islands to the north including New Guinea; second, Temperate or Antarctican, including species also found in Antarctica, South America and the colder highlands of New Guinea; and third, Tropical or Malaysian, including species found in the islands to the north and the Asian Continent. For the insects a similar pattern has been recognised.

These groupings, substantiated by the occurrence of common species, have been interpreted as evidence for the migration of species into the continent from the separate areas at different times. Thus Burbridge (1960) suggested that 47 per cent of the plant species of the central Eremaean Zone were endemic to Australia; while only 31–47 per cent in the Temperate Zone and 14 per cent in the Tropical Zone. She argued therefore that the northern Tropical Zone showed most evidence of later invasion by alien (i.e. non-Australian) plants.

The concept of plant and animal invasions might explain some of the variation in patterns of species since maps of species might be interpreted as showing 'tide-marks' of the advance and retreat of different genera. They also might show evidence of a contest not only between rival life-forms but between those life-forms and the environments – what Laseron picturesquely described as a 'grim and relentless war of the plants, a war that has gone on ceaselessly for some 50 million years'. He distinguished only two main combatants however, 'the massed battalions of the jungle and the guerilla forces of the Xerophytes' – the plants adapted to the warm humid tropics and those adapted to the hot arid tropics. Like most wars, however, reality was probably much more complex than that.

Whereas the broad patterns of genera might reflect the history of plant and animal migration – the duration and extent of the continental exposure to these influxes, the detailed patterns are more likely to reflect the adaptation of life-forms to the local environment. This environment was not climatically stable, however, and the increasing aridity of the last 40 000 years in the interior may have killed off all but the Palm Valley and Mt Olga's remnants of the humid tropical flora and fauna which once covered the whole area, reduced the numbers of invading animal species and encouraged the spread of endemic species better able to cope with the arid conditions.

The negative anomalies of vegetation too poor for the climate might reflect accessibility with regard to the sources and routes of migration of richer floras or the inherently infertile nature of most of the continental soils. The latter seems the stronger explanation, since most of the poorer stands (shrubs such as mallee on potential southern woodland sites, and grasses in potential shrublands in northern Australia) are in fact on highly leached sandy soils, deficient in trace elements as well as nitrogen and phosphorus.

However, not all of the anomalies – particularly these negative anomalies – can be explained in this way and for other possible factors we must look to the human population of the continent in 1770 and the history of their evolution and possible environmental impact.

5
The Indigenes

Although to a casual observer the continent may have seemed empty of human life, in reality a complex pattern of cultural groups were making successful use of the continental resources. Their numbers were small, perhaps 300 000 but their activities appear to have ranged over the whole continent, finding enough to sustain life in all the major ecosystems. Their adaptation to the contemporary resources, their impact on the resources themselves, their character as the original inhabitants of the continent prior to European occupation, and their role as the ancestors of the present-day Aborigines are worth investigation.

The problem of reconstruction

To establish the character of the Indigenes prior to the arrival of the first permanent European settlers poses several problems. In the first place very little material evidence of the original population has yet been discovered; this has been partly the result of the lack of material goods in the original culture, partly the result of the extremely rapid collapse of the indigenous cultures after first contact with the European invaders, and partly the youthful nature of archaeology in Australia. The evidence which has remained has survived often by the accident of remoteness, as the case of the rock drawings and paintings which are now concentrated in the central and northern areas but probably were much more widespread originally. Survival also may have resulted from the very unobtrusive nature of the evidence itself, as the case of the coastal shell middens (Fig. 5.1) and inland archaeological sites which are only now being recognised. In effect the reconstruction is based on very scanty evidence, although archaeological discoveries in the 1960s and 1970s have suggested that there is much more to be learned from this source than previously believed. As a result the comments here may be 'dated' very rapidly in the later 1970s.

Lack of recorded evidence is but one problem. Another is the fact that over the years since first European contact official attitudes to the Indigenes and Aborigines have tended to deliberately isolate them from the white settlers and to reduce contact to a minimum. In effect therefore the collapse of the indigenous culture has been allowed to go unrecorded for the general public, being noted only in the brief reports of the few responsible

Fig. 5.1 Aboriginal hearth and shell midden, Younghusband Peninsula, S.A. The fire-blackened stones (brought some distance into the site) form the core around which are the white fragments of mussel-shells. The ocean is *c.* 328 ft (100 m) to the left of the picture. Similar middens have been dated as *c.* 2000 years old. Preservation appears to have been after burial under the mobile sand dunes, with reappearance as the sand moves on to the right of the picture.

(*Source:* K. L. Bardsley)

Government officials and the private accounts of the missionaries. The official reports of the Protectors, appointed early in the nineteenth century to 'protect' Aborigines from Anglo–Australian exploitation, in fact were rarely more than administrative accounts of expenditure on items supplied to the Aborigines, doles of food or blankets, and the condition of the people themselves was usually ignored or indicated only by inference. The same can be said for much of the missionary files, although here at least was some attempt to describe the condition of the people, if only as background material to moral judgments on their condition.

The physical and mental isolation of the Indigenes and later Aborigines from the general body of the settlers was emphasised by the difference in the official policies towards them. Each colony faced the same problem of how to cope with the population, but each tackled it differently, in detail if not basic intent. As a result, the factual records in the official archives vary according to the policy towards these people: here a concern for the dwindling numbers and increasing distress is illustrated by returns of population and location by districts, there the lack of interest is marked by a blank in the records or by a few sheets of official accounts for handouts of food and woollen blankets. Not only the material facts of the indigenous occupation are few, but the potentially useful secondary sources are basically uneven in value and often very limited in scope.

Were the sources themselves to be abundant, interpretation would still have to be cautious because it is evident that in many cases the facts which have survived have been in part preserved for a specific reason. The reactions of the observers and the policies of governments and missionaries carry evidence of preconceived standards against which the Indigenes were measured and usually found wanting. For some the indigenous life was Hell on earth, for others that Eden from which the Fall had precipitated civilised man. In neither case was the result an objective account.

Indigenous culture in 1770

Although the most recent investigations are tending to stress regional differences in the indigenous culture, some basic generalisations are relevant and useful for an appreciation of the continental scene in 1770. The first basic point, and one which impressed all observers immediately on first contact, was the paucity and simplicity of the material effects of the Indigenes. Not only were their tools and equipment simple – 'primitive' by European standards – but they had a range of skills and artifacts more limited than their neighbours in New Guinea or New Zealand. Thus, although they possessed knowledge of fire, they knew nothing of the cultivation of plants, or the herding of livestock. In essence they were hunters, gatherers and fisherfolk. Further, their dependence upon their knowledge of the indiscriminate occurrence of natural foodstuffs was heightened by a lack of knowledge of food preservation. Periodic famine was endemic from the hunters in the desert interior to the coastal fishermen. Without any adequate buffer against the vagarities of the food resources of any one location the cultures were forced to be nomadic, for the natural surpluses occurring irregularly in time and space could only be used by highly mobile consumers. In extremity, when mobility alone had proved insufficient answer and food supplies were inadequate, there is evidence that infanticide and abortion were practised, although whether as an immediate or long term relief measure has not been established.

Environmental stresses and the limitations of a nomadic resource use system appear to have kept the population densities low. If the figure of 300 000 is tentatively accepted as the most logically appealing of the many guesses which have appeared, this would give a continental density of one person per 10 square miles (1 per 25 km^2), much lower than the Maori two per square mile and New Guinea highlands over 100 per square mile. Recent research has suggested that nomadic land use particularly of the hunting–

gathering type is a relatively efficient means of resource use – in terms of energy inputs and returns, but whether the lack of agriculture was a deliberate negative decision (contact across Torres Strait apparently exposed Indigenes in the Cape York to Papuan agriculturalists) or lack of opportunity is still debatable.

In recent years also there have been suggestions that the population in 1770 was not in as harmonious a balance with its environment as was previously thought. A decline in numbers from diseases (among them smallpox), possibly caught in the contact with Malay fishermen operating off the northern coasts for about 300 years prior to 1770, seems to have been evident even on the southeast coast at first European contact, and the Indigenes appear to have made a significant impact on their environment as we shall see.

The pattern of people

Allowing for a possible decline, already evident by 1770, there is no doubt that the overall low density was considerably varied in the different ecosystems. Large areas of the interior were probably uninhabited for most of the time, being visited only after exceptionally heavy rains had left abundant surface water and drawn in wildlife.

This empty interior must have contrasted with a relatively densely populated periphery, with pockets of above-average densities along the coast and some of the more reliable interior watercourses. In what was to become New South Wales, one estimate put the original population at 55 000, of which 40 000 were located in coastal valleys, 10 000 on the western slopes of the tablelands and only about 5000 along the Murray–Darling River frontages (Bell, 1962). This kind of ratio between fringe and interior seems to have been borne out elsewhere.

Bearing in mind the limitations of the method and data used, the map showing the density of Indigenes (Fig. 5.2) suggests several significant variations in the pattern of population distribution over the continent prior to the disruption from European intrusion. For the bulk of the continent, densities were less than the average for the whole, hence most of the population was concentrated in relatively few and limited areas. The pockets of densities more than twice the average occur particularly along the northern, eastern and southern coasts, but there are interesting exceptions to this rule in the pockets of the subtropical highlands of east central Queensland and the Murray Valley. The coastal fringe of high densities, however, is not continuous and it is possible to see a major gap in Queensland which separates the north-eastern from the south-eastern high density core areas. Just why is difficult to say. Elsewhere in the continent densities are only above average in areas where water was a reasonably certain resource, as by the water holes in the Channel Country, the Darling River tributaries and north-western Australia. The Indigenes seem to have been found in greatest numbers in the eastern half of the continent, within the richest ecosystems

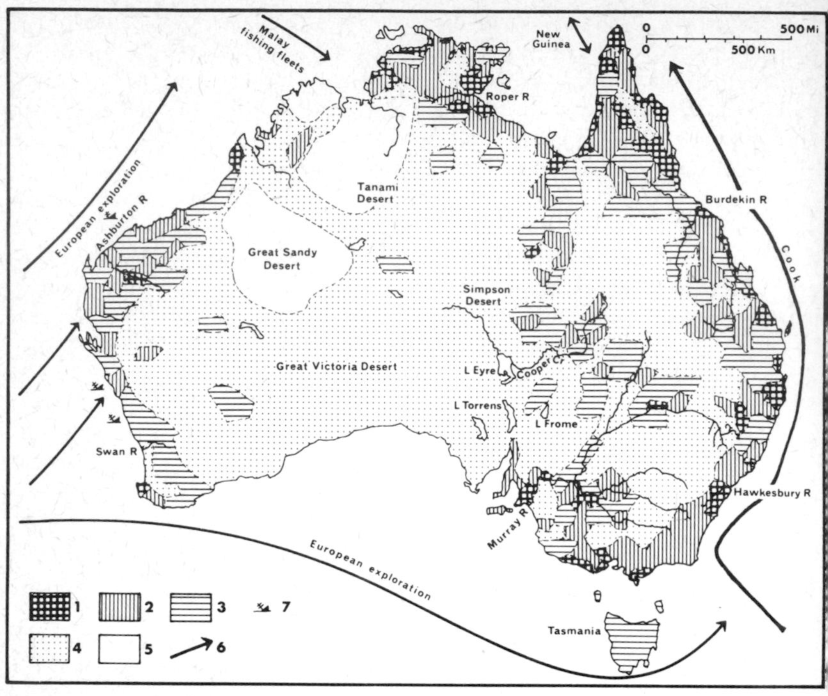

Fig. 5.2 Australia 1770: the quiet continent
Indigenous population densities shown as: **1**, More than twice continental average; **2**, Less than twice the average; **3**, Below the average but not below half the average; **4**, Less than half the average; **5**, No data. Densities calculated assuming each varying tribal area (Tindale, 1940) supported 450 people. Intrusions: **6**, Lines of external contact or approach of intruders by 1770; **7**, Major European wrecks pre-1770.
(*Source:* See text)

and the areas most heavily wooded, where in fact the European intruders were to make their most significant mark.

The explanations for this pattern seems to lie partly in the nature of their origins and their detailed and varied responses to the challenges of their habitats. The origins of the Indigenes is still uncertain. What is agreed is that they do not appear to have evolved in the continent, but immigrated into it from Asia via the island chains of southeast Asia and New Guinea, using the same routeways as did much of the continental flora and fauna at earlier dates.

Traditionally, two indigenous cultures – groups of peoples with similar technologies, social organisation and physiological traits – have been recognised. The oldest, or Tasmanoid, was thought to have existed only in Tasmania and a pocket in the Atherton Tableland of Queensland in 1770. Of more negroid features and shorter stature, they were physically distinguishable from mainland Indigenes, and this combined with their less sophisticated array of weapons and hunting–gathering techniques and their limited and remote locations, suggested an earlier arrival and retreat in the face of land invaders. The younger, Australoid culture included a wider range of weapons, the semidomesticated dingo, and seemed to have been a later arrival in the continent. Recent discoveries of rock carvings in central Australia and of burials in Victoria have suggested the possibility of two other groups, but the full examination of the finds has not yet been completed.

If we accept the invasion hypothesis and recognise, as now seems likely, that at least four separate cultural groups entered the continent, possibly at different times, the fundamental question remains, when? Geologists and geomorphologists currently hypothesise that during the last major world ice ages the associated shrinkage of sea-levels would have lain bare land bridges between Asia, the islands and the Australian continent sufficient to facilitate plant, animal and human migrations into a continent whose moister climates would present an even more attractive array of ecosystems. Recent archaeological evidence has suggested remains *c.* 30 000 years old in Australia and the most recent, 1973, find has been of so-called relatives, some 10 000–20 000 years old, of Java Man, who was supposed to have died out in Java 100 000 years ago. If correct, then the land bridge concept is plausible since sea-level falls sufficient to bare the continent shelf north of Australia have been estimated as *c.* 17 000–20 000 years ago, 40 000–50 000 years ago, and 130 000–140 000 years ago. Which group came when, however, is still uncertain.

Nevertheless, by 1770, only two of the four cultures had apparently survived, yet within the broad divisions of the Australoids and Tasmanoids a variety of socio-economic patterns and population densities had evolved in response partly to the varied ecosystems within which the groups were existing.

The organisation of the various aboriginal groups appears to have been on a tribal structure and anthropologists have estimated that from 500 to over 700 tribes originally existed. The definition of tribes is basically on linguistic affinities but there is evidence that they had a physical expression in that they usually compromised about 450 people (although the figure could range from 150 to 1500) and had a territory peculiar to the tribe, within which the tribe had exclusive hunting and gathering rights and which it was prepared to defend against intruders. The boundaries of the tribal areas appear to have been generally vague, and in times of plenty may have overlapped those of adjacent tribes. In times of stress, however, a core area seems to have been recognised in which trespass was seen as justification for conflict between tribes. Within this tribal area were located the special sites for communal meetings, initiation ceremonies, dance grounds and totem sanctuaries for the tribal gods. Few, if any, artificial structures were associated with these sites; to the Anglo–Australian eye only an occasional circle of undressed stones, or a suspiciously artificial clearing in the scrub, or an 'unnatural' collection of tree branches, grass, bark or stones, possibly daubed with ochre, was any indication of human occupation. The tribe itself had physical unity only on the ceremonial occasions, when most of the members would be gathered in one place at the same time. Otherwise the tribe was split up into family groups or hordes of fifteen to twenty people wandering over the tribal territory as loose-knit units. Leadership was not fixed on any one person for any length of time; for the day-to-day decisions the best hunter had authority, but for the ceremonials and rites the elders were consulted.

With a nomadic culture, evidence of permanent occupation would not be expected, and with the exception of the features of the special sites mentioned above, there was no evidence of any permanent occupation of the land when the first white settlers landed. The only settlement site was the temporary camp, where a hearth of charcoal and burnt stones, a group of decaying windbreaks of bark, leaves and timber, with scattered refuse and animal bones, marked the site of a brief halt in the perpetual march in search of food. Of evidence of permanent villages there was none.

Equipment was simple by comparison with European technology but showed a variety fully adequate for the limited needs of hunting–gathering. Lacking the wheel or any form of draught or domestic animal except the dingo, all transport was by man power and as a result only the essentials, weapons, fire, and occasionally small containers of bark, woven grass or bone for the seeds, fruits, roots and possibly water, were carried. For clothing there was generally little need and locally less regard. Weapons were of wood and local stone and included spears, clubs, throwing sticks, digging sticks, hand axes and hammers, and in the fishing communities, fish nets of grass and fibre, and crude bark canoes cut in one piece from suitable trees. The weapons of wood, bone and stone were, however, handled with great skill and this, together with their bushcraft in the chase, enabled the Indigenes to achieve considerable efficiency within the limits of their economy.

Against the apparent paucity of their material impedimenta should also be set the considerable knowledge of the environment in which they lived. For certain parts of the continent it may be no exaggeration to say that the Indigenes knew all the available edible plants, animals and insects. In the northeast some 240 species of edible plants were known, a list which included some only edible after treatment with lime to neutralise the toxic acids, and a further ninety useful species of molluscs were common knowledge. Knowledge went beyond the mere occurrence of foods however. In north central Australia from five to nine different climatic seasons were recognised, times when supplies of game and plant foods varied, when certain routine jobs had to be completed, weapons made or repaired, when certain ceremonies and initiations had to be observed, and when certain parts of the tribal areas were more attractive for occupation than others.

In the details, the response to the environment seems to have reflected the local resources and produced a regional variation in the basic culture and economy, divided into four basic types of economy (McCarthy, 1959). A mixed hunting, fishing and collecting economy was found in the areas where the range of immediately edible foodstuffs was most extensive; that is, the subtropical forest of the northern and north-eastern coastlines. South and east of these, but still coastal in location, were the fishing and shell-collecting economies of the east coast and Tasmania, where, in contrast with the first type, there was a seasonal winter food shortage. Inland from both economies was a third type, the collectors of the mountains and forests, relying only upon honey, fruits and roots, and only found on the Atherton Tableland. The final type was the hunters and collectors of the dry interior of the continent, stalking all forms of animal life, often trailing the wild dingoes to their prey and sharing it with them, and adding to their diet by roots, seeds and fruits in season. Of the types, McCarthy suggested that the third was the most primitive and may have reflected an island of the earlier Tasmanoid occupation surrounded by later Australoid invaders. Certainly the sequence of occupation of the continent may have affected the distribution of the various economies as much as it seems to have affected the cultural patterns. Significantly, the most varied and sophisticated economy was that closest to the much more highly sophisticated neighbours of Melanesia to the north, and in general the complexity of the economies tended to be reduced away from the supposed points of original entry in the north.

Indigenous environmental impact

With such a limited material economy, range of tools and technical skills, it might be argued that the landscape inhabited by the Indigenes differed little from that prior to their arrival in the continent. The extent of their effect on the landscape indeed is the subject of a debate not yet resolved. On the one hand it is argued that whatever impact there may have been locally, the overall picture remained unchanged by their occupance, whereas on the other hand it has been suggested that indigenous man and his dingo 'for a time may have assumed dominant roles in the faunal assemblages of the Australian Continent' and that the Aboriginal influence on plant life was considerable (Tindale, 1959). Both arguments have force. The hunting economy could make a direct impact only on the game and that in proportion to the number of the hunters, which we know to have been small. Similarly it would be difficult to prove that the fishermen made any significant impression on the supplies of salt or freshwater fish on a continental scale, nor would the gathering of seeds or fruits be anything but of local significance, even where the tribes were in closest competition, for in these locations the resources were naturally most varied and abundant. Yet the impact of prehistoric hunters on the large (by 1770 extinct) marsupials has been claimed to have so significantly depleted numbers by indiscriminate slaughter – what has been recognised elsewhere in the world as 'Pleistocene Overkill' – as to aid their final extermination. An equivalent argument for as significant an impact on the flora would be more difficult to substantiate.

Of probably greater significance were the indirect efforts of indigenous occupation, particularly through the deliberate or accidental use of fire. Both the preparation of food and the chase involved the use of fire and charcoal has been found associated with human remains, at least 18 000 years old. For the early Anglo–Australian explorers one of the clues as to the presence of Aborigines in the country ahead was the sight of smoke from their fires. Where such fires were allowed or encouraged to spread, the effect upon the vegetation must have been locally considerable. It has been suggested that much of the grassland of Australia could have been brought into being as a result of indigenous action. Some of the post climax (optimal) rain forests may have been destroyed in favour of invading sclerophyll (drought tolerant) forests, as the effects of his firestick were added to the changing climate in Early Recent time (10 000–20 000 years ago) (Tindale, 1959). The effects must have varied in significance from place to place. The Aboriginal smokes were most frequently remarked upon in the interior plains and occasional evidence of their burning of the vegetation is most common here, where the transition between the grasslands and the open woodlands probably provided the most suitable conditions for the use and effectiveness of fire against game and enemies, among them the explorers themselves. The evidence of use of fire in woodlands, which would be necessary to bear out Tindale's hypothesis, is less abundant although suggestions have been made of the burning of coastal swamp forests in Victoria (Gunson, 1968). Further, considering the possible time span and the supposed routeways of the indigenous groups into the continent from the north, it might be hypothesised that the northern lands would have had the longest exposure to this form of modification and here the presence of large areas of grassland in 1770 where woodland might have been expected climatically (Chapter 4) is a remarkable coincidence. By 1770 indigenous man may have already made an indelible mark upon the continental landscape.

Summary

Thus, by 1770, the continent was inhabited, albeit sparsely, by a variety of tribes showing evidence of at least two major cultural groups and a complex variety of adaptations to the local environments. Some of these northern tribes had experienced brief contact with other cultures, whether shipwrecked Europeans, camping Malay fishermen or bartering New Guinea tribesmen. But there is no evidence that the southern tribes who opposed Cook's landfall in 1770 had any idea of the danger or strength of these new invaders, or of the weaknesses of their own cultures in the face of the external stresses to come.

Part two

Australia 1970

6
The unquiet continent: Australia 1970

Were our observer of 1770 in his satellite to be transported in time to 1970, he would probably notice little change in the overall view of the continent. The basic shapes, the broad patterns of colour – red-brown core and dull-green fringe, the main movements of air and ocean – were all unchanged, at least at first glance. A closer look, however, would show many significant modifications.

The form of the land

While the basic patterns of land forms had not changed there were significant changes in local landscapes, particularly in the south and east of the continent. Here river channels had been straightened, estuary mud-flats reclaimed, swamps drained, shifting dunes along the coast stabilised, new man-made promontories built-out into the sea. Inland, new channels led river waters out across the dry plains in new lines of drainage and tunnels through the eastern rim of the continent added water from the short coastal rivers to the long meandering inland drainage systems. This additional water inland was supplemented by the flows of often hot and brackish subterranean water brought to the surface by artesian bores and pumps and allowed to flow unchecked along man-made bore drains until lost by seepage and evaporation.

Locally, even the surface of the land had changed. New man-made drainage patterns had created new valleys in miniature, but there were many other areas where the old smooth surfaces had been stripped away and the ground scarred by gullies, ditches, pot-holes and spoil-heaps. Beside these scars, new gravels had filled up old water holes and river courses and added new alluvial layers to the river flood plains.

New colours

In detail, the green girdle of the continent was broken in the south and east by patches of lighter tones, yellows and browns – new areas of grasslands and the seasonal changes of croplands. Here the dense green tree cover had been thinned and the lighter green grassland cover thickened and extended; there the trees had been replaced by cultivated land in cereals or new grasses. On the coast, patches of white showed new man-made salt pans and inland the blue of new lakes. Pinpoints of reds and blues linked by lines of grey-blue (macadamised) and white (gravel) roads showed the clusters of new settlements. At night, the lights from these were a broken circlet of diamonds along the southern and eastern fringes of the continent. Often, during the daylight hours, the larger of these settlement clusters would seem to give off a blue-grey haze, which rose first from the city and then plumed slowly out to sea on the land breeze. Occasionally, also, the rivers which ran close to or through these centres would be stained bilious shades of yellow and brown as the effluents they carried seeped away to the sea. Inland, the white plumes of bush fires would still be seen occasionally, while on the northeast coast in autumn were the pinpoint flares of sugar-cane fields burned of undergrowth before harvest, and inland the flares of burning gases lit the remote natural gas fields in the deserts.

New shapes

By 1970 such new shapes as had appeared were dominated by the regularity of surveyed grid lines. The new colours were in fact a lattice-work of browns and greens representing the surveyed blocks of fields and farms (Fig. 6.1). The edges of the scrublands were now clearly marked, the 'frontier' of farming was a patchwork, but of regular rectangular patches with fence lines marked by cardinal points and surveyors' compasses. Even the new pine woodlands – patches of darker denser green – were in regular regimented blocks. In the clusters of settlements the grid of roads and houses was a miniature of the grid in the country, and between these centres stretched the lines of surveyed road and railways, the poles and wires of telegraph, power and telephone links (Fig. 6.2). Only in the interior was regularity of new shapes less precise. Here, local roads and bush tracks wound less certainly across the countryside and from the air the radials of sheep and cattle tracks converged on the isolated watering points and bore drains.

New movements

Some old patterns of movement had disappeared by the 1970s. While the mutton birds still migrated along the coasts, whales and seals were rare in the bays and fewer in overall numbers offshore. On land, the numbers of most species of kangaroos, wallabies and emus had been drastically thinned and the smaller mobs were restricted generally to the inland areas.

In detail, however, the dominant impression was of new, more intensive and more rapid human movement. The leisurely migrations of nomadic hunters and gatherers had been replaced by the hustle of a technological society. Movement and contact between Australia and the rest of the world had markedly increased. The bark canoes of the Indigenes and the sailing prahas of the visiting Malay fishermen, had been replaced by the ocean liner and jet aircraft. In 1770 the visitor would have taken six months by sailing

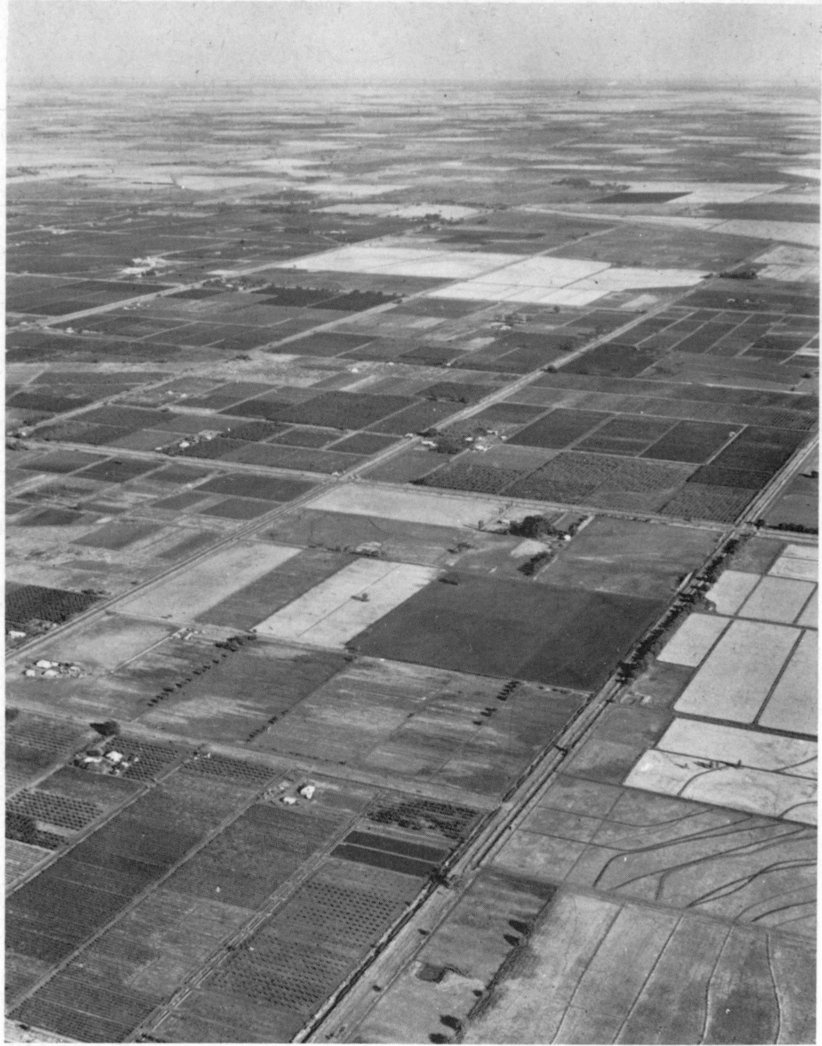

Fig. 6.1 The surveyor's imprint
The grid pattern of irrigated lands in the Murrumbidgee Irrigation Area, N.S.W. Both tree crops, vines and field crops (rice in right foreground) are illustrated.

(*Source:* Department of Tourism, N.S.W.)

ship from London to Sydney; in the 1870s the time by sailing clipper was down to just over two months; steamers cut that to just over one month by the 1920s and just under one month by the 1970s; and jet air flights had cut the travel time to just over thirty hours by 1970. The distances are still the same and for example the sea routes are enormous: 12 396 nautical miles

Fig. 6.2 Dalby, Darling Downs, Qld.
A regional centre for the wheatlands and expanding gas and oil fields of the Darling Downs.
Main shopping street in foreground, with railway link to Brisbane, and grain silos in centre. Most buildings are of one storey except for occasional shops in the main street and wide street grid-plan is obvious, as well as the ever-present cars.

(*Source:* State Public Relations Bureau, Qld.)

(22 300 km) Sydney to London, 6467 nautical miles (11 640 km) Sydney to San Francisco, 9704 nautical miles (17 460 km) Sydney to New York, 6279 nautical miles (11 340 km) Sydney to Cape Town and 4316 nautical miles (7880 km) Sydney to Tokyo. Yet they no longer mean remoteness, only a question of costs and these, both economic and psychological, are being reduced.

As a result of this conquest of what one Australian writer (Blainey, 1966) has called 'The Tyranny of Distance' the volume of movement to and from, as well as within, the continent has increased markedly (Fig. 6.3). To the west, north and east, the oceans are dotted by liners, refrigerated cargo ships and oil tankers carrying the raw materials, fuels and manufactures of the complex technological society which now inhabits the continent. The

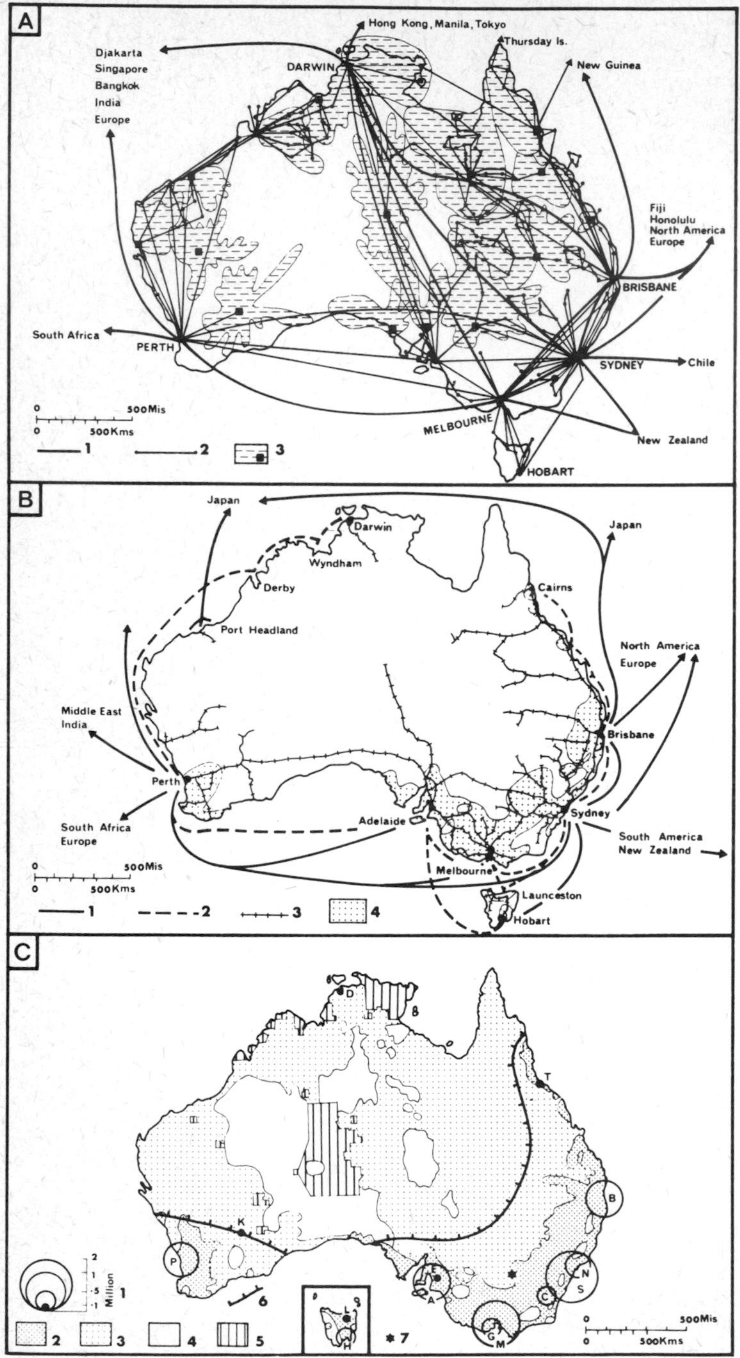
A
Hong Kong, Manila, Tokyo
Thursday Is.
Djakarta
Singapore
Bangkok
India
Europe
DARWIN
New Guinea
Fiji
Honolulu
North America
Europe
BRISBANE
South Africa
PERTH
SYDNEY
Chile
MELBOURNE
New Zealand
HOBART
0 500Mis
0 500Kms
1
2
3
B
Japan
Darwin
Japan
Wyndham
Derby
Port Headland
Cairns
North America
Europe
Middle East
India
Brisbane
Perth
Adelaide
Sydney
South Africa
Europe
South America
New Zealand
Melbourne
Launceston
Hobart
0 500Mis
0 500Kms
1
2
3
4
C
D
T
B
K
P
E
A
N
S
C
G
M
L
H
2
1
.5
.1
Million
1
2
3
4
5
6
7
0 500Mis
0 500Kms

major lines of these movements are across the southern Indian Ocean to Europe via the Cape (as long as the Suez Canal remains closed), diagonally across the Pacific Ocean to the west coast of North America and via the Panama Canal to the east coast, and finally, in increasing volume, north to Singapore, Japan and Hong Kong. To the south move only the foreign whaling fleets and the occasional supply ship for the Antarctic bases.

Above the oceans, in the air lanes at 30 000–35 000 ft (9000–10 000 m), move the international passenger aircraft to and from Australia. From Sydney or Melbourne, where most international flights terminate, local air services use the air space up to *c.* 30 000 ft (9000 m) to link the continental centres of settlement. Beneath the oceans by submarine cable, above the oceans by radio wave and television signal, move thousands of messages per year between the continent and the rest of the world. Sporting events from the other side of the world, latest share prices of local mining companies, orders for wool, meat and wheat, personal news from immigrant families, all now tie the continent to the rest of the world.

Within the continent the movement of people and goods has multiplied over the years since 1770. Where indigenous movements were local or at most regional, modern movements combine local, regional and continental scales. The daily journey to work of a suburban commuter by private car or public transport is perhaps up to 10 or 20 miles (16–32 km) each way, his holiday trip by car or public transport might cover 1000 miles (1600 km) each way. Within the farm or pastoral property movements might be from a few hundred yards to 50 100 miles (80–160 km), between farm or property and local market might be a journey of up to 2000 miles (3200 km) and to ultimate market beyond the continent over 11 000 miles (17 000 km). Despite the distances (Perth–Sydney, 2461 miles (3938 km) by train, taking sixty hours; 2120 miles (3392 km) by aircraft, taking five hours) the shuttle of people and goods by car, lorry, train and aircraft is a ceaseless movement across the continent in the 1970s.

Fig. 6.3 Australia 1970: the unquiet continent

A. Patterns of air communications
1, International air routes; 2, National air routes; 3, Royal Flying Doctor Service areas with radio headquarters

B. Patterns of land and sea communications
1, Main international sea routes (freight); 2, Main national sea routes (freight); 3, Main railway systems; 4, Road density >0.5 mile (km)/mile^2 (km^2).

C. Population
1, Largest and next largest city populations in each state: P, Perth; K, Kalgoorlie; A, Adelaide; E, Elizabeth; M, Melbourne; G, Geelong; H, Hobart; L, Launceston; C, Canberra; S, Sydney; N, Newcastle; B, Brisbane; T, Townsville; D, Darwin. 2, Population density >1/mile^2; 3, Population density <1/mile^2; 4, Uninhabited; 5, Main Aboriginal reserves; 6, Outer edge of area dominated by Aboriginal population; 7, Mean centre of gravity of total Australian population.

(*Source:* Australia, 1962)

The new relevance of the seasons

The seasons, although apparently unchanged, had a more varied impact and relevance in the 1970s. The coming of the rains is still relevant to the seasonal flooding of the draining patterns, the rhythms of local ecosystems and the few nomads still dependent upon them, but they have a wider relevance – to pastoralists awaiting a break in the seasonal drought and new forage for their livestock, to wheat farmers trying to sow before the heaviest downpours make the loamy soils unworkable, to proprietors of ski-resorts in the southern 'Australian Alps' gauging the snowfalls, to city water engineers watching the storage levels of their mountain catchments.

The dry northern winter is the period of greatest activity not only for native animals in search of dwindling water and forage, but as the clay plains become trafficable once more it is the period of maximum human activity. Pastoralists are out repairing fences, grading their tracks, cleaning out bores and stock-watering troughs. It is the fieldwork season for scientific research teams from universities and Government agencies; the travelling season for southern-based politicians to inspect the 'underdeveloped north' when the environmental problems seem less depressing; the travelling season for the tourist buses raising the dust of remote bush-tracks, grinding over the rock ledges of Palm Valley and through the sands of the Finke River in temperatures which are warm but tolerable.

The dry southern summer coincides with the annual school holidays and from late December to end of January it seems as if at least half the country's population is camped on the beaches or along the few inland lakes and waterways. At night the gleams from thousands of tents and holiday shacks dot the coast between the constant sodium-orange and magnesium-blue glow of the major cities' street-lights. In the city centres, the offices are closed or at least at half-strength, the streets still crowded but mainly with visitors. In the suburbs the hoses are playing on the emerald green lawns beneath cobalt blue skies and iced beer glasses sweat quietly on the shady verandah tables.

Landscape modifications, 1770–1970

Two hundred years had witnessed marked changes in the continental landscapes. In essence these changes were the result of the invasion of a continent with an indigenous population of *c.* 300 000 by an alien and technologically more sophisticated people whose numbers by 1970 had reached 12 million. The results were first the modification of original ecosystems by new uses of the land and its resources, and second the redistribution of the original and invading populations.

The basic pattern of changes to the continental ecosystems are summarised in Table 6.1 and for comparison equivalent data for the continental USA are included. Comparing the areas indicated on this table, it is apparent that Australia has almost a third of the original landscapes and ecosystems of 1770 still intact, whereas the USA has lost all but a tenth of her pre-

Table 6.1 Environmental impact, Australia and USA by *c.* 1970

Impact	*Percentage of total area*	
	Australia (a)	*USA (b)*
1. Ecosystems pre-European settlement relatively intact in 1970	31.3	12.2
2. Ecosystems modified in detail by 1970:		
forests thinned or replanted	1.7	22.4
grasslands under grazing	57.4	15.2
3. New ecosystems or land cover by 1970:		
cultivated and orchards, etc.	9.5	41.9
urban areas	0.1	8.3
Total	100.0	100.0

Sources: (*a*) 'Land Use', *Atlas of Australian Resources*, 1973; (*b*) *US Book of Facts, Statistics and Information*. Data for mid-1960s

European settlement landscapes and ecosystems. Different areas have had detailed modification of the landscapes in both countries (59% Australia, 37% USA) and here the larger area of original forest in the USA is apparent, whereas Australia had a larger area in original grasslands. A major contrast, however, which points up the shorter history of European settlement and less significant spatial impact of that settlement in Australia is the much smaller area from which all trace of the original landscapes have been removed, i.e. the cultivated and built-up areas. Australia's proportion is only a fifth that of the USA and less than a tenth of the continent has completely lost the original landscape and its associated ecosystem.

These basic changes, however, hide a complex variety of new land uses and increased population densities. Scott's estimates for the mid-1960s (Table 6.2) suggest a gradation of intensity of land use from 'vacant' (supposedly unused land, but in fact because of the scale of his original inquiry including the Aboriginal Reserves and isolated mining and military settlements) to the major urban centres. The 29 per cent of the continent still 'vacant' carries only 0.6 per cent of the total population and that at the lowest overall density of less than 0.1 persons per square mile. But as a result of renewed interest in the resources of this area, both for tourist use and for minerals, it is experiencing a recent population increase which is second only to the major cities and which locally will bring marked modifications to the landscapes in new settlements and mines. As yet, however, the small absolute totals of this increase, less than 10 000 people 1961 to 1966, has not made any other than local impact and the visual scene has not greatly changed since 1770.

Beyond, mainly south and east of these vacant lands, is a girdle of lands where the impact of European and Anglo–Australian settlements has been

Table 6.2 Land use and population trends in 1960s

	Area		*Population 1966*					
						Trend 1961–66 (%)		
Land use	*Total 000/sq. ml.*	*% continent*	*Total (000s)*	*Total (%)*	*Density/sq. ml. (sq. km)*	*Urban*	*Rural*	*Total*
Vacant (a)	*865*	*29.1*	*76*	*0.6*	**0.1 (0.2)**	+7	+12	+12
Forest and woodlands (b)	*93*	*3.1*	*656*	*5.6*	**7.0 (17.5)**	+9	+1	+3
Pastoral:	*1924*	*64.8*	*2546*	*20.4*	1.5 (3.7)	–	–	–
Extensive sheep	797	26.8	333	2.9	0.4 (1.0)	+7	–1	+3
Extensive cattle	883	29.9	229	2.0	0.3 (0.7)	+19	–2	+8
Intensive sheep	86	2.8	648	5.6	8.0 (20.0)	+7	–5	+1
Intensive cattle	17	0.6	143	1.2	8.0 (20.0)	+6	+2	+4
Dairying	48	1.6	993	8.7	21.0 (52.5)	+13	–6	+6
Agricultural:	*177*	*5.9*	*1121*	*9.8*	6.3 (15.7)	–	–	–
Intensive cropping	15	0.6	532	4.6	37.0 (92.5)	+26	–12	+9
Wheat and sheep	162	5.3	589	5.1	4.0 (10.0)	+7	–2	+2
Major urban (c)	2	*0.1*	*7325*	*63.6*	**3368.0 (8420.0)**	–	–	+13
Totals	*2968*	*100.0*	*11524*	*100.0*	4.0 (10.0)	+11	–2	+10

Notes

a. Includes isolated mining areas, military establishments, aboriginal reserves.
b. Includes most hydro-electric power schemes, and some mining centres.
c. Federal and State capitals and Launceston.

Source: Scott (1968). Note the slight differences between these per cent areas and those given in Table 6.3

evident in some detail. Forest and woodlands, pastoral and agricultural lands, together comprising 74 per cent of the continent, contained 36 per cent of the total population in 1966, at densities which reflected the intensity of land use and by implication the intensity of modification of indigenous landscapes. Thus the highest densities of rural population (37 per square mile) were found on the most intensively cropped areas while a smaller density (21 per square mile) reflected the most intensive form of pastoral land use – dairying. Landscape modification on the cropped lands would have replaced native vegetation by exotic crops, grains, fruits and fibres, while on the dairy lands native vegetation has generally been replaced by exotic grasses. Such areas were relatively small by comparison with the much larger area of extensive sheep and cattle operations where the population density was not much more than that in the 'empty' core, and where landscape modification was limited to encouragement of native grasses. Throughout this girdle of modified landscapes, populations were increasing only slightly prior to 1966 and locally showed significant decreases with movement of people out of the rural areas.

In contrast to the two major landscape categories above, the final urban category, although covering only 0.1 per cent of the continent, contained 64 per cent of the population and contained landscapes from which the 1770 components had been generally removed. Here were the highest population densities in the continent – over 3300 per square mile: here were the man-made environments of bricks and mortar, steel, concrete and macadam.

The landscapes of 1970: old and new

The general pattern of landscape modification showed spatial distortions over the continent and for explanations of these distortions and the variety of new landscapes which resulted in the years 1770 to 1970, we need to examine the sequence and results of the changes in some detail. In the sequence – the evolution of the 1970 landscape – will be seen the efforts of individual settlers, activated by a variety of motives from religious fantacism to private commercial profit; official policies of land settlement based upon contemporary political platforms and philosophies of man's role in nature; the influence of technology and technological innovations in opening up new possibilities of resource uses and widening the scope for landscape changes; and overall – because the bulk of settlement has been so based – the compelling problems of commercial profit and loss. At different times different themes seemed to dominate the explanations, but throughout there was a theme of 'development' – of the change of prior situations to new possibilities by the inputs of human energies and skills – a developmental process which by implication brought with it modification of existing ecosystems and landscapes.

The process of this development through time was achieved by the introduction of a series of new production systems. The definition of these systems, as noted in the Introduction, was the processes by which the resources of the continent were recognised and used. Incorporated in these systems were the themes noted above and it will be suggested that each of the new systems has produced at least one major new landscape type in the 1970 scene. Thus, while it is possible to distinguish on the one hand *Relict Landscapes* little changed in 1970 from 1770, an array of at least five new major landscapes and their associated resource use systems can be identified (Fig. 6.4 and Table 6.3).

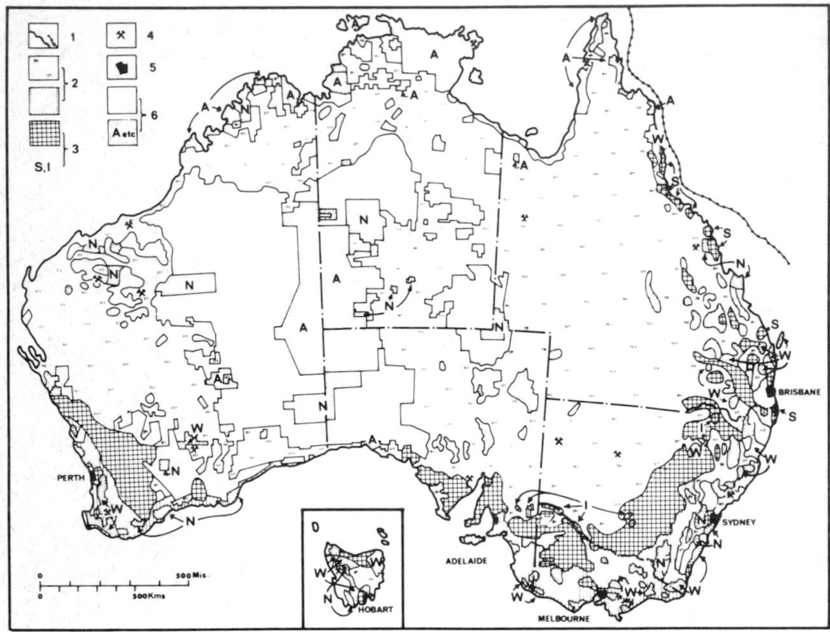

Fig. 6.4 Australian landscapes 1970
1, Maritime landscapes (coastline and reefs); **2**, Pastoral landscapes: extensive and intensive (lined); **3**, Agricultural landscapes: (hatched)-grain farming; S, sugar farms; I, irrigated farms; **4**, Mining landscapes; **5**, Urban landscapes; **6**, Relict landscapes: (blank)-vacant lands; A, Aboriginal Reserves; N, National Parks, scientific and recreation reserves; W, Woodland (mainly native but including some exotics).

(*Source:* Land use map, Australia, 1973)

Of the new major landscapes the first to appear was that associated with the development of the marine resources of the continental coast and offshore islands – the *Maritime Landscape*. Here, the invading Europeans exploited the juxtaposition of land and water to harvest the seas, establish long distance ocean navigation links for supplies and trade, and to site their major settlements and later recreation centres. Second in time was the creation of pastoral production systems which created *Pastoral Landscapes*

Table 6.3 Detailed environmental impact in Australia *c.* 1970

Landscape (a)	*Continent area (%) 1970 (b)*	*Percentage of area affected and type of impact*					
				Complete replacement			
				New biotic cover			
		None	*Selective (c)*	*Similar (d)*	*Different (e)*	*Non-biotic (f)*	*Total*
Maritime	0.1	?	?	?	?	?	
Pastoral:							
Extensive 'stations'	57.4	<2	98	0	0	0	100
Intensive grazing farms	3.3	3	21	70	6	0	100
Intensive dairy farms	0.5	?	26	45	29	0	100
Agricultural:							
Grain farms	5.2	1	32	41	26	0	100
Sugar farms	0.1	0?	43	0?	52	0	100
Irrigated farms	0.1	0?	0	15	85	0	100
Other farms	0.3	?	?	?	?	?	
Mining	<0.01	?	?	?	?	?	
Urban	0.1	0	5	5	40	50	100
Relict landscapes	32.9	75	25	0	0	0	100
Total	100.0						

Notes

a. Landscape categories.
b. *Atlas of Australian Resources*, 1973, land use map.
c. Impact from selective timber cutting (past or present), grazing of native pastures (past or present).
d. Native pasture or woodlands replanted to 'improved' exotic pastures.
e. Cultivated land, crops, orchards, fallow.
f. Built-up areas, roads, etc.

Figures are intended to show relative rather than absolutely accurate values.

Sources: Topographic maps and land use data from Sinden (1972); Alexander and Williams (1973)

inland by grazing introduced livestock on first native and then introduced pastures to provide export products. Closely associated with this in time came the first widespread cultivation of the soil and the creation of a series of *Agricultural Landscapes* where exotic crops were produced for remote, often overseas, markets. Of less continuous importance, but all important for brief periods, has been the episodic revival of mineral production systems leading to the creation of *Mining Landscapes*. Finally, the combined effects of these production systems, together with the basic environmental complex of the continent and the nineteenth-century context of most of the formative stages of resource appraisal and development, has led to the dominance of a fifth component, the *Urban Landscapes* where, as we have seen, can be found the bulk of the population and the most impressive environmental modification of the 1970s. In the chapters which follow, these new landscapes and the isolated relics are described and analysed in some detail before the overview and prospect of the final part of the book.

7
The maritime landscapes

Bearing in mind the origin and the approach route of the first permanent European settlement in 1788, it is not surprising that the first years of that settlement should be dominated by the new oceans rather than the new lands. Indeed, the traditional explanation of the motives for the first British settlement at Sydney Cove – that it was to establish an outlet for the crowded prisons of Britain – has been recently challenged, and it now seems more likely that the settlement was to combine the function of a gaol with that of a political and commercial base for operations in the South Pacific.

Whatever the rationale, there was no doubt that the settlements were from their initial years dominated by, and oriented to, the sea. The coastal nature of all the first sites for settlement; the necessity for each, be it colonial capital or smallest hamlet, to have a landing place for ocean-going shipping; the complete dependence upon such shipping, first for supplies, information and instructions from Britain, secondly for the return of produce and home-going passengers, and third for the Pacific Ocean trade; and the winning of resources from the sea itself – all these illustrated what might be called a Maritime System. This system, comprising coastal settlement sites linked by ocean shipping to the home country for trade, fresh settlers (free or convict), institutions and government, and dependent upon local and remote Pacific marine resources for its first commercial profits, created a land and seascape, elements of which are still apparent in 1970. It was from over the ocean that the first settlers came; it was by the ocean that they explored the rim of the continent and maintained their subsidiary outports along it; it was from the ocean they gained their first livelihood. In the 1970s it is still from over the ocean that half of the annual increase in population comes; it is still by the ocean that 90 per cent of the continental produce is exported and trade received; all the state capitals are still basically ports; probably 80 per cent of the continental population still live within 20 miles of the ocean and for most, the ultimate vacation is a coastal beach. What has been the continuous attraction of this 'Maritime Landscape'? In part the answer is historical, in part geographical and *in toto* a complex interplay of the two.

Exploring the maritime resources

The recognition of potentials for European settlement in the Australian continent was the result of relatively late marine exploration. The discovery

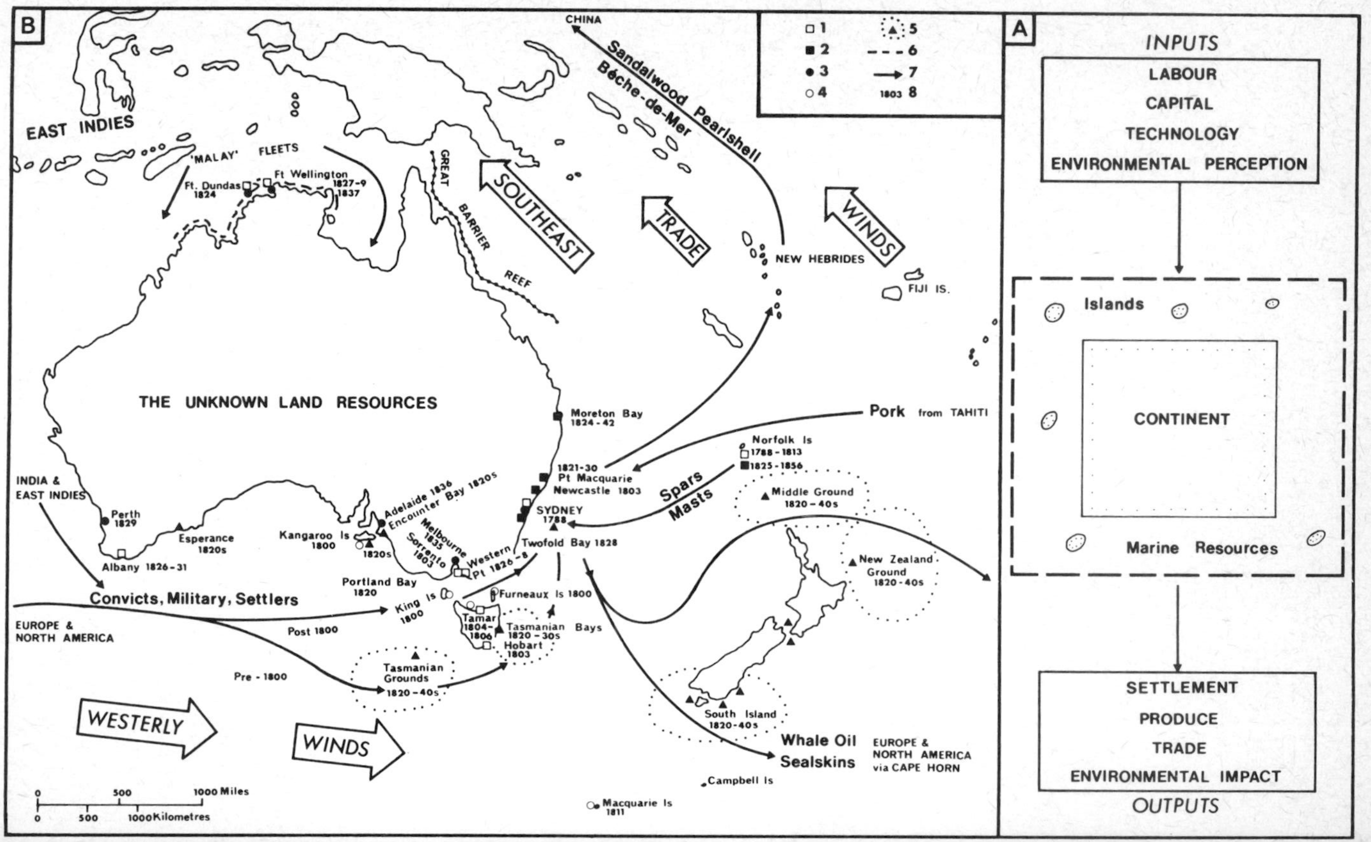
B
EAST INDIES
'MALAY' FLEETS
Ft. Dundas 1824
Ft Wellington 1827-9 1837
CHINA
Sandalwood Pearlshell
Bêche-de-Mer
1
2
3
4
5
6
7
1803 8
GREAT BARRIER REEF
SOUTHEAST
TRADE
WINDS
NEW HEBRIDES
FIJI IS.
THE UNKNOWN LAND RESOURCES
Moreton Bay 1824-42
Pork from TAHITI
Norfolk Is 1788-1813 1825-1856
1821-30 Pt Macquarie
Newcastle 1803
Spars Masts
Middle Ground 1820-40s
INDIA & EAST INDIES
Perth 1829
Esperance 1820s
Albany 1826-31
Kangaroo Is 1800
1820s
Adelaide 1836
Encounter Bay 1820s
Melbourne 1835
Sorrento 1803
Western Pt 1826-8
SYDNEY 1788
Twofold Bay 1828
New Zealand Ground 1820-40s
Portland Bay 1820
Convicts, Military, Settlers
EUROPE & NORTH AMERICA
King Is 1800
Furneaux Is 1800
Tamar 1804-1806
Tasmanian Bays 1820-30s
Hobart 1803
Post 1800
Pre - 1800
Tasmanian Grounds 1820-40s
South Island 1820-40s
WESTERLY
WINDS
Whale Oil Sealskins
EUROPE & NORTH AMERICA via CAPE HORN
Campbell Is
Macquarie Is 1811
0 500 1000 Miles
0 500 1000 Kilometres
A
INPUTS
LABOUR
CAPITAL
TECHNOLOGY
ENVIRONMENTAL PERCEPTION
Islands
CONTINENT
Marine Resources
SETTLEMENT
PRODUCE
TRADE
ENVIRONMENTAL IMPACT
OUTPUTS

of the eastern coast in 1770 by Captain James Cook of the British Navy was not the discovery of a new continent, but the verification of the boundaries of a continent whose western shores had been known to European navigators at least from the early seventeenth century. While there is a strong suspicion that Portuguese sailors discovered the north-western coast as early as 1522, there is no doubt that between 1606 and 1644, by a combination of deliberate exploratory voyages and accidental shipwrecks, virtually two-thirds of the northern, western and southern coastlines were discovered by the Dutch. The combination of a waterless coast in the south and west, and hostile Indigenes in the north, seem to have deterred any lasting Dutch interest in the land, and the resources of the ocean were not at that time even considered. Brief British contact with the northwest coast by shipwreck in 1622 and Captain William Dampier's voyages in 1688 and 1699, brought a few plant specimens back to Oxford but generally confirmed the negative assessment of the land and its inhabitants. Prior to 1770, the European impact had been merely a litter of flotsam around the coast, brief contact and often physical conflict with the Indigenes, and the assemblage of the names of several European notables on the nautical charts of the coasts.

By contrast, the favourable reports from Cook's voyage along the east coast were used to identify the site for the first permanent British settlement – a port, with good water, plenty of building materials, pleasant climate and good soil (or so it was hoped). Once this settlement had been established, the first job was detailed exploration of the adjoining coasts for further settlements. The various voyages from Sydney provided not only charts of the coasts, but also notes on the abundant fish, seals and whales. By 1804 the bulk of the coastline and its marine resources were at least sketched in and the evolution of the maritime landscape was under way.

The early maritime bases

The settlement at Sydney Cove was the first of a series of bases established for varying motives around the Australian coast (Fig. 7.1). One immediate problem of the first settlement was what to do with convicts guilty of further offences in the settlement itself. From 1803 to 1825 this was met by the creation of places of secondary punishment, along the coast away from Sydney (Newcastle, 1803; Moreton Bay, 1824), or on nearby islands

---

Fig. 7.1 Maritime systems 1788 to 1840s
A. Model of maritime systems
B. Patterns of maritime resource use
Key
Types of settlement: 1, Strategic; 2, Gaols; 3, Free colonies; 4, Sealing stations; 5, Whaling grounds; 6, Trepang (*bêche-de-mer*) grounds; 7, Main shipping routes; 8, Dates of initial settlement.

(*Sources*: See 'A note on the sources')

(Norfolk Island, 1825) (Fig. 7.2). In most cases the convicts were to provide the labour for the construction of the settlement – the jetty, storehouses, barracks and gardens which were common to all. In addition, they worked the exposed coal seams at Newcastle, felled the Norfolk Island pines for ships' masts and spars and cleared the land for agriculture at Port Macquarie and Moreton Bay.

Apart from secondary gaols, several bases were set up for strategic motives to establish territorial claims to portions of the continent. European rivalries, particularly between France and Britain, had been transferred to the Pacific Ocean, and the few French naval explorers and traders to visit Australia in the wake of Cook were sufficient to cause London and Sydney to plan defensive outposts on remote portions of the coasts. Thus successive 'panic' reactions led to the Tasmanian settlements of 1803 and 1804; Fort Dundas, 1824; Western Port and Albany in 1826; and Fort Wellington, 1827 (later Port Essington). Essentially these were 'show the flag' outposts not initially intended as bases for exploration or occupation of the inland.

Other bases had trading functions. Fort Wellington was in part projected as a future 'Singapore' for the East Indies trade and several bases were set up by private capitalists as headquarters for their commercial activities. Thus the settlement of free British colonists at Swan River (Perth) in 1829 and Adelaide, 1836; had, among their intended functions, a base for trade with India and the East Indies and as depots for fishing and whaling operations. The function of these relatively late arrivals had in fact been suggested by successful experiences in the older gaols and strategic bases.

Of the six ships which brought the first convicts to Sydney Cove, five returned to Britain with cargoes of whale oil from catches off the east coast of Australia. This was the first of a lucrative trade which attracted whalers from North America as well as Britain, and which was responsible for many temporary camps on headlands along the south-eastern coasts, where whales killed at sea or in the bays were brought ashore to be flayed and boiled down for oil. At the height of the trade, in the 1820s and 1830s, before the bays and inshore breeding grounds were fished out, Hobart and the bays of the Tasmanian east coast were crowded by whalers loading oil or landing carcases to be flayed. Until 1835 whale oil was the most valuable export of Australian produce and at its height at least seventy-six local whaling ships were operating from the British settlements. After the exhaustion of local supplies in the 1840s operations had to be extended to Antarctic waters and the returns declined significantly.

Paralleling the whaling activity in time and often in locality was the sealing trade, whereby the fur seals coming ashore to breed on the offshore islands of south and east coasts were clubbed and stabbed to death and their skins exported to Europe. Again, temporary working camps were established ashore, where the skins were prepared for export at the end of the season. Occasionally gangs would stay over from one year to the next but the settlements never became anything more than rough huts of flotsam, driftwood and earth, smoke blackened, tucked into the foot of cliffs or

Fig. 7.2 Kingston, Norfolk Island
Well-preserved buildings of original convict settlement mainly constructed between 1825 and 1850s: 1, Original commissariat store, now church; 2, New military barracks, now administration centre for island; 3, Stores and jetty area; 4, 'New gaol' site. Within the wall was a pentagonal building for the convicts; 5, Site of convict barracks; 6, Governor's residence; 7, Surf breaking on reefs which surround the island.

dunes and surrounded by the discarded skeletons of seals, broken storecases and bottles. The peak of activity was passed earlier here and by the 1820s sealers were having to turn to whaling to eke out their profits.

Trade with the Pacific Islands, the East Indies and China also contributed to the economic success of the first settlements. From 1793 to 1830 the Sydney settlement was importing pork from Tahiti to feed the convicts and garrison, and was making profits not only from whaling and sealing, but from the sale of New Zealand flax to English linen manufacturers, sandalwood from Fiji and the New Hebrides, and *bêche-de-mer* (for trepang), pearl shell and edible tropical birds' nests to the Chinese market (Fig. 7.1). As late as the 1870s the islands still offered profitable enterprises. At that time cotton plantations were established in Fiji following the closure of the 'Deep South' cotton supplies during the American Civil War. When the bottom dropped out of the cotton market with the resumption of the American supplies to Britain, the same men transferred their capital and their indentured island labourers (many forcibly recruited or 'blackbirded') to the Queensland sugar industry (Chapter 9). A historian recently described the varied activities of three of the most eminent local personalities of the first half of the nineteenth century as John MacArthur 'sheep-breeder and sandalwood trader', Rev Samuel Marsden 'chaplain, magistrate, sheep-breeder, pork trader and missionary', and Robert Towns 'sandalwood trader, sugar planter and "blackbirder"' (Young, 1967). Such men were continuing to exploit the maritime resources long after the extent of the land resources of the continent had been established.

In fact, although production from marine resources fell rapidly in relative importance in the latter half of the nineteenth century, it has never disappeared entirely, and remains a significant item both economically and in the landscapes associated with it up to the present day. The relative decline in the late nineteenth century was a result of the massive expansion of production from the land resources on the one hand, and the absolute decline of marine production on the other. This latter resulted from the exhaustion of local whaling and sealing supplies, increased resort to remoter Pacific and Antarctic fishing grounds where competition from especially American shipping was fierce, and the collapse of the world whale oil market in the 1870s in the face of competition from cheaper kerosene oil from the petroleum fields of the USA. The reduced attraction of this major component in the marine resource use system helped to divert capital and enterprise into the already expanding pastoral, agricultural and mining activities on land. In the 1970s marine resources were still being used, but the scale and location of activities showed significant changes.

Maritime landscapes in the 1970s

The rapid relative reduction of investment in marine resources of the latter half of the nineteenth century did not result in the disappearance of the maritime landscapes, only the reduction of their spatial and economic significance in comparison with the other land-based resource use systems. Thus, in the 1970s most of the landing sites used by the first European settlers are still in use as major entry points, fishing ports are still active and a component which was beginning to appear in the 1860s, namely the coastal resort town, has been considerably expanded in the twentieth century.

The first European settlers brought ashore their equipment and supplies at locations which immediately acquired the status of ports through which the land settlements could be linked by overseas communication lines to the home country. Such ports were established for various reasons as we have seen, but by the 1970s there was evidence not only of the modification of the original rationale for their establishment and the modification of the original associated landscapes, but also the creation of new types of landing places, new sites where the population sought to exploit the juxtaposition of land and sea (Fig. 7.3).

From the first landings by small rowing boats ferrying people and goods to be carried ashore through the shallows from the large ocean-going vessels anchored in deeper waters, was but a short step in time to the first wharves where such vessels could moor alongside. On the wharves were built warehouses, to which first ox- and horse-drays, then railway wagons and then the motorised trucks and container vans could be drawn and the transhipment from land to water transport more efficiently managed. Apart from the offices of the merchant traders, the official harbourmaster's home, customs officers' quarters and bondstores and labour office for the dock workers came to be standard components among the structures built to serve and supervise these transhipments. From Sydney's steel, concrete and asphalt 'jungle' of wharves and buildings centred upon Circular Quay (Fig. 2.7) to the battered wooden shed labelled 'HM Customs' and the sagging wooden pile pier of the smallest ports (Fig. 7.4A), the components are there, if at a different scale and a different level of activity.

The size of the transhipment ports appears to have been increasing through time as their overall numbers appear to have declined. Certainly, fewer ports now dominate the trading patterns than before, for with the technological innovations both in land transport and in bulk handling of commodities, it is now cheaper to send produce of the land to fewer central ports where it can be bulk-loaded by containers or bulk-storage handling. When transhipment was mainly by hand 'lumping' of bagged goods with perhaps the aid of the ship's winches, the smallest jetty was an effective port, serving an immediate hinterland, but the capital costs and efficiencies of bulk handling require fewer, more central points with greater volumes of traffic to justify themselves and the small ports had to change their function or wither away.

Thus in South Australia, the old wheatport of Edithburg on the Yorke Peninsula retains both jetty and old rail-line to its massive but now empty stone warehouses, filled from the 1870s to the 1950s each year by bagged wheat, while 50 miles (80 km) north along the coast stand the concrete

Fig. 7.3 Kwinana industrial complex, W.A.
Begun in 1955, the complex includes, looking south: (1) an alumina refinery using ores from the Darling Range; (2) oil-fired power station; (3) blast furnaces of iron and steel complex; (4) oil refinery and (5) CSBP. Note location on land/sea junction zone with ocean shipping jetties on one side and road and rail links on the other.

(*Source:* Department of Development and Decentralisation, W.A.)

silos, loading gear and jetty of the new wheat terminal of Ardrossan, which can pump 400 tonnes of wheat per hour into the bulk wheat carriers lying offshore (Fig. 7.4). Some half-dozen men in the 1970s do the job which took some thirty men 100 years earlier.

The same basic pattern is reflected in the sugar-exporting ports of northern Queensland where earthmoving equipment has been adopted to move the mountains of raw sugar from bulk store warehouses to the ships' holds, especially at Townsville, the largest sugar export centre in Australia. For the minerals, the volumes of traffic, extent of mechanisation and impact on settlements are even more spectacular. Port Hedland in 1961, with a population of less than 1000, a sleepy distribution centre for the

Fig. 7.4 Old and new grain export facilities
A. Edithburgh jetty and warehouses, S.A.
B. Ardrossan grain silos and jetty, S.A.
(See text for explanation)

pastoral northwest of Western Australia, has been transformed by the export of iron ore from the Pilbara area into a hastily assembled complex of private caravans, company-built housing estates, and renovated fibrous-asbestos shacks, housing some 10 000 people in 1973. Ore brought in by rail is stockpiled in mountains of fine ore from which mechanical loaders transfer up to 8000 tons per hour into the 100 000 ton Japanese ore carriers lying at the wharves. On the other side of the continent, at Altona, some 10 miles (16 km) west of Melbourne, a petro-chemical complex based upon the adjacent refinery, processing imported crude oil, employs over 700 workers on a site of 527 acres (211 ha). Here $66 million of capital has been invested by seven corporations in by-product processing plants which are highly integrated in their planned 'industrial estate'. Such facilities here and at Kwinana (Fig. 7.3) are a far cry in time and technology from the first primitive jetties.

The fishing ports of the 1970s are widespread in their location, extremely varied in function and are the bases for over 16 000 commercial fishermen. From the remaining whaling station at Albany, Western Australia, where Sperm whales from the Indian Ocean are brought ashore for processing, through the tuna and abalone fleets based on Port Lincoln, South Australia, the Gulf of Carpentaria prawn boats based on Cairns and northeast Queensland ports to the crayfish boats operating out of Robe, Port Macdonnell and Portland, and the oyster beds of the Hawkesbury and Pittwater estuaries north of Sydney, the variety of capital investment, workers employed, methods of resource use and the associated character of the port itself are considerable. The wood and steel grids, bared at low water, on which oysters are raised, contrast with the ramps up which the whale carcases are dragged to be processed, while the freezing works are the sole indicator, apart from the boats in the harbour, of the fishing industry of Port Lincoln. For many crayfish and prawn ports only the chalked sign 'fresh crays' at the local grocery shop or 'deli' is any indication of what is the dominant income earner, for the catch may be landed on the beach and trucked immediately to the nearest freezing works for export or to the nearest local metropolitan market.

Within the urban areas one is never far from perhaps the most persistent reminder of the maritime resources – the ubiquitous 'fish and chip' shops. Here is maintained a cultural link with traditional British food preferences, although the eyebrows of the purists might be raised at the proprietors – usually Greek or Italian-born immigrants – and the fish, often including (until recent banned because of its mercury content) 'flake', which is in fact shark!

Paralleling, if somewhat later in time, the development of the seaside resort in Britain, the Australian seaside resorts were beginning to appear as identifiable units in the 1860s. The state capitals each had their sea-bathing beaches – patronised at weekends and on the newly introduced public holidays. As early as the 1850s special ferries were running from Circular Quay to Manly for the 'Sydneysiders', special trains ran to St Kilda beaches for Melbournites from 1857, and by 1880 at weekends twenty-six trains a day were taking Adelaidians back along the track of the first settlers to the first landing point at Glenelg, which by then was a thriving resort (Fig. 7.5). The patronage was considerable; it was claimed for example that over 1 million passengers a year made the latter trip in the early 1880s.

Such were merely satellites of the largest centres of population, but in the latter half of the nineteenth century and particularly the 1950s and 1960s, coinciding with periods of increasing local wealth and mobility (initially by railways, most recently by motor car, coach and air transport),

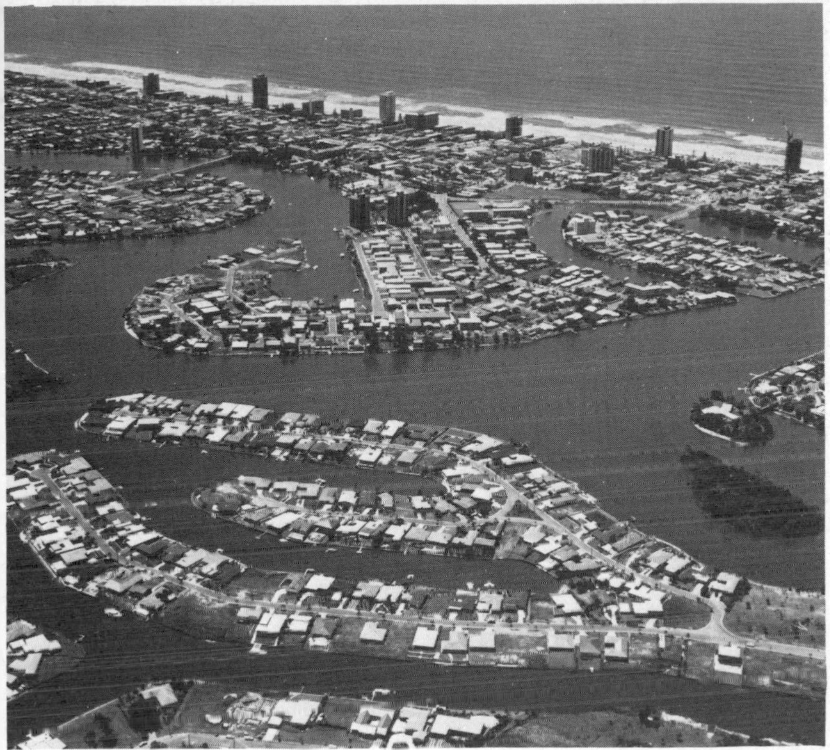

Fig. 7.5 Surfers Paradise, Qld.
The 'marinas' of the house lots each with its boat ramp built on reclaimed swamp land behind the original line of dunes on which the multi-storey hotels, motels and apartment complexes have been built. The marinas are dangerously close to the tidal high water mark and erosion of the coastal sand beach has necessitated expensive sea defence measures. An example of real-estate promotion of an average surfing beach which has produced a highly sophisticated tourist centre, very vulnerable to flooding by either river or sea.

(*Source:* State Public Relations Bureau, Qld.)

came the growth of the independent resort towns. Some, especially Katoomba in the Blue Mountains of New South Wales, were inland health resorts, particularly used for their cooler summer temperatures, but the majority were coastal and the 1950s to 1960s in particular saw the expansion of tourist facilities along the Great Barrier Reef of Queensland. Here the combination of winter warmth, a tropical vegetation and the variety of coral formations and marine life on the reefs has been rapidly exploited (Fig. 4.2, p. 36). Even the periodic summer cyclones and destructive storm surges fail to deter the predominantly Australian tourists. As yet, the remoteness from Sydney, which is their main port of entry, and lack of

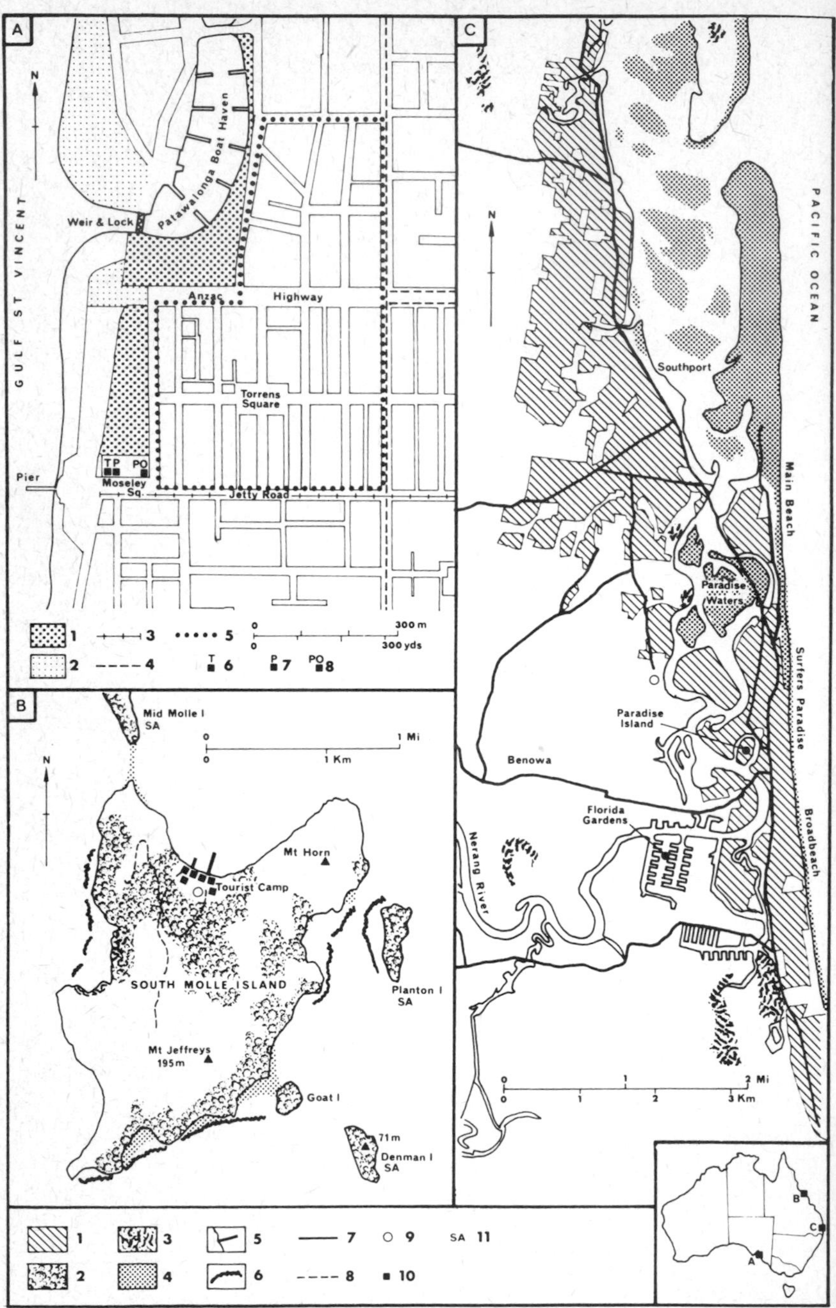
A
Patawalonga Boat Haven
Weir & Lock
GULF ST VINCENT
Anzac
Highway
Torrens Square
Pier
Moseley Sq.
Jetty Road
1
2
3
4
5
6
7
8
300 m
300 yds
B
Mid Molle I SA
1 Mi
1 Km
Mt Horn
Tourist Camp
SOUTH MOLLE ISLAND
Planton I SA
Mt Jeffreys 195 m
Goat I
71 m
Denman I SA
C
PACIFIC OCEAN
Southport
Main Beach
Paradise Waters
Surfers Paradise
Paradise Island
Benowa
Florida Gardens
Broadbeach
Nerang River
2 Mi
3 Km
1
2
3
4
5
6
7
8
9
10
SA 11

publicity, seems to have kept the international tourist component down to about 6 per cent of those visiting Australia, but this may be expected to rise with plans to build international-class accommodation on the various resort islands.

At the opposite end of the scale to the complex of commercial accommodation, communication systems and organised 'enjoyment' of the 'Miami Beach' mimicry of Surfers Paradise, Queensland (Figs. 7.5, 7.6), the beach shacks which seem to be the optimal 'holiday homescape' of the average Australian family present a much less spectacular picture. Dotted, often indiscriminately, on beach-dune or among mangrove or ti-tree swamps, serviced by unmade roads, perhaps by electricity, certainly not piped water or sewerage, many have a derelict air which hints at their long periods of non-use. Others, close to the metropolitan centres, may be on fully serviced subdivisions linked by metalled roads with neat gardens and lawns and a corner grocery store but all empty during the week, only busy at weekends with families at work on their gardens or setting off for the adjacent beach.

The maritime landscapes therefore remain in the 1970s a significant component in the Australian landscape, but we need to examine more closely the land-based resource patterns to explain the dominant characteristics of the continental landscapes.

Fig. 7.6 Maritime landscapes: the coastal resorts
The nineteenth-century resort

A. Glenelg, S.A.
1, Reserves; 2, Car parks (post 1950s); 3, Tram line to Adelaide; 4, Bus routes; 5, Edge of first town survey (central square mirrored Adelaide's plan); 6, Town Hall; 7, Police Station; 8, Post Office. Outline of streets indicated. Patawalonga Boat Haven added 1960s.

The twentieth-century resorts

B. South Molle Island, Qld.

C. The Cold Coast, Qld.
1, Urban area; 2, Dense forest; 3, Mangroves; 4, Sand dunes and flats; 5, Jetty; 6, Reef; 7, Main roads; 8, Tracks; 9, Golf course; 10, Buildings; 11, Scenic area (reserve). Note 'marinas' at Florida Gardens and proposed marinas at Paradise Waters.

(*Sources:* A – Glenelg Sheet, 1:7920, 1956; B – Molle Sheet, 1:31 680, 1966; C – Burleigh and Southport Sheets, 1:50 000, 1967)

8
The pastoral landscapes

If the Maritime System can be identified as the means by which the 'limpet ports' of the European settlements were established and maintained, the Pastoral System must be credited with the opening up of the land resources and the transfer of the focus of attention into the interior rather than the periphery of the continent. In essence the system had the same basic components of European labour and capital, but in this case directed to the production of raw materials and foodstuffs from the land instead of the sea. These products were derived from the grazing of imported domesticated livestock on first the natural and then the modified ('improved') pasture lands of the continent. As the result of this production system, a series of distinctive 'Pastoral Landscapes' were created. At one end of the spectrum were the extensive cattle and sheep 'stations' producing wool, hides and meat; at the other the small family dairy farms providing first for local and then international markets.

Origins

By the 1830s the decline of whaling and sealing was being paralleled by expansion of pastoral production and the nature of the pastoral system and its associated landscapes were already becoming apparent. The techniques and livestock were dominantly of British origin and usually straightforward transfers to the new grazing grounds.

The British pastoral system of the eighteenth and early nineteenth centuries, from which the Australian system was drawn, incorporated the grazing of cattle for beef, hides and dairy products; sheep for wool and mutton; pigs for pork; and fowls for their eggs and meat. Horses were raised as the draught animal to supplement the basic use of bullocks for land freight transport. The grazing grounds for beef cattle tended to be remote and rough northern and western moorland pastures from where the surplus would be walked each autumn along the traditional 'drove roads' east and south to market for slaughter. Dairy cattle needed daily supervision and had to be closer to cottages and dairies, often grazing well-watered alluvial meadows. Milk would not keep so that the product was usually butter or cheese for the local market town. Sheep were grazed on the short grasses of the limestone uplands and downs, the edges of the heather moors of the north and west and were being introduced onto the new crops of turnips and clovers which were reclaiming, with the help of sheep-dung and compaction by their treading of the loose sandy soil, the heathlands of eastern England. Each day the shepherd would take his flock from their night yards around his cottage or wagon to their daily grazing grounds. Shearing and lambing were springtime activities. Pigs, the traditional small farmer's standby, were grazed daily on cottage commons or waste land, which might include beech or oak woodlands providing 'mast' and acorns, or grasslands with roots and seeds. Fowls were ubiquitous around small and large farms and foraged where they could with a minimum amount of supervision. Of distinctive breeds, as we would now recognise them, there was scant trace. The evolution of the famous Shorthorns, Angus, Hereford and Jersey cattle was just beginning. The ancestors of the Romney, South Down and Leicester sheep breeds were the treasured darlings of a few progressive flockmasters, who were already showing interest in King George III's flock of Spanish merinos, smuggled from the semi-arid plateaus of central Spain and currently in the 1780s struggling with the cooler and moister summers of Windsor Great Park.

The technology and equipment outlined above were the sources upon which the British capitalists drew when, impressed by the reports of good natural grazing lands in Australia, the increasing demands for wool by English manufacturers, and the uncertain supplies from a Europe torn by Napoleonic Wars, they began to export their capital to set up new pastoral systems in Australia.

The grazing resources of the continent had not been immediately apparent to the settlers in the coastal bases for they faced the sclerophyll and rain forests, which offered timber and relatively well-watered lands but little grazing potential until the trees were cleared and European grasses sown. Not until a local drought and a plague of caterpillars in 1813 drove the first pastoralists to seek fresh grazing lands beyond the western barrier of the Blue Mountains were the best *natural* grasslands discovered (Fig. 8.1A). Once official permission to occupy these lands was given in the 1830s, the expansion of the pastoral system became a march of cattle and sheep herds across the mountains to the crescent of grasslands fringing the arid core of the continent. Initially, the better-watered denser grasslands of the southeast interiors were occupied, but pressure of increasing stock numbers soon spread the herds onto the shrublands and poorer grasslands of the interior where surface water was scarce and seasonally non-existent.

The evolution of the pastoral landscapes

The development of the Pastoral System and the landscapes it produced were the work of both private and official agencies. The original idea of supplying the expanding British wool market from Australia at the end of the eighteenth century, for example, seems to have been in the minds of several local residents. Among them, John MacArthur, an Army officer

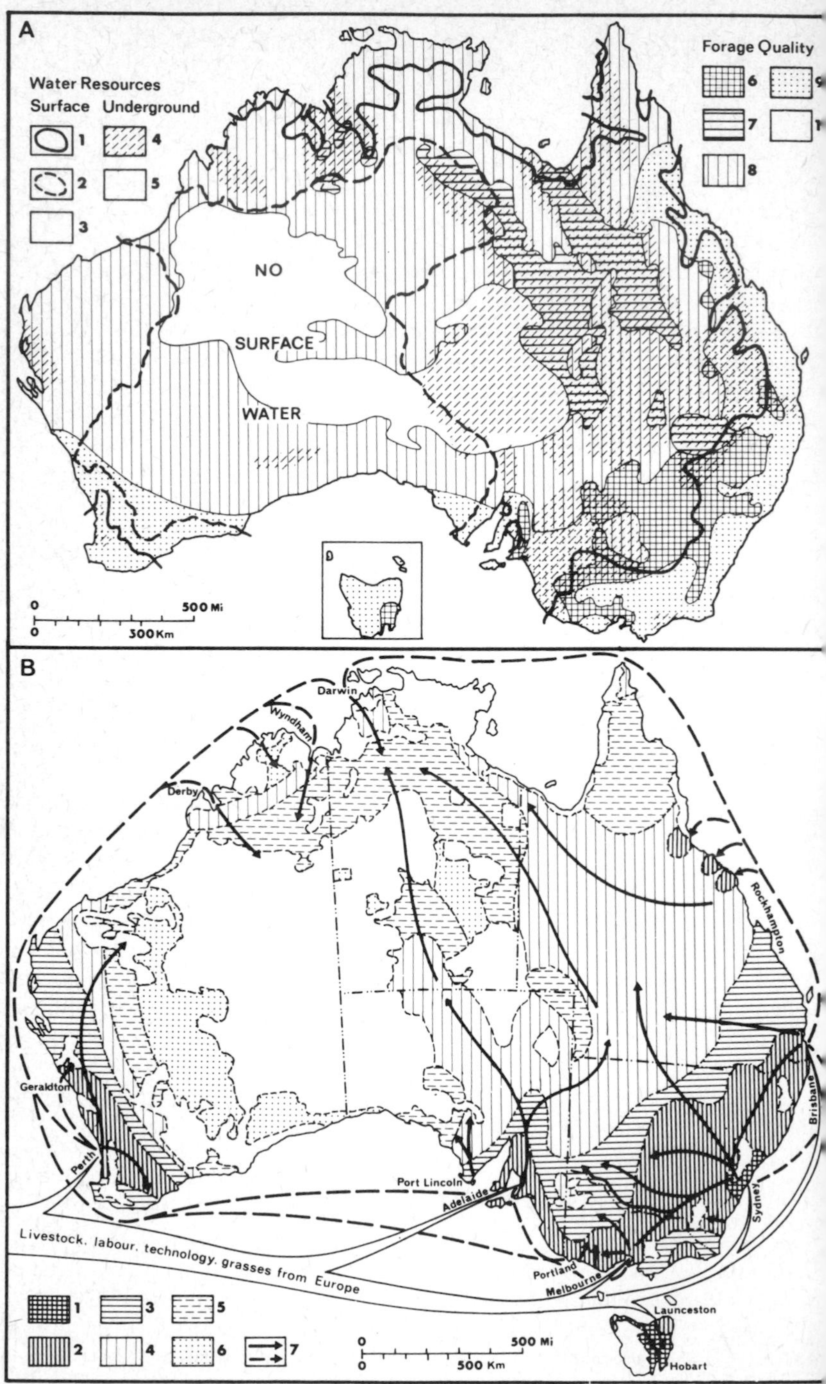
A
Water Resources
Surface Underground
1
2
3
4
5
Forage Quality
6
7
8
NO
SURFACE
WATER
0
500 Mi
0
300 Km
B
Darwin
Wyndham
Derby
Rockhampton
Geraldton
Brisbane
Perth
Port Lincoln
Adelaide
Sydney
Livestock, labour, technology, grasses from Europe
Portland
Melbourne
Launceston
Hobart
1
2
3
4
5
6
7
0
500 Mi
0
500 Km

stationed at Sydney, has been traditionally recognised as a leader, both for the flocks of sheep, principally merinos, which he bred up on his estate, and for his part in the formation of the first major capital investment in the land resources of the continent – the Australian Agricultural Company. Set up in 1824 with a capital of £1 million sterling and the aim of 'raising fine wool and subordinate to that object, cultivating the vine, olive, flax, and other productions now imported [in 1824 to Britain] from the shores of the Mediterranean', the company eventually obtained good grazing lands beyond the mountains and these, together with purchase and operation of the Government coal mines at Newcastle, provided a profitable investment.

Indeed, the grazing of sheep on the natural grasslands rescued other capital investments when the original non-pastoral resource uses proved unprofitable. Thus, the Van Dieman's Land Company, founded in 1825, was an attempt to set up an agricultural colony in northwest Tasmania, but only paid its way when the farmers turned first shepherds and then, in the 1870s, miners of copper and tin. Similarly, the South Australian Company found that in the first decade after its settlement had been established at Adelaide in 1836, the main income came not from whaling (they were ten years too late as we have seen) but from wool and beef.

Most of the first pastoralists were men of independent means, sons of aristocratic families or yeomen farmers and graziers who brought families, labourers, wagons, livestock and techniques as well as their savings to the new grazing lands. Later, their sons in turn took up new pastures in the interior and the imported traditions were gradually tempered by local experience as settlement pushed inland. Only later, after the expansion of agriculture and under the umbrella of Government-sponsored settlement

---

Fig. 8.1 Pastoral landscapes: evolution 1830s–1970s

A. Pastoral resources

Water resources: 1, Perennial surface water available; 2, Intermittent surface water available; 3, No surface water; 4, Underground water available; 5, Underground water absent or too brackish for livestock.
Forage quality: 6, Best perennial and annual grasses, Woodland Ecosystem (grazing capacity 1–2 acres per sheep); 7, Second quality perennial grasses of Grassland Ecosystem (5–10 acres per sheep); 8, Poor quality grazing, highly variable seasonally, mainly annual grasses and herbs of mixed Woodland–Grassland ecosystems on fringe of Desert (over 20 acres per sheep); 9, Rare grazing resources – some pockets of natural grasslands, but mainly dense woodlands of Sclerophyll and Rain Forest ecosystems;
10, No grazing resources except for occasional short-lived herbs after rains, Desert Ecosystem.

B. Expansion of pastoral land use

Inputs from Europe produced the initial occupation for pastoral use by:
1, 1830; 2, 1845; 3, 1860; 4, 1880; 5, 1900; 6, Post 1900; 7, The main lines of advance of the pastoralists by land and sea.
The blank areas were not used for pastoral use in *c.* 1970 but include some areas which may have *been* used and subsequently abandoned.

(*Sources:* CSIRO, 1960; Roberts, 1968 and 1970; Australia, 1962–73)

schemes, did the small capitalists, or in some cases labourers, become pastoralists – usually as dairy farmers.

Officially, after the 1830s, opinion came to see pastoral land use as an effective form of pioneer land settlement, in the tracks of which the farmers could follow in turn. Official exploration of the interior, beginning effectively in the 1830s, began to expose the apparently limitless grasslands to the public view, and private explorations by intending graziers and land speculators added to the private knowledge of the pastoral resources. By the late 1880s, as a result of both efforts, the major pattern of pastoral resources of fodder and surface water supplies in the continent had been established (Fig. 8.1B) and was common knowledge for anyone able to read the official reports in the *Government Gazettes* and newspapers, and the books and pamphlets beginning to appear from private pens.

From the 1880s onwards, the colonial and state Governments began to take a more active role in promoting actual pastoral settlement – previously, as we shall see in the next chapter, their efforts had been directed only towards agriculture. After the 1880s, existing pastoral holdings could be subdivided, one-half remaining with the previous owner, while on the surrendered portion several new pastoral holdings were surveyed and new settlers with smaller capital backing encouraged to take up the smaller units. In this way one large holding supporting one family was to be divided up so that the same area would in future support several families. The justification for this official process – to be called later 'Closer Settlement' – was that extensive pastoralism was but the first stage of the sequence to more intensive pastoral operations and eventually to intensive agricultural settlement. Each stage in theory represented an increase of capital investment and of productivity per unit area, and a parallel increase in human population carrying-capacity. In fact different pastoral and agricultural landscapes did come to reflect these contrasts by the 1970s (see Figs. 8.2, 8.4, 9.3) although the most intensive uses were not as widespread as was originally hoped, as we shall see.

After the Second World War the same principle of 'Closer Settlement' was used, in combination with scientific research, to improve yields from the Ninety Mile Desert of southeast South Australia and allow extensive pastoral and some vacant lands to be subdivided into 1000-acre blocks for 'intensive' family pastoral operations. When the trace element deficiencies (cobalt, copper, molybdenum, and zinc) of the local soils were remedied, instead of a sheep needing 20 acres (8 ha) to support it the year round only a tenth of that area was now required. Settlement had indeed intensified the returns from the land.

The spread of the extensive pastoral stations

The surge of alien livestock into the interior was not without setbacks. The points of entry onto the grazing lands were initially in the southeast (pre-1830s) and thereafter from the south (Adelaide) and southwest (Perth)

(Fig. 8.1). While the initial stimulus was for sheep for wool, both cattle (for local beef needs and hide exports) and horses (as remounts for the British Indian army, 1840s to 1850s, as well as the steady demand for local draught and riding animals) were raised on the new ranges. By the 1860s, most of the more reliable southern (winter rain) grazing lands had been occupied, mainly by either cattle or sheep, and by the 1890s most of the less reliable northern (summer rain) grazing lands. Thereafter, the overall pattern of pastoral land use was modified only by isolated expansions and retreats on the edge of the desert core, the filling-in of some gaps in humid country and the retreat of extensive grazing before the advancing waves of intensive pastoral and agricultural land use. These latter were spreading out in the tracks of the pastoralists from the south and east from the 1860s onwards.

The pattern of expansion reflected both the continuing demand for wool and later protein in the British and European markets, and the transformation of legal and technical framework inherited with the introduced pastoral system.

While there were no real physical barriers to pastoral land use once the Blue Mountains had been crossed, there were considerable legal barriers until 1847 and the system then adopted was to remain the feature of pastoral land use until the 1970s. Initially any occupation of the interior had been forbidden by the British Government in order to concentrate the energies and security of the small population close to the coast. In the face of successful illegal settlement in the interior from mid-1830s onwards, stockmen were granted temporary six-month permits to graze their animals on the interior grasslands. They were in fact 'lessees' of the grazing rights and that was all. To buy the land they would have had to pay 5 shillings per acre in 1831, 12 shillings in 1838 and £1 sterling after 1840. With natural grazing capacities on the better lands often hardly a sheep to 2–3 acres (*c*. 1 ha), the capital needed to amass sufficient land for an economically viable flock (several thousand) was not available. MacArthur and some of the earlier pioneers had been granted their estates free – for official services rendered, but that system was abolished in 1831, so that avenue was also closed. The result was a continuation of mainly illegal occupation until the innovations of 1847.

In 1847 a system of leases for pastoral lands was begun, which enabled land to be leased for up to fourteen-year periods in units sufficient to carry 4000 sheep or cattle equivalent. Again the pastoralist who had refused to buy his range outright was given leave to graze his stock, use the natural waters and cut such timber as he needed for building, fencing and fuel, in return for payment of an annual rent – less than a farthing an acre usually – for up to fourteen years. This same principle, modified in the rent and terms, was later adopted by all states for their pastoral lands and is retained in the pastoral leases which cover 99 per cent of the lands used for extensive pastoral purposes in the 1970s. The relatively low capital investment and yields per unit area, which originally made the fixed price of the land too high for the pastoralist, have come to be recognised and, in return for

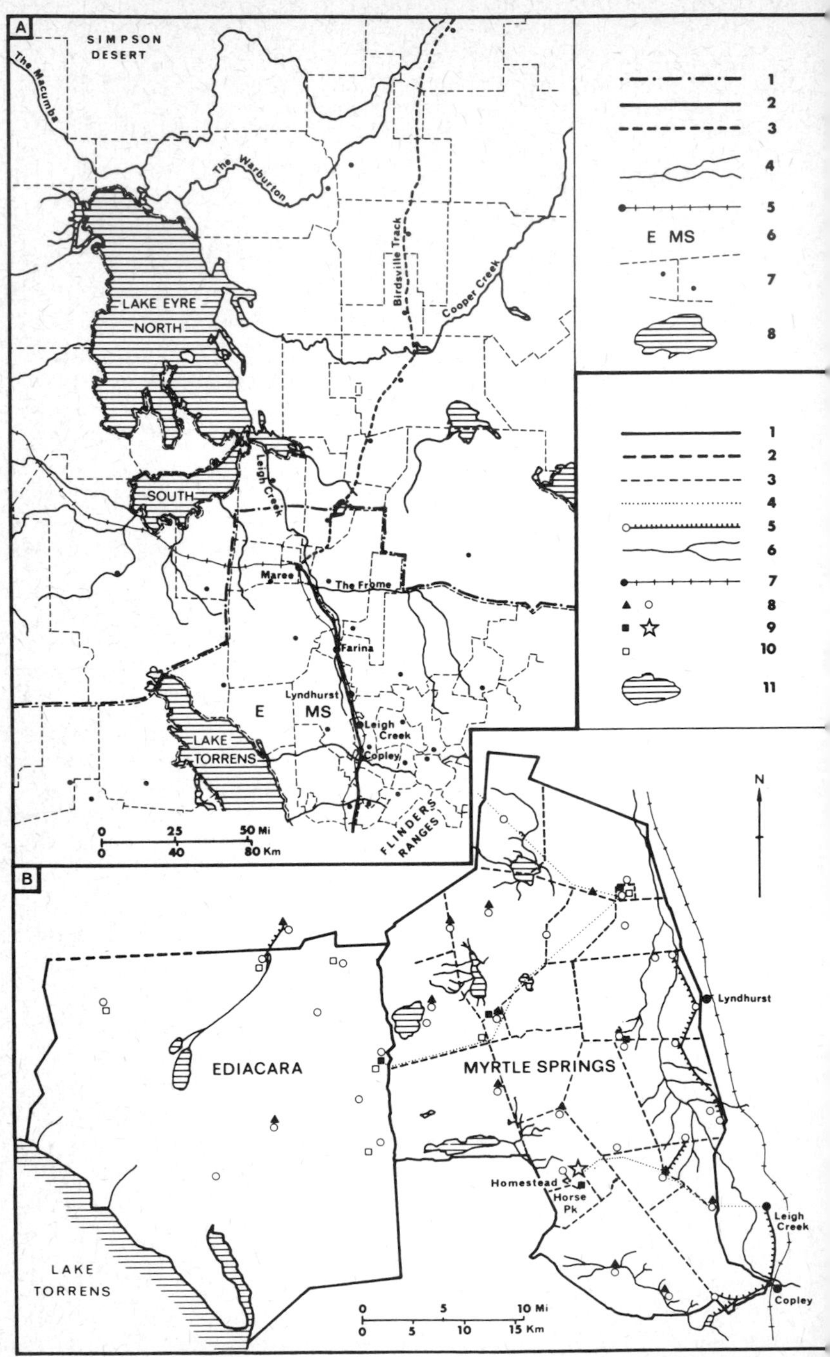
A
SIMPSON DESERT
The Macumba
The Warburton
Birdsville Track
Cooper Creek
LAKE EYRE NORTH
SOUTH
Leigh Creek
Maree
The Frome
Farina
Lyndhurst
E
MS
Leigh Creek
Copley
LAKE TORRENS
FLINDERS RANGES
0 25 50 Mi
0 40 80 Km
1
2
3
4
5
E MS 6
7
8
1
2
3
4
5
6
7
8
9
10
11
B
N
EDIACARA
MYRTLE SPRINGS
Lyndhurst
Homestead
Horse Pk
Leigh Creek
Copley
LAKE TORRENS
0 5 10 Mi
0 5 10 15 Km

occupation without ownership, he has been granted use by lease of only a limited range of the land's resources. If he wishes to change his land use to agriculture, he was and still is usually required to give up his pastoral lease and *purchase* his land. In fact from the 1860s onwards the competition for the better south-eastern pastoral lands, between the older established pastoralists and the new advancing farmers (see Fig. 9.2), forced the pastoralists either to buy their leased lands and intensify their production system to give a higher income per unit area if they wished to stay, or retreat inland beyond the limits of agricultural potential of the land and leave their ranges to be bought up for agriculture. By the 1970s, therefore, the extensive pastoral stations which remain are in fact occupying land not yet considered capable of more intensive land use (Fig. 8.2). They lie on the arid frontier, beyond them is the desert (Fig. 2.2).

Competition from agriculture did not always result in the eviction of livestock however, and two types of intensive pastoral resource uses evolved, usually where rainfalls were too high for grain crops, the fattening of livestock for slaughter and the development of dairying.

The spread of the intensive pastoral farms – the grazing landscapes

Until the current boom, generated by the massive United States purchases of meat beginning in the 1960s, the overseas market for Australian beef had never been as successful a stimulant to pastoral production as the market for wool. Despite equal opportunity, competition from North America and the Argentine effectively seems to have cornered the European markets from the first successful ocean transport of refrigerated beef in the 1880s. Australian beef producers therefore tended to be the poorer cousins of the sheepmen, with markets limited more to local consumption. Yet cattle fattening was one of the successful alternatives to agriculture where high tablelands had natural grasslands with a frost hazard (the Eastern Highlands) and there was scope to improve cattle carrying capacities by introduction of

---

Fig. 8.2 Pastoral landscapes: extensive sheep/cattle stations

A. Pastoral stations in Lake Eyre Basin, S.A.
1, Dingo-proof fence basically separating unprotected cattle stations to north from protected sheep stations to south; 2, Main road; 3, Birdsville track to Queensland; 4, Watercourses, mainly dry; 5, Railway and settlement; 6, Ediacara and Myrtle Springs station (see B below); 7, Boundaries of pastoral properties with homesteads (not all permanently occupied); 8, Salt lakes or clay pans.

B. Ediacara – Myrtle Springs station
1, Fenced boundary; 2, Unfenced boundary; 3, Internal paddock fences; 4, Telephone lines; 5, Water pipelines; 6, Watercourses, mainly dry; 7, Railway and settlement; 8, Windpump for underground water, storage dam; 9, Dwelling or shed, airstrip; 10, Livestock yards; 11, Salt lake or clay pan.

(*Source:* S.A. Department of Lands and Sale Brochure for Ediacara – Myrtle Springs)

exotic higher yielding grasses such as rye grasses (*Lolium* spp.) from southern Europe, and paspalums (especially *Paspalum dilatum*) from South America. Here, and on the tropical tablelands of Queensland where Rhodes (*Chloris gayana*) and Kikuyu (*Pennisetum clandestinum*) grasses from Africa have improved yields, 'store' livestock raised on the pastoral stations of the Northern Territory, western Queensland or New South Wales are fattened up for the city and export abattoirs (Fig. 8.3).

In contrast, the sheepmen who have survived in the higher rainfall country have been able to combine the traditional wool raising with fatten-

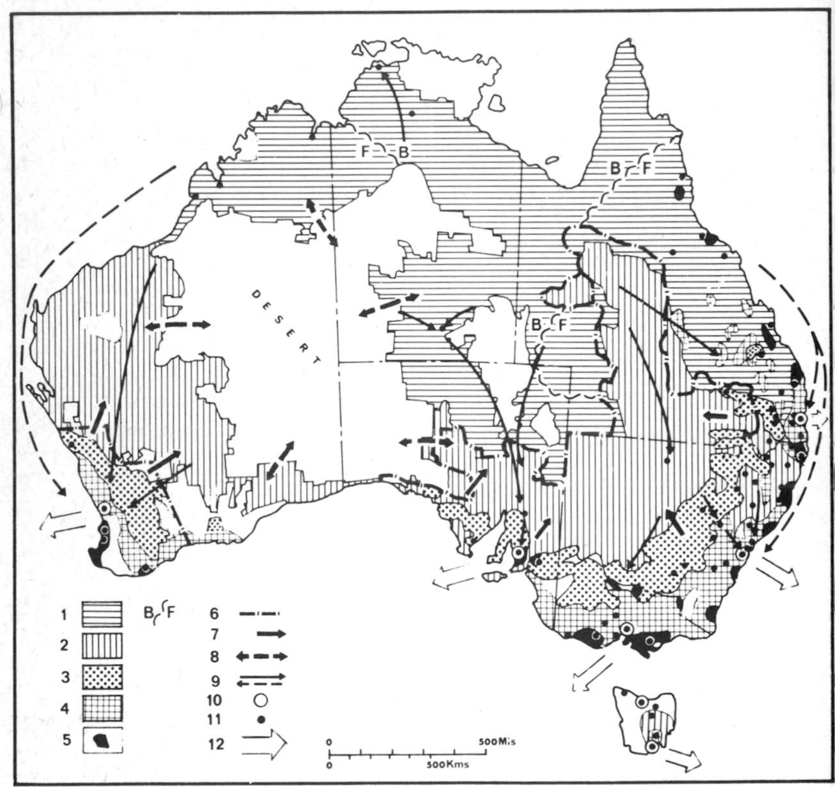

Fig. 8.3 Pastoral production patterns 1970
1, Extensive cattle stations: B, mainly breeding; F, mainly fattening; **2**, Extensive sheep stations; **3**, Grain landscapes – mainly wheat and sheep farms; **4**, Intensive grazing farms (sheep or cattle); **5**, Intensive dairy farms; **6**, Dingo-proof fence; **7**, Boundaries of land use under pressure from more intensive uses; **8**, Boundaries of actual land use vary according to seasonal drought severity; **9**, Internal movement of livestock by land and sea; **10**, Main domestic meat markets; **11**, Exporting meat works; **12**, Main export outlets.

(*Source:* See text)

Fig. 8.4 The traditional pastoral landscape
The original woodland of the ridge in the background contrasting with the exotic vegetation of the foreground, the introduced grasses of the paddock, the ornamental willow and fir trees and the artificial water storage dam in the original creek bed, show this to be part of an intensive grazing property. The horse probably still makes sense in rugged terrain; but on the plains it has been replaced by the motor cycle.

(*Source:* Australian News and Information Service)

ing of lambs and wethers (emasculated rams) (Fig. 8.4). They were prevented from occupying the eastern tropical tablelands of Queensland by the native spear grasses (*Stipa* spp.) which affected wool quality and often caused flesh wounds by their barbed seedheads, but by careful 'dipping' and 'drenching' of their livestock to control parasites, the pastoralists have extended their activities on the south-eastern tablelands up to the alpine ecosystem of the Kosciusko plateau. Once again they have found themselves occupying land well beyond the environmental range of the agriculturalists – in this case on the 'frigid frontier', beyond them are the winter snowfields.

The spread of the intensive pastoral farms – the dairy landscapes

A taste for butter and cheese came ashore with the first settlers but the popularity of liquid milk had to await the coming of refrigerated transport by rail and road and the urgings of the nutrition experts in the twentieth century. Before refrigeration began to be adopted in the 1880s, the sale of liquid milk was in any case limited to areas within a day's journey of the farm, and even cheese and butter production had been restricted to the local demands of the larger towns, each served by its own dairying area. Thus Sydney's butter and cheese came from the Illawarra Coast where Scottish Ayrshire cattle had been established on river flats cleared of timber and sown down to English grasses which thrived year-round with the mild winters. The impact of refrigeration and standardisation of the cream content by the Babcock Tester was to open up both local and international markets. By 1901 over one-third of Australian butter was exported and the future of dairying seemed certain.

Officially, dairying was a popular method of land settlement, since it was argued that it lent itself to production from small family operated units, and provided one of the highest densities of rural population (Table 6.2, p. 66), which would itself support country towns and a satisfactory level of rural services and amenities. Several of the Closer Settlement Schemes, which resettled soldiers returning from the First World War, were intended as settlements of potential dairy farmers and even earlier private estates had developed dairying as a livelihood for their tenants.

By 1850, as one example, the Bega Valley landscape of southeast New South Wales was still largely wooded pastoral country crossed by ridge-top bridle tracks and dotted by shepherds' huts, occasional stockyards and stone walled sheepfolds. A few small wheat-fields clustered around the small settlement of Bega. By 1870 two capitalists in partnership had bought up 400 000 acres between them and had recreated an English country estate, complete with the trees, hedges and tenant farmers of England. Sheep gave way to dairy cows in the 1860s and by 1880 a third of the estate farms were supplying milk to a local cheese factory which began a local dairy production famous still in 1970.

The dairy farming settlements, mainly hacked out of the sclerophyll and rain forests, would in theory provide a rapid return on investment as cattle could graze within a year on the grasses sown in the ashes amid the blackened stumps of the burnt timber, and an interim income would be provided by the sale of the larger trees (Fig. 4.4). Many of the official schemes failed, however, because of the unskilled management of the settlers, their lack of sufficient capital backing to tide them over for the first lean years, the high cost of land clearance and the lack of adequate marketing organisation. In addition, the collapse of prices and world trade in the 1930s hit dairymen and wheatmen alike. Many small operators on slender profits went bankrupt, farms and herds were amalgamated to give economies of scale and diversification through sheep and beef cattle helped. Improvement of herd quality, the development of Jersey and Guernsey stock and the improvement of pasture qualities by fertilisers, nitrogen-fixing legumes and successful exotic grasses such as paspalum improved efficiency and profits.

The landscapes of 1970, however, retain much of the character of the earlier periods (Fig. 8.5). Within the 'milk-shed' of each of the state capitals, at dawn and late afternoon herds congregate patiently at paddock gates to the clank of churns and automatic milking gear. Gleaming steel road tankers crunch into farmyards, load up and pull away, past the small wooden platform at the gate where the churns used to stand and still do on some of the smaller properties, on down the bitumen roads winding through the hills to the creamery in the valley below.

Changing pastoral techniques

Traditional pastoral techniques had to be adapted to cope with environmental hazards unknown beforehand. Not all the native grasses were edible, some were poisonous to all livestock, others only to sheep, others only to cattle; some of the grass seeds had sharp barbs which worked their way into the flesh of sheep in particular, other seed 'burrs' caught in the fleece and reduced its value by requiring expensive treatment before spinning was possible. Such were only discovered after tragic experiences and the names the stockmen gave them are eloquent, their Latin names dispassionately objective: Paterson's Curse (in New South Wales) or Salvation Jane (in South Australia) (*Echium plantagineum*) reflecting differing interpretations of its historic role as poisonous plant or drought feed, Stinkwort (*Inula graveolens*), Bathurst Burr (*Xanthium spinosum*) and spear grasses (*Heteropogon* spp.).

Apart from the arid interior where the stations still run stock on the native grasses and shrubs, most of the more humid grazing lands have had their grazing resources improved by the sowing of exotic grasses – the rye grasses and paspalums of the temperate winter rain areas and the Rhodes and Kikuyu grasses of the tropical summer rain areas. In addition, partly benefiting from research for legumes for use in rotation cropping for the adjacent crop lands, the less humid rainfall ranges have often been sown down to subterranean clovers (*Trifolium* spp.) and medics (*Medicago* spp.) which both provide livestock feed and soil nutrient replenishment where cropping is practised.

In the periodic droughts, however, even the native grasses died off and only the leaves on the shrubs remained as feed. As this time, the cattle, being taller, had the advantage over sheep and were able to range further from water, 15 miles (24 km) as opposed to 3–5 miles (5–8 km) according to some opinions. For the sheepmen, they could either let their stock die, which might prove cheapest in the long run, evacuate them to rented 'agistment' grazing or buy feed – both of which were very expensive measures, or hire labour to cut down the edible branches so the sheep could get at them. In the eastern semi-arid grass and shrublands in the droughts of the 1890s as an example, gangs of Chinese labourers (often ex-gold miners) 'cut scrub' wherever mulga (*Acacia aneura*) or kurrajongs (*Brachychiton* spp.) were available to keep starving sheep alive until the rains came. In the droughts of the 1960s the same effect was achieved by various mechanical implements, from the blade of a bulldozer to homemade 'scrub-bashers' of logs lashed

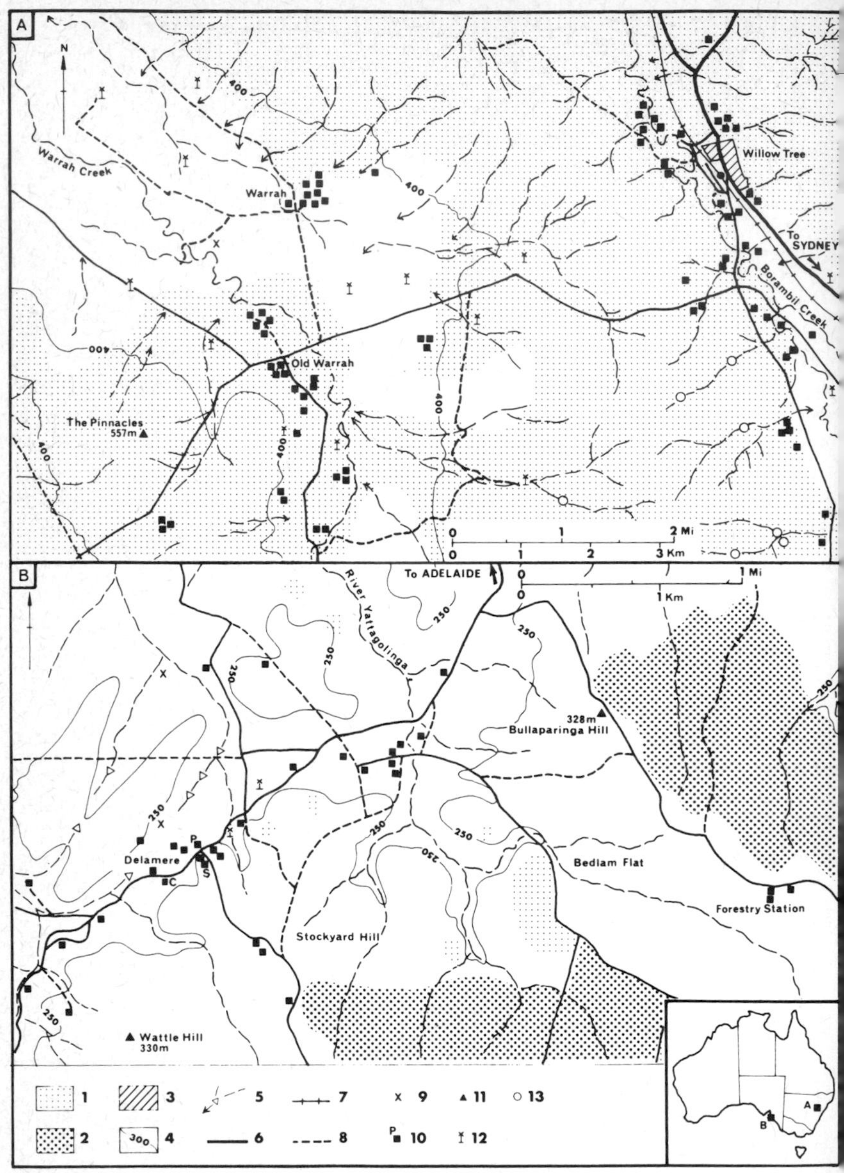

Fig. 8.5 Pastoral landscapes: intensive farmscapes
A. Intensive improved grazing: Warrah, N.S.W.
B. Dairy farming: Delamere, S.A.
1, Open woodland; **2**, Pine plantation; **3**, Urban area; **4**, Contours (metres); **5**, Watercourse with dam; **6**, Main road; **7**, Railway; **8**, Secondary road; **9**, Ruins; **10**, Buildings (generalised) mainly farms, but P, post

onto old horse wagons pulled now by tractors. On the intensive grazing lands farmers bought more hay and wheat and handfed their stock as long as they could afford it.

Not only the vegetation posed problems, for the most serious deficiency, which became more obvious as the pastoralists pushed inland, was the scarcity of surface water. Already in the 1860s in the relatively well-watered southeast, small dams had been made and small reservoirs (tanks) excavated on the clay plains to catch run-off. These were of some value in a good rainy season, but often worse than useless in a drought when livestock tended to bog themselves in the stinking mudhole at the bottom of the empty tank.

From the earliest years, wells had been sunk in the beds of dry creeks and likely low spots, but not until the introduction of diamond tipped drills and power-driven gear adapted from the deep oil-prospecting in North America in the 1880s was the existence of potable water discovered at depths of 2000–3000 ft below the plains. Not only was this potable, it was part of the Great Artesian Basin and flowed to the surface and indeed several feet above it under hydraulic pressure, eliminating the need for any lifting engines. The discovery opened up vast areas of the northern grasslands and shrublands which otherwise were waterless for most of the year. Water from these artesian 'bores' was led over the plains in ditches – 'bore drains' – to open up new areas to livestock. By 1900, most of the useful artesian basins had been discovered (some waters were too saline even for livestock) yet the droughts of the period still caused losses of up to half the livestock. Why? By 1900 the stock were dying of starvation along the full bore drains, the fodder within travelling distance of water having been either eaten or destroyed by the drought.

Competition for the grazing resources from native herbivores, such as kangaroos, wallabies and emus, was locally a problem since they tended to bunch on the remaining feed in the droughts and this led to the extermination policies of many pastoralists. A far greater problem was competition from the European rabbit, which had been introduced as a game animal in Victoria in the 1860s and by the 1890s had occupied the eastern rangelands and was beginning to appear in the southern and northern rims of the desert country. The impact of this grazing competition was again worst in the stress of droughts, when mobs of thousands ringbarked the remaining shrubs and edible scrublands and, weakened like the cattle and sheep, drowned in the tanks and watering troughs, fouling with their carcases the vital water supplies. Despite extensive poisoning by hand, digging up of warrens, and rabbitproof fencing of state and property boundaries, not until the introduction of the virus 'myxomatosis' in the 1950s was some kind of control

---

Caption to Fig. 8.5 – continued

office, S, School, C, Church; **11**, Spot height; **12**, Windpump; **13**, Spring or well.

(*Sources:* A – Murrurundi Sheet, 1:100 000, 1970; B – Cape Jervis Sheet, 1:50 000, 1958)

over their numbers effective and the pastoralist could ride out over his paddocks without a portion of the grey-brown foreground suddenly taking to its heels in front of his eyes. The seasonal reoccurrence of the disease, transmitted by summer mosquitoes, plus continued poisoning, appears to have confined the rabbits to manageably small colonies.

The only other significant indigenous hazard, apart from the Aborigines, who acquired a taste for beef and mutton early in the history of settlement, was the dingo which attacked young cattle and especially sheep. Poisoning has been only of limited success and trapping has been a highly skilled and hence expensive solution. It is significant that even in the 1970s the division between cattle and sheep properties in the central grazing lands is the dingo-proof fence from South Australia to Queensland (Fig. 8.3). Inland from the fence the dingo is king and sheep are generally absent; outside the fence the dingo is officially controlled and sheep can thrive.

Apart from attempting to cope with environmental hazards, technological innovations within the pastoral system have been tried to improve the efficiency of production, often by means which have left significant imprints in the landscape. In the 1850s when shepherds deserted for the goldfields, fencing of the ranges became essential if production was to continue. Experience of livestock in fenced paddocks soon convinced pastoralists that the stock benefited from being left alone, without the daily 'forced marches' to and from night yards. In effect, on a fenced property the stock could be left alone for virtually eight to twelve months until the annual muster and/or shearing, when the surplus stock were drafted out for sale off the property, young stock were 'branded', inferior animals picked out or 'culled', the wool baled and the annual balance sheets worked out. Mechanisation was extended to shearing itself in the 1880s, and the slap of leather drive-belts and the chatter of toothed mechanical clippers drowned out the click of the manual shears in the woolsheds thereafter. Lambing times were changed from spring to autumn on the arid ranges, where the milder winter sun took less heavy toll of young lambs and weaning ewes, particularly where pastures were bare before the irregular summer rains greened them up again. The time of shearing here was also changed in the same way, for experience showed that unshorn sheep withstood the searing temperatures much better than their shorn brethren, as the unshorn fleece was a very effective solar heat shield.

To adapt the introduced livestock to the varied ecosystems of the interior, original breeds were gradually modified. Part of the change was accidental, in the best biological tradition by survival of the fittest*, but part was deliberate, the crossing of the survivors with higher yielding breeds. Thus British sheep breeds became dominant in the cooler wetter southeast, while on the inland more arid plains roamed the descendants of His

* Several instances of the survival of wild sheep have been reported. The most recent was in 1964, when sixteen sheep, descendants of a flock lost in the Kimberleys in 1924, were recaptured, to be tested by the CSIRO for genetic adaptations of value to domestic flocks.

Majesty's Spanish (and later Saxon) merinos. By 1850, there were more merinos in Australia than in Spain and from the 1860s onwards sheep studs in the Riverina were breeding for quality of wool and carcase and their prize-winning products were providing progeny to upgrade 'outback' (interior) flocks. The same process for beef cattle seems to have been delayed virtually 100 years, for British breeds (the Shorthorn and Hereford) (*Bos taurus*) were introduced overland from the south-eastern entry points to the tropical north with minimum efforts at selective breeding. Not until the 1950s were Indian humped Zebu (*Bos indicus*) cattle and variants developed in the United States (particularly Santa Gertrudis) introduced into the tropical ranges for serious breeding purposes to attempt to cope with the summer heat stress, the ravages of cattle ticks and parasite diseases such as 'red-water fever'.

On the cooler wetter pastures of the south-eastern highlands and Tasmania, a form of transhumance was established by which both cattle and sheep were grazed on the lower valley pastures in the winter but sent up to the sub-Alpine pastures of the plateaus in the spring. Such spring and summer grazing lands came to be occupied as 'snow leases' by lowland pastoralists, who returned their flocks to the safety of the lowland each autumn.

In the arid interior, special concessions of low rents and larger leases were given to pastoralists who improved the quality of the grazing resources. 'Scrub leases' encouraged them to clear inedible shrublands in favour of colonisation by grasses (native or exotic), while 'improvement' and 'artesian well' leases encouraged the search for underground water. In the droughts, extention of leases were given to allow the recouping of losses in the good seasons which were assumed to follow, while reduction of the annual rents and cheaper rail freights for stock feed in or stock evacuation gave some immediate financial relief. The result, at periods of stress, could be a 'deserted' pastoral landscape.

Pastoral landscapes in the 1970s

Beneath the broad generalisations of Fig. 8.1 lie many contrasting details of individual properties resulting from contrasting histories of land use, ownership and managerial skills. Some idea of the scope of these contrasts is given in Tables 6.2 (p. 66) and 8.1 (p. 100) and by Figs. 8.2 and 8.5. Thus the extensive pastoral stations might be over 1 million acres (400 000 ha) in size if a cattle property and yet be as small as 41 000 acres (16 400 ha) if mainly a sheep property. Investment of labour will vary from over ten to an average of three to four men; capital investment per property might average $400 000, but would represent the lowest per unit area figure of the whole pastoral landscapes. Profits per unit area would be the lowest also, but profits per property and the net return on capital could be the highest.

Myrtle Springs–Ediacara, a cattle and sheep property lying on the edge of the Lake Torrens salt flat (Fig. 8.2B) in South Australia is one example

Table 8.1 Organisation of pastoral and agricultural production units in 1960s

Type	*Size (ha)*	*Labour (men)*	*Capital ($000)*	*Return ($ net/ha)*	*Stock density (seu/ha)*
Extensive pastoral:					
Cattle station	441 680	10–15	409	0.05	0.2
Sheep station	23 430	3–4	170	2	0.3
Intensive pastoral:					
Cattle farm	1400	2	129	7	3.0
Sheep farm	513	1–2	75	18	5.6
Dairy farm	145	1.5	35	55	
Agricultural:					
Grain (wheat) farm	978	1–2	85	13	2.2
Irrigated farms:					
Rice and sheep	406	?	84	20	?
Cotton	809	3–5?	505	114	?

Note
Seu-sheep equivalent units of eight sheep to one cow.
Sources: Alexander and Williams (1973); Davidson (1967); BAE (1970 and 1971)

of such an extensive property. Some 966 square miles (2512 km^2) of 6.6 inches (165 mm) rainfall country, comprising low tablelands, saltbush plains and cane grass swamp and clay pans, crossed by dry watercourses, is rated officially to be able to carry one sheep on every 29 acres (12 ha). Annual rent for this fifty-year leasehold in 1973 was approximately one-tenth of a cent per acre or about 3 cents per sheep carried. While the eastern half (the original Myrtle Springs) has been subdivided into paddocks averaging 24 square miles (58 km^2) each, the western half (Ediacara) remains 'unimproved' apart from the isolated surface catchment dam and the two bores. In mid-1973 the whole was sold at auction for $725 000 or *c.* $1.17 per acre ($2.93 per ha).

Warrah Homestead in New South Wales (Fig. 8.5), the core area of the Australian Agricultural Company's original 1833 grant of 249 600 acres (99 840 ha), was in 1969 some 5784 acres (2314 ha) of alluvial flats and basalt hills on which some remnants of the original savannah woodland of white box and kurrajong timber provided shade for the stud Shorthorn cattle. Subdivisions for closer settlement had so reduced the size by 1969 that the Company finally decided to sell out. Underground water at 20–30 ft (6–9 m) depth was drawn upon by eight bores which irrigated a small area of lucerne, grown in rotation with the wheat crop for fodder. Average stock numbers for the district would be *c.* 1 sheep per acre (2.5 per ha) and the land prices were about $50–80 per acre ($125–200 per ha).

At the most intensive end of the spectrum of pastoral land-use, the dairy farms present a contrasting picture. In size they vary from 150–400 acres (60–160 ha) with herds of about sixty cows (Jerseys, Friesians, Illawarras and Ayrshires), but for over half the farms – practising mixed crop farming – the herd might be as low as fifteen animals. They are, as originally intended, family farms, operated usually by man and wife, and produce almost invariably only the liquid milk, which is then processed in the local creamery for urban liquid milk (about $\frac{1}{4}$ of output), preserved as butter ($\frac{2}{3}$ of output), or cheese. In appearance, the farms vary from neat trim properties with gravelled tracks, clean pastures and tight wire fences, to dishevelled broken-down homesteads, surrounded by mud and tussocky, weed-ridden, pastures with decrepit post and rail fences. Many are too small, barely economic units, and claims were made in 1970 that net incomes off the smaller properties could be as low as $1000 a year.

The environmental impact of pastoralism

This variety of production unit and intensity of land-use has had an environmental impact which has varied usually with the intensity of capital investment. As suggested by Table 6.3 (p. 69) the extensive grazing on the large stations has had only a selective effect on the vegetation, whereas on the more intensively stocked grazing and dairy farms the original cover has been replaced on over a third to three-quarters of the area. Rather surprisingly, a fifth of the dairy landscapes seem to have been relatively unaffected: that is, remain more or less in the original vegetation cover. Much of this area, however, represents country in the Highland Zone which has been so far too steep or rugged to be cleared even for grazing lands.

The impact of grazing on the extensive pastures of the interior has been generally to reduce the quality of the most edible and accessible species, especially around permanent watering points, and to indirectly encourage the spread of inedible species by removing their competitors. Variations in local stocking densities over time make any continental generalisations suspect, but one recent estimate (Newman and Condon, 1969) has suggested that loss of virtually half of the 'pristine' condition of the vegetation had occurred over 65 per cent of the shrublands (bluebush and saltbush communities) and 30 per cent of the woodlands and more rugged grazing areas, whereas the original grasslands and spinifex country were only 15 per cent and 10 per cent so affected. These latter figures are surprising, but might be the result of the need to remove all livestock from the grasslands in the severe droughts, as no feed at all is left, and delays in re-stocking allowing regeneration from seeds after the drought breaks. In the other vegetation communities in contrast there would always be some growth above ground and stockmen would be tempted to leave stock on the ranges longer into droughts, thus possibly causing more significant damage to the vegetation. Until much more detail of past stocking practices is known, however, all such explanations can be only speculative, for 'range management' is still in its infancy in Australia.

Overgrazing in the past has been commonly blamed for evidence of soil erosion of the grazing lands – wind erosion in the interior and water erosion in the humid fringe of the continent. Wind erosion did not suddenly appear with the first pastoralists – the first explorers reported it in dry seasons well before the appearance of any cattle or sheep – but there is no doubt that the rate has locally been accelerated by the reduced vegetation cover. Studies of intensive grazing areas in the Highland Zone suggest that water erosion is evident but as yet affecting only limited areas. Thus while 47 per cent of the catchment area above Canberra shows some erosion, only approximately 6 per cent is classed as moderate or severe gullying or sheet erosion, the remainder being of minor significance despite the fact that this area has up to 33.5 inches (850 mm) of rainfall annually and has been grazed for 130 years. The environmental impact of pastoralism is more subtle than immediately obvious, certainly when compared with the impact of agriculture, as we shall see.

9
The agricultural landscapes

The first fleet bringing convicts to establish the first permanent settlement in 1788 carried seeds and seedlings which were to establish a local food supply for the colony. The intention was that the settlement should become self-sufficient as soon as possible, but not until over fifty years later was the local agriculture able to meet local needs. For these first fifty years agriculture absorbed only a small portion of local energies, which were directed more to maritime and pastoral activities as we have seen. From mid-nineteenth century onwards, however, agricultural production expanded to meet not only increasing local demands but also to take up a share of an increasingly international market. From the initial concern for basic foodstuffs, the trend was towards specialisation of production and the creation of distinctive landscapes as a result. The farmers began to leave their lands around the south-eastern coastal bases and press first inland on the heels of the pastoralists and then north along the tropical coasts, modifying old and evolving new crops to exploit the new and generally superior lands.

The evolution of agricultural landscapes before 1850

The pattern of agriculture which evolved before 1850 was basically one of attempted local subsistence in food supplies and very limited production of raw materials, despite early hopes. The farmers faced considerable initial difficulties.

Around the first settlement at Sydney was a broad ring of barren sandy soils carrying a deceptively dense stand of sclerophyll forest; no river entered the harbour and no large river flats bordered it. Here farmers tried and failed to produce a colonial food supply and their successors in 1970 have made more sense out of it as suburban housing and a National Park. The first thirty years of farming in the new colony were in fact a search — often desperate as local foodstocks ran low — for sufficient fertile land close enough to provide a food supply at minimum cost. The search was successful only in certain of the larger coastal valleys — on the mainland the Hawkesbury (first farmed in 1794) and the Hunter (first farmed in 1823) and in Tasmania, the Derwent (first farmed in 1804). Here fertile lands were located alongside navigable waters and this combination allowed Tasmanian grains to supply Sydney some 633 miles (1013 km) away.

Fertile lands were essential because the lack of livestock reduced organic fertilisers to a minimum (chemical fertilisers were only just being thought of in Europe), and because of the need to crop the minute cleared lands continuously to obtain immediate yields. Methods and the landscape which resulted were initially rough. An eyewitness (Dawson, 1830, pp. 394–5) described the systems operating in the Hunter Valley about 1830:

> The first crop which a settler takes from this *newly* cleared land is maize, which is planted from September to December [i.e. spring], generally after one ploughing; and sometimes the poorer settlers do not plough it at all merely making holes with the hoe, and planting the seed. A crop of wheat succeeds the maize, and alternates with it as long as the land will bear it; and where the settler can afford to go on clearing, the first patch as soon as it becomes exhausted, is abandoned for the more newly cleared lands, while the former is left to nature and time to restore its fecundity.

The crudity of such methods, coupled with the energy which had to be diverted into the process of clearing the heavy stands of timber from the river flats before any cropping could take place, and the fact that the warm and moist conditions favoured bacterial fungoid diseases, especially 'rust' and 'smut' in the wheat, meant that yields were disappointingly low. In addition, the floods, which had replenished the natural fertility of the river flats before the settlers arrived, continued after their arrival and indeed seem to have increased in volume over the years as a result of forest clearance in the upper watersheds. Thus, the Hawkesbury harvests of 1799 and 1801 were destroyed and the Hunter Valley harvests were obtained irregularly in the face of periodic serious flooding. Yet not until a disastrous Hunter Valley flood in 1955 were effective measures taken to control seasonal flood peaks and the Hawkesbury still floods its lower floodplain in the 1970s.

The first 'farmers' were convicts, working in gangs under supervisors, often hired or lent to landowners to help the initial land clearance – felling, carting logs, grubbing roots and burning-off the trash, all with limited hand tools and limited man-power. Later they were convicts who had served out their sentence, had been freed – 'emancipated' – and offered small plots of land to start life afresh. Finally, they were free men with some capital who had immigrated as settlers from Britain, especially after 1831, when assisted passages began to be offered from the revenues of colonial land sales. Such men, particularly the second and third types, would have been found along the Hunter Valley in the 1830s and upstream from Hobart along the Derwent in the 1840s. From 1829 and 1836 the third type began to establish themselves in the new colonies of Western and South Australia respectively.

Not until the 1820s was the colony self-sufficient in bread grains: not until 1830 could it afford to discard the pork imported from Tahiti. By

1850, however, agriculture had proven itself in terms of food supply. Wines and tobacco were being produced in the Hunter Valley and vineyards were appearing amid South Australia's wheatlands. Sydney's butter and cheese were being supplied by Hawkesbury river and coastal boats from Hunter Valley and Illawarra farms, while inland each settlement had its own small circle of farms supplying its needs for wheat, potatoes and other vegetables. Only water transport was cheap enough to allow any other than local movement of foodstuffs, and in a continent already recognised to be deficient in water inland no one seriously thought the British canals would be worth copying.

The evolution of agricultural landscapes after 1850

From about the mid-nineteenth century the agriculture of Australia underwent significant changes, first to meet an increasing demand for food products at home and overseas and second as a result of political policies on the process of land settlement itself. The results on the landscape were the rapid expansion of farmlands but within a framework delimited by official settlement policies.

A sudden increase in local demand for all foodstuffs was a direct result of the influx of foreign miners on their way to the gold and other precious mineral 'rushes' beginning in 1850. In 1857 the non-Aboriginal population of Australia was 400 000, by 1901 it had increased almost ten-fold and by 1970 the internal needs of the total population of 12 million was a significant stimulus to agricultural production. By 1901, however, while the production of wheat had similarly increased ten-fold, half of this was already being exported to Europe and the proportion was to increase in the twentieth century.

The increase in international trade in Australian farm products came from a combination of circumstances. The repeal of the protectionist Corn Laws in 1846 opened the British market to the international wheat trade; higher living standards in Europe in the late nineteenth century brought increased demands for food and traditional suppliers appear to have failed to cope. In addition, however, there was a basic economic reason; it was cheaper to buy bread grain produced in Australia and the Americas and shipped to Britain than it was to buy British. Again, the details were complex but worth considering when we try to explain what was grown and where in Australia.

Several technological innovations in the latter half of the nineteenth century made possible the coordination of agricultural production and marketing from one side of the world to the other. In the 1860s information of supply and demand began to flow across the world along the expanding network of international telegraph lines. By 1872 the major cities of Australia were linked to London by a copper wire looped across the central deserts and then by submarine cables to Europe.

The flow of goods was generally speeded up over this same period. Fast sailing clippers, built to bring gold miners to Australia, sailed back to Europe via the newly discovered Great Circle routes across the southern Pacific and by Cape Horn to the Atlantic, running before the westerlies with their holds full of wool bales and wheat bags. From 120 days in the 1840s, the trip to London was cut to sixty to eighty days in 1860s. By comparison the ocean-going steamships, which dwarfed locally built coastal steamers alongside the wharves at Sydney and Melbourne by the 1860s, were initially slower but benefited from the opening of the Suez Canal in 1869, since the Red Sea winds were unreliable, and began to provide a tolerably swift and regular cargo service to Europe. By the 1880s their cargoes were larger than the clippers and they never looked back.

None of these means however could cope with perishable cargo. Wheat as grain or flour, salted and pickled beef and pork could survive the trip alongside the wool bales, but not until refrigeration of cargo holds began in the 1880s, could unprocessed meats or dairy produce survive the time and the high tropical temperatures of the voyage. Salted meats had a limited market – mainly as military and naval stores – but cooked meats had been shut out of the British market by tariffs on manufactured products in the 1840s. Salted butter in wax-tight jars had been exported to California in the 1849 gold rush but did not long survive local American competition.

Chilling of perishable cargoes was followed by careful grading and standardisation of produce for the international market place. For wheat, assessments of the quality of annual harvests began to be made by the official department of agriculture at the turn of the century and coincided with official encouragement to improve yields. Chemical analysis of samples from the main producing areas each year gave officials 'fair average quality' (FAQ) standards by which all crops could be measured and buyers assured of quality.

A final factor in the pattern of world demand was the sequence of world events. Continental European suppliers of grain to Britain had their trade disrupted by the wars of the nineteenth century and their rivals in Australia benefited. The American Civil War encouraged Queensland as well as Fiji in the 1860s to attempt to produce cotton to fill the demands of British mill-owners who could no longer trade with the Confederate States. Imperial preference agreements between Britain and her colonies and dominions after the First World War gave a protected market to Australian agriculture, for from wheat and sugar to fruit and dairy produce. The food and raw material scarcities of the two world wars, later the Korean and to a lesser extent the Vietnam Wars have stimulated demands, and the Communist Revolution in China so disrupted that country's domestic agriculture as to force her to become one of the leading importers of Australian wheat surpluses in the 1960s to 1970s.

To satisfy this increasing demand, a range of factors has enabled the volume of agriculture production to be expanded and an increasing area of the continent to come under the plough. Initially, existing farms were more intensively used, but until the introduction and widespread use of chemical fertilisers after the 1890s, any increase was of only a few years' duration, the main increases had to come from *new* farmlands.

From *c.* 1850 to 1914 Australian farmers began to occupy some of the best agricultural soils in the continent (Fig. 9.1). The wheat farmers moved out into the red-brown earths of the southeast and the dairy and sugar farmers began to occupy the remoter eastern coastal alluvials on both sides of the Tropic of Capricorn (see Fig. 9.5). After 1914, the extensions inland began to reach the arid limits of the required growing season, although a renewed extension in Western Australia has come since the 1950s with a reappraisal of the capacities of the sand plains and careful use of fertilisers to offset the soil trace-element deficiencies. This latter expansion in the 1960s was bringing into agricultural production approximately 750 000 acres (300 000 ha) of previously pastoral lands annually.

While much of the land first occupied after 1850 was grassland or savannah woodland, where ploughing could begin almost at once, by the 1880s these areas had generally been occupied and farmers faced the extensive shrublands, where dense stands of mallee and acacia scrubs defied all traditional clearing methods (Fig. 4.5, p. 41). Individual farmers solved the clearing problem by a combination of hard labour with grapnel and horse teams and inspired inventions. Trees were felled and the stumps dragged out and fired, to smoulder for days in great heaps amid the clearings; scrubs were knocked down by massive rollers, often old steam boilers filled with rocks and pulled by a horse team (used first in South Australia in 1876) and, by the 1950s, two caterpillar tractors pulling heavy anchor chains attached to a large steel ball. The roots of the mallees heated homes in Melbourne and Adelaide suburbs where the factories were turning out the new stump-jump ploughs which jigged across the cleared lands, the blades bouncing on springs over the hidden roots which would have snapped traditional implements. Behind came the clumsy 'strippers'. First pushed and later pulled by horses, these large metal boxes on wheels chewed off the ears of wheat too short on the stalk to be cut, bound, stooked and threshed in the traditional way.

Commercial production and the export of a surplus crop was impossible from inland Australia until the cost of land transport was significantly reduced by the spread of the colonial railway networks, which were one of the major items of public investment in the 1860s to 1890s. During this period, investment produced not one network but several — at least one for each colony; not one gauge but an incredible range of gauges from 3 ft 6 inches (1.05 m) to 5 ft 8 inches (1.70 m); a variety of rails from wood to steel, and a variety of motive-power from horse-drawn tramways in 1880s for the wheatlands on the coastal plains of South Australia, to the multiple-engined steam giants hauling the wheat trucks over the 'Zig-Zag' tracks of the eastern highlands to the coast. The least variety, significantly, was in the railway ownership, which devolved onto the governments when the few private ventures (apart from mining lines which were a special case as we shall see) were bankrupted and the American land-grant system was turned

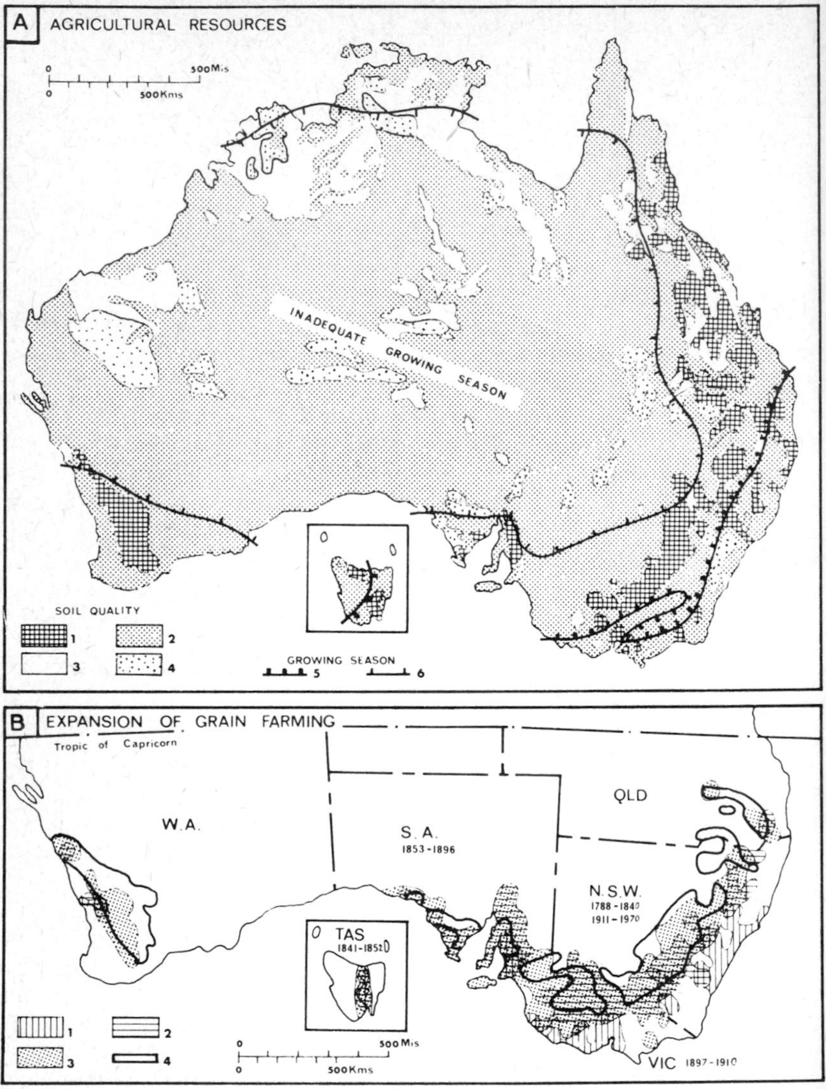

A AGRICULTURAL RESOURCES
0 500Mls
0 500Kms
INADEQUATE GROWING SEASON
SOIL QUALITY
1
2
3
4
GROWING SEASON
5
6

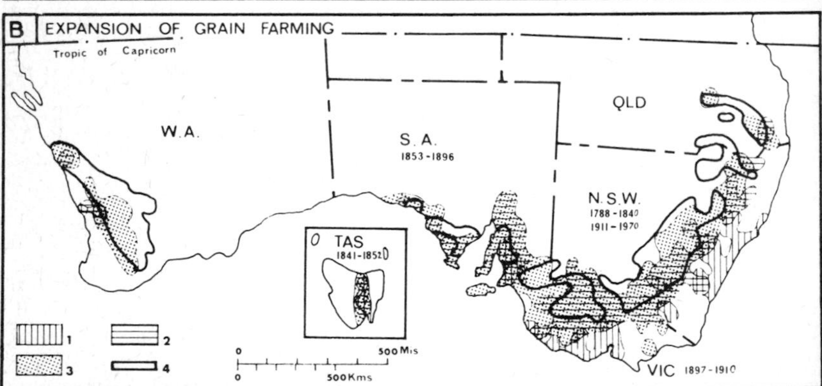

Fig. 9.1 Agricultural landscapes: evolution 1788–1970s

A. Agricultural resources
Soil quality: **1**, Good; **2**, Deficient in either fertility or moisture; **3**, No effective soil; **4**, Mixed quality.
Growing season: **5**, Less than nine consecutive months; **6**, Less than five consecutive months.

B. Expansion of grain farming
Areas under crop in: **1**, 1860; **2**, 1892; **3**, 1910; **4**, 1970. Dates show periods when state production was highest in Australia.

(*Sources:* Australia, 1962; Dunsdorfs, 1956; Callaghan and Millington, 1956; CSIRO, 1960)

down. The latter was rejected because the amounts of land needed to compensate a company for railway construction would have created land monopolies to dwarf even the American transactions.

Despite bureaucratic control, however, the railways were built and were continuing to be built up to the world depression of the 1930s. The details of the pattern reflected different state Government policies. Queensland tended to see her railways as pioneering ventures to tap the pastoral resources of the interior and built long isolated tentacles in from ports on the eastern coast. New South Wales and Victoria saw the railways as more important for agriculture and laid out parallel tracks 20–30 miles apart in the inland wheat country. South and Western Australia had patterns of both and a more complex picture resulted. In each case, with the exception of Queensland, all systems deliberately converged on the state capital and by tapered freight rates encouraged even the remotest producer to truck via his state system and divert movements from shortest to cheapest routes.

By the combination of new lands, new methods of production and new transport systems the interior farmlands were finally able to compete in the world market. But when last we looked at the inland the pastoralists were in full control; it was a pastoral landscape. We need now to consider how that was transformed into an agricultural landscape.

So far, we have assumed that land was there for the taking – in any way one chose. In fact it was not so and not only the timing but to some extent the diversion and certainly the detailed form which the farms took depended upon the legal disposal of land ownership.

We have seen that pastoral land use evolved its own form of land holding – large estates of land either acquired free or for a trifling sum in the early years of settlement or, more usually, held as leases for quite long periods of time on payment of nominal rents per acre. This 'extensive' land-use and its associated tenure system was the direct antithesis of the agricultural land use encouraged by the various colonial and state Governments. In this latter case the intention, firmly stated in all the local parliamentary debates on the bills to enforce it, was to break the land monopolies and 'socialise' this national resource by the establishment of a 'yeoman' farming settlement: the pastoral estates were to be replaced by small, family operated farms. This concept was implicit in legislation in Western Australia in 1850, 1860 and 1872; in New South Wales in 1861; in Victoria in 1859, 1862 and 1869; Queensland, 1860 and 1868; South Australia, 1869; and Tasmania, 1868. Land was to be taken out of pastoral lease and made available in small blocks (usually from 80–320 acres (32–130 ha) with 160 acres (65 ha) a most common size) at low prices and on long-term credit, provided certain qualifications were met.

Although intended to produce agricultural use of pastoral land, the concept was wedded to the 'Closer Settlement' policies mentioned in Chapter 8. The intensification of numbers of settlers on the land, achieved by what was in each case a subdivision of large into smaller production units, was thought to lead to intensification of capital investment and consequent production. In fact, the legislation was less effective than had been hoped. A combination of careless legal drafting, inefficient supervision of its enforcement and blatant frauds enabled monopolists to maintain or build up control of 'divided' estates, and many *bona fide* settlers (both pastoralists and farmers) to be blackmailed off their lands. There can be no doubt, however, that without this legislation agriculture would have developed much later and in a vastly different manner, and the present patterns of rural Australia could have been significantly changed.

The combination of demand for Australian produce from outside the continent and the technological and legal innovations which encouraged that demand to be met from within the continent, provided a changing kaleidoscope of landscapes which had by 1970 resolved itself into three major types. Each of these needs to be examined separately.

The grain landscapes

After the excess moisture and fertility problems of the coastal valleys, the search for new wheatlands led across the Highland Zone on to the drier but fertile red-brown soils of the interior. The only location where these soils occurred at the coast was at Adelaide, South Australia, and this coincidence helped the colony establish major interstate export in wheat in the 1840s (Fig. 9.1). By 1861 these soils in South Australia carried 40 per cent of the continent's wheatfields and quintripled that area by an expansion of farmlands in twenty years. A legal barrier, Goyder's Line, checked expansion briefly in the early 1870s but was removed in 1879 and the only other checks to expansion prior to 1890 were the limits of the fertile soils, the ever present threat of drought and the mallee shrublands.

By 1895 Victorian wheat acreages, expanding into its portion of the 'fertile crescent', had taken the lead from South Australia; by 1911 the lead had passed to the New South Wales portion. This shift of the peak of wheat acreage from west to east around the fertile crescent resulted from the initial transport advantage of the coastal farms of South Australia being eroded by the railway networks set up by the Victorian and New South Wales Governments (Fig. 9.2); the opening up of new areas for settlement by legislation and some decline in yields from the older South Australian farms. In Western Australia, a late mining boom triggered off a local wheat boom in the 1890s to 1900s but an even greater expansion has come since the 1950s, when as noted above trace elements and fertilisers brought previously useless sand plains into wheat production.

Droughts, the world economic depression and falling wheat prices of the early 1930s brought first a voluntary and then Government subsidised reduction in wheat acreage from the peak of 18 million acres (7 300 000 ha). The amalgamation of less successful into more successful farms had been a logical process ever since the land had been subdivided and opened to agriculture, but the 1930s and 1940s saw official amalgamations of small and uneconomic, into larger, economic, production units. This

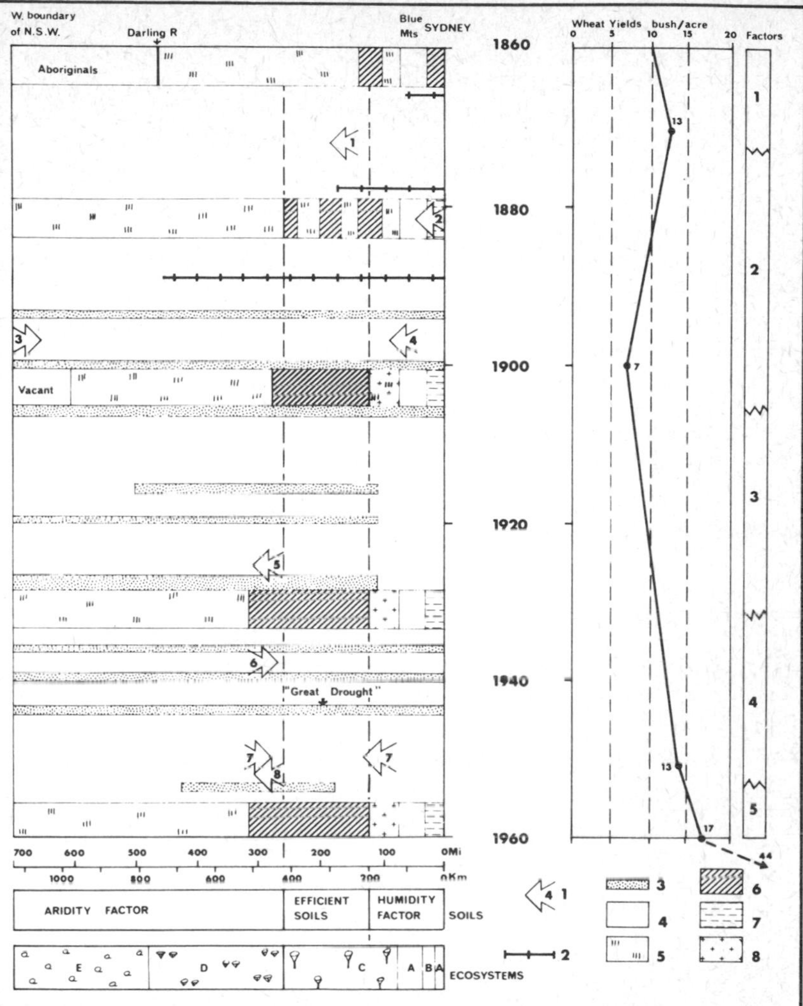

Fig. 9.2 Pastoral–agricultural frontiers, N.S.W., 1860–1960

The expansions and retreats of pastoral and agricultural land use along a line from Sydney to the north-western border of N.S.W. are indicated by means of cross-sections of land use at twenty-year intervals, with the variables which appear to have affected these patterns indicated, and the trends in yields of wheat and factors which affected those trends shown for the equivalent period of time.

General key:

1. Variables which affected pastoral–agricultural land use patterns. Within the diagram these are indicated as: 1. (1860s) Legislation 'unlocks' the pastoral lands for agriculture, local demand for grain increases, expansion of rail network across Blue Mountains and favourable seasons of 1870s. 2. (1880s) Retreat of wheat farming from coast because of experience of

'Marginal Lands Scheme' operated mainly at the arid limit of the wheat areas and used Government money to buy out bankrupt smallholders to offer their farms to larger neighbours as additional areas (Fig. 9.3). Production need not be altered but the survivors were encouraged to diversify to mixed grain and livestock farming. This was the first official recognition that there might be environmental and economic limits to continued intensification of land-use.

From the period of the 1930s, not only did the size of most grain farms expand, but their production became more varied. For many years there had been the coastal production of maize as a livestock feed and a general sowing of oats to add to the wheat chaff for the horses, while from about the 1820s onwards maize lost favour as a raw material for the local brewers who instead provided an expanding market for malting barley and Tasmanian hops. Even the continuous cropping of the dominant crop wheat, was replaced by more mixed production, and from the 1930s what came to be known as the wheat–sheep complex began to emerge. Encouraged by fluctuating wheat prices and the Marginal Lands Scheme, farmers began to buy sheep to graze the young wheatfields, the fallowed land and

---

Caption to Fig. 9.2 – continued

rust diseases, declining yields and competition from dairying. 3. (1890s) Retreat of remotest pastoralists in face of droughts 1895–1902. 4. (1890s) Retreat of farming from highlands because of frost and competition from dairying and intensive grazing. 5. (1920s) Advance of wheat farming into dry country aided by Government policies, Soldier Settlement Schemes, new wheat breeds, use of artificial fertilisers. 6. (1930s–40s) Retreat of wheat farmers from 'Marginal Lands' with drought and World Depression.
7. (1950s) Retreat of monoculture wheat in face of high wool prices of 1950s, Government support for diversification, emergence of 'wheat–sheep' farms. 8. (1960s) Expansion of wheat–sheep farms into dry country with aid of subterranean clovers and superphosphate fertilisers.

2. Railway expansion (little development along section post-1900).
3. Droughts.
4. Unoccupied Land.
5. Pastoral land use (extensive).
6. Agricultural land use (mainly wheat farming).
7. Intensive agriculture (horticulture) with dairying.
8. Pastoral land use (intensive).

Factors affecting trends in wheat yields

1, Initial cropping using inherent fertility; 2, Decline from continuous cropping and monoculture; 3, Improvements from use of fallowing, and new higher-yielding grains; 4, Greater use of artificial fertilisers and rotation of nitrogen fixing legumes; 5, Advent of 'scientific' farming with greater knowledge of precise growth requirements and soil management.

Ecosystems

A, Sclerophyll forest; B, Rain forest; C, Woodland; D, Shrubland (Mallee); E, Mixed grassland (with saltbush) and shrubland (mulga).

Soils

Aridity and humidity factors indicate which climatic characteristic reduced the potential for grain cropping.

(*Source:* See text)

Fig. 9.3 **Marginal land, near Peterborough, S.A.**
A deserted farmhouse originally built on pastoral land opened up for wheat farming in the 1870s. Abandoned in 1930s after a combination of droughts and world economic depression of wheat prices forced the governments to buy out bankrupt farms and to create pastoral lands once more. Now grazing land, cropped occasionally after a good season's rainfall. Average rainfall *c.* 11.5 inches (*c.* 300 mm).

the occasional paddock of sown pasture. An income from wool and mutton gave alternatives to wheat, and careful husbandry could use the sheep as natural fertilisers and soil-compactors on the loose sandy wheat fields. Fallowing, to build up nutrients and moisture from one season to the next, was extended and supplemented by chemical fertilisers such as superphosphate after the 1890s and rotation planting of nitrogen-fixing legumes from the 1940s to the 1950s.

What would the typical wheat and sheep farm look like? Using a detailed sample survey of conditions in 1967 (BAE, 1969), we can build up a reasonable statistical picture to supplement Fig. 9.4. The average size of a farm would be around 2500 acres (1000 ha) with the largest in Western Australia (and including some of the most recent *new* lands) of 5800 acres (2300 ha) and the smallest (1200 acres (480 ha)), in some of the oldest farmed lands of South Australia. Most of the land would be flat or undulating and less than 5 per cent hilly or too rugged to cultivate. On the farm almost a fifth of the land would still have some timber standing on it, over half of it as yet

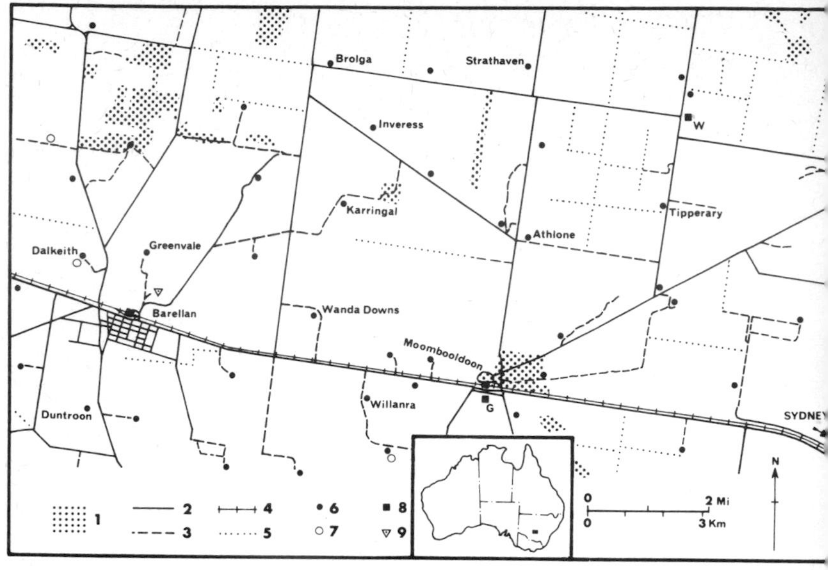

Fig. 9.4 Grain farmscapes
The N.S.W. wheat–sheep country.
1, Woodland; **2**, Main roads; **3**, Secondary roads; **4**, Railway; **5**, Planted windbreaks; **6**, Farm homesteads; **7**, Silos; **8**, G, Grainshed; W, Woolshed **9**, Showground.

(*Source:* Ardlethan Sheet, 1:100 000, 1971)

uncleared, the remainder ringbarked and dead with probably reasonable grass growth beneath. This is an average only, for in the most under-developed farms in the north of New South Wales half the farm (which itself would be bigger than the national average) would still carry timber, and half of that as yet untouched! In South Australia, by contrast, a longer history of clearance is reflected in the virtual absence of timber stands.

At any one time only approximately a quarter of the average farm would be under grain crops, mainly wheat or barley. Sown pastures would be also about a quarter but 42 per cent of the area would still be in unimproved pasture or waste (timber) lands, and 8 per cent would be fallowed each year. On these pastures, about 1400 sheep, a small herd of cattle and a handful of pigs might be found.

True to history, three-quarters of the land would have been or was being purchased outright by the owner, and the remainder on perpetual lease of ninety-nine years or more (a reminder of some modifications to the Closer Settlement Schemes). The yeomen farmers would still be there, for 62 per cent of the farms were owned by family partnerships and 22 per cent by sole owners, with only 11 per cent by private company or some other type. The management was even more a family affair with 75 per cent by family members and 21 per cent by the owner himself.

The sugar landscapes

At the other end of the climatic spectrum, the cultivation of sugar cane produced a successful tropical export industry and a variant on the agricultural landscape. Sugar cane was one of the tropical crops first considered for commercial production in Australia. A convict plantation at Port Macquarie (1823–28) and a free-labour plantation on the Clarence River (1858–61) were the first (and most southerly) of a series of centres of production which, over the next century, were to leapfrog northwards from one coastal valley to another searching always for moister and warmer (frost free) conditions (Fig. 9.5). By 1870 most of the 10 000 acres (4000 ha) of sugar was in Queensland and by 1900 85 per cent of the 133 000 acres (53 200 ha); by the 1950s over half of the production came from north of Mackay.

The first sugar farms in New South Wales (except for the abortive plantations above) were small, independently owned and operated, and supplied cane to both private and cooperative crushing mills for the local market only. The traditional 'plantation' system was imported from the West Indies and Mauritius and adopted most extensively in Queensland where the Government encouraged the import of an indentured labour force (Kanakas) from the Pacific Islands, labourers who by 1885 numbered 11 000 – roughly one for every 6 acres ($2\frac{1}{2}$ ha) of cane. Complaints of kidnapping (blackbirding) of unwilling recruits brought official disfavour and the Federation of the Australian States in 1901 brought the exclusion of 'coloured' labour and an enforced changeover from a plantation system with wage labour on a large unit to a small holding (leasehold tenant or freehold owner) producer supplying a central company mill (from system 1 to system 4 or 5 of Fig. 9.5).

The spread of the sugar production in the twentieth century was the result of an expanding and guaranteed Australian market (the reward paid the sugar growers and Queensland for phasing out their Kanaka labour force), together with technological and scientific innovations which maintained and even increased yields. Even as late as the 1950s croplands were still being extended into original subtropical forest lands and, followed up by widespread use of phosphate fertilisers and high-yielding hybrid canes bred locally on Government experimental stations, production was being maintained despite the exhaustive nutrient demands of the crop.

The sugar landscape at the height of the plantation period differed markedly from the picture in 1970. One of the most spectacular early landscapes was the Pioneer Plantation on the Burdekin Delta, owned by a Scottish family. About 1889 the scene was described as follows (Laut, 1968, I, p. 219):

> The plantation buildings consisted of the manager's house, an office, a field manager's house, men's huts to provide single men's accommodation for thirty, the plantation store, seven cottages for married mill employees, four large grass huts for the Kanaka labourers, stables to

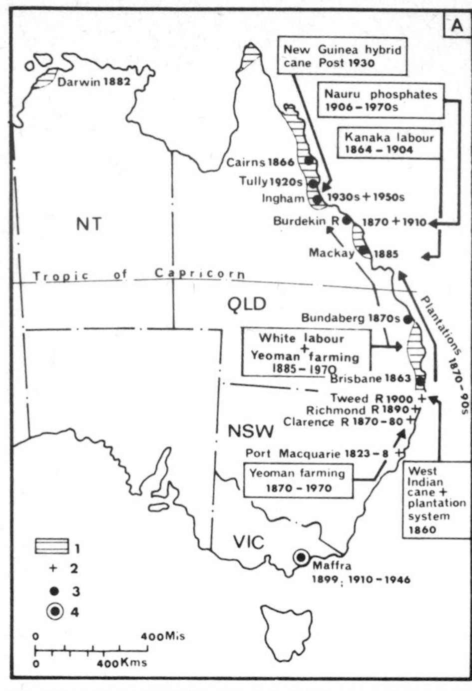

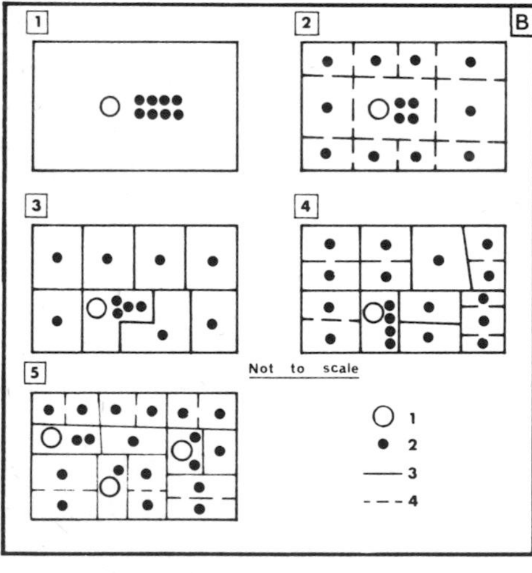

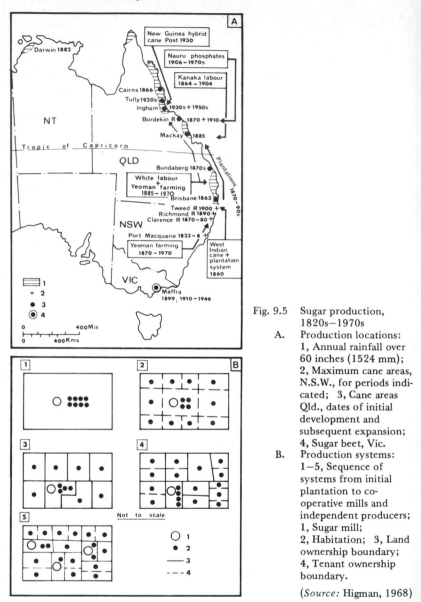

Fig. 9.5 Sugar production, 1820s–1970s
A. Production locations: 1, Annual rainfall over 60 inches (1524 mm); 2, Maximum cane areas, N.S.W., for periods indicated; 3, Cane areas Qld., dates of initial development and subsequent expansion; 4, Sugar beet, Vic.
B. Production systems: 1–5, Sequence of systems from initial plantation to co-operative mills and independent producers; 1, Sugar mill; 2, Habitation; 3, Land ownership boundary; 4, Tenant ownership boundary.
(*Source:* Higman, 1968)

accommodate 117 horses, a blacksmith's shop, a cart shed and a carpenter's shop.

Among the equipment were 100 draught horses and 17 hacks for overseers, 54 working bullocks and 36 milk cows, together with 4 steam ploughs and the crushing mill. At that time the area under crop was slightly over a

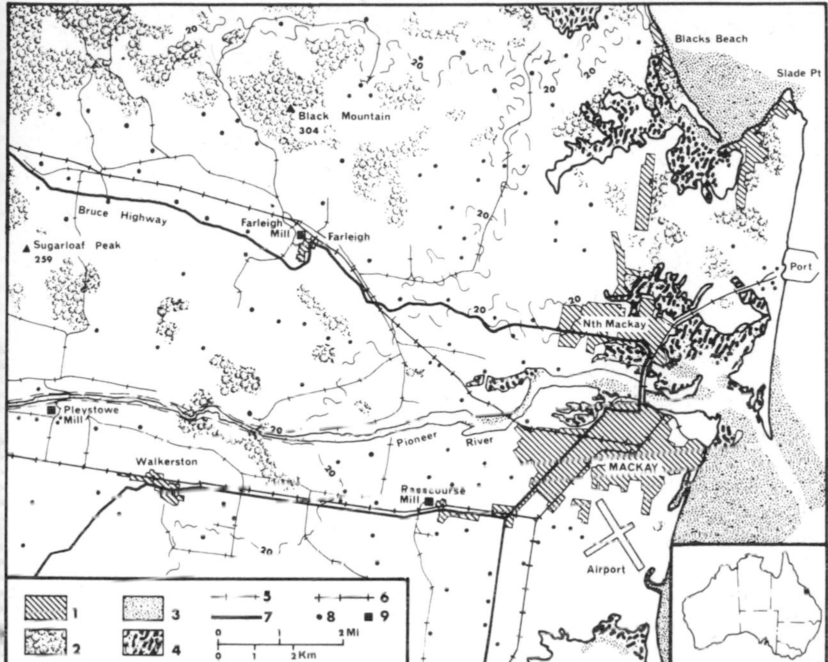

Fig. 9.6 Sugar farmscapes
Pioneer Valley, Qld.
1, Urban area; **2**, Woodland; **3**, Sand flats bare at low tide; **4**, Mangroves; **5**, Light railways and tramways to sugar mills; **6**, Main railways; **7**, Main roads; **8**, Clusters of buildings, mainly sugar farms; **9**, Sugar mill. Secondary roads not shown. Contour and spot heights in metres.

(*Source:* Mackay Sheet 1:100 000, 1971)

quarter of the 5800 acres (2320 ha). The field hands were 290 Kanakas, the mill workers 113 Japanese, the 22 ploughman, 5 stable hands and 6 engine drivers mainly Australians.

By 1970 the sprawling central villages had disappeared although the mills remained, now often in cooperative ownership (Figs. 9.6 and 9.7). Instead the cane came from independent farms of *c*. 70 acres (*c*. 30 ha) each, owned often by one-time cane cutters who had saved their seasonal pay and invested it locally. Many, over half, were of Italian origin, with Maltese and Greeks sprinkled among them. At any one time three-quarters of the cropped land might be under cane as the system of four-year rotation gives three cane crops and then the fields are sown down to legumes to recover fertility.

The irrigated landscapes

Despite the aridity of the Australian interior, the use of supplementary crop water in farming operations came relatively late. Not until 1885 and then in

Fig. 9.7 Pleystowe sugar mill and countryside, Mackay, Qld.
Alluvial flood plain of the Pioneer River is mainly under sugar cane, with surrounding hills (background) in sclerophyll forest. See also Fig. 9.6.

(*Source:* State Public Relations Bureau, Qld.)

one of the better watered states – Victoria – were extensive irrigation works constructed under the supervision of engineers imported from California. These first major projects on the Murray River, first at Mildura then at Renmark, had resulted from a combination of events. Some local experience of river divertion for gardens after 1865, a tentatively enthusiastic report in 1881 on the feasibility of larger irrigation schemes, drought in the early 1880s, the individual leadership of the Victorian Minister for Water Supply, later Premier, Alfred Deakin, and the rivalry of the South Australians – all played a part in the final decision making.

These first projects were of the 'intensive' type – watering a small area for high yielding crops, but by the turn of the century another, 'extensive', type was under consideration. Here on the dry plains away from the river, water from high country run-off was led by canals to tanks and surface storages in the plains as livestock drinking water. The latter scheme had greater success initially as lack of expertise among the first 'intensive' farmers, inadequate knowledge of soil reactions to irrigation, high water losses through evaporation and seepage from the unlined open canals caused heavy wastage. Again a lack of concern about marketing the new produce brought economic and practical problems to the intensive scheme.

After 1905 a further Californian expert, Elwood Mead, suggested concentration of efforts on the intensive schemes under Government patronage and integrated with the closer settlement policies. The states bordering the Murray encouraged a variety of intensive schemes, which raised by 1970 a wide range of products, from the traditional vines and stone fruits to improved pastures for dairying, fat lamb production and even rice (Figs. 6.4 and 9.8). Overseas trade took the dried and canned fruits, some of the butter and cheese, and some of the mutton; the Australian market took table and wine grapes, some dairy products, the fat lambs and the rice.

Outside the Murray Valley irrigation has not been extensive, despite available water supplies. Exceptions are the Gascoyne River flats near Carnarvon (Western Australia) where bananas and vegetables for Perth are grown, and the Burdekin River delta, Queensland, where irrigation supplements the 40 inches (1016 mm) of rainfall for the sugar-cane fields. Both these are using underground supplies in contrast to the Murray Valley. The most recent expansion of the irrigated landscapes have been in the Namoi River area of New South Wales where American cotton farmers have introduced highly mechanised production methods, and the Ord River of Western Australia (Fig. 9.8), where construction is still under way of storage to irrigate approximately 200 000 acres (80 000 ha) by 1975 for cotton and probably sorghum as cattle feed.

Although the products grown in the irrigated areas vary enormously, there is a unity in the landscapes which is striking to the careful observer. As might be expected, to make most efficient and even distribution of water the terrain has to be generally flat or at most undulating. It varies in fact from the Burdekin delta flats backed by the Dividing Range to the low swells of the stabilised sand dunes carrying the orchards along the Murray River, and the imperceptible fall of the apparently dead flat plains of Namoi and Ord Rivers. Most of the water comes from surface storages and the internationally recognisable concrete and earth-walled dams lie mainly in the Highland Zone storing surplus run-off for the arid plains. On the plains, weirs pond up the regulated flows along the natural watercourses and from here the waters are led or pumped through open, not always concreted, channels and siphons to the individual farms where a gauge at the boundary measures individual flows. In the paddocks, or orchards, open earth channels or orchard sprinklers bring the water finally to the plants.

The need for outside overall control of water supply and allocation, together with the history of mainly officially sponsored, surveyed and developed settlements, gives the irrigated landscape a regularity and neatness

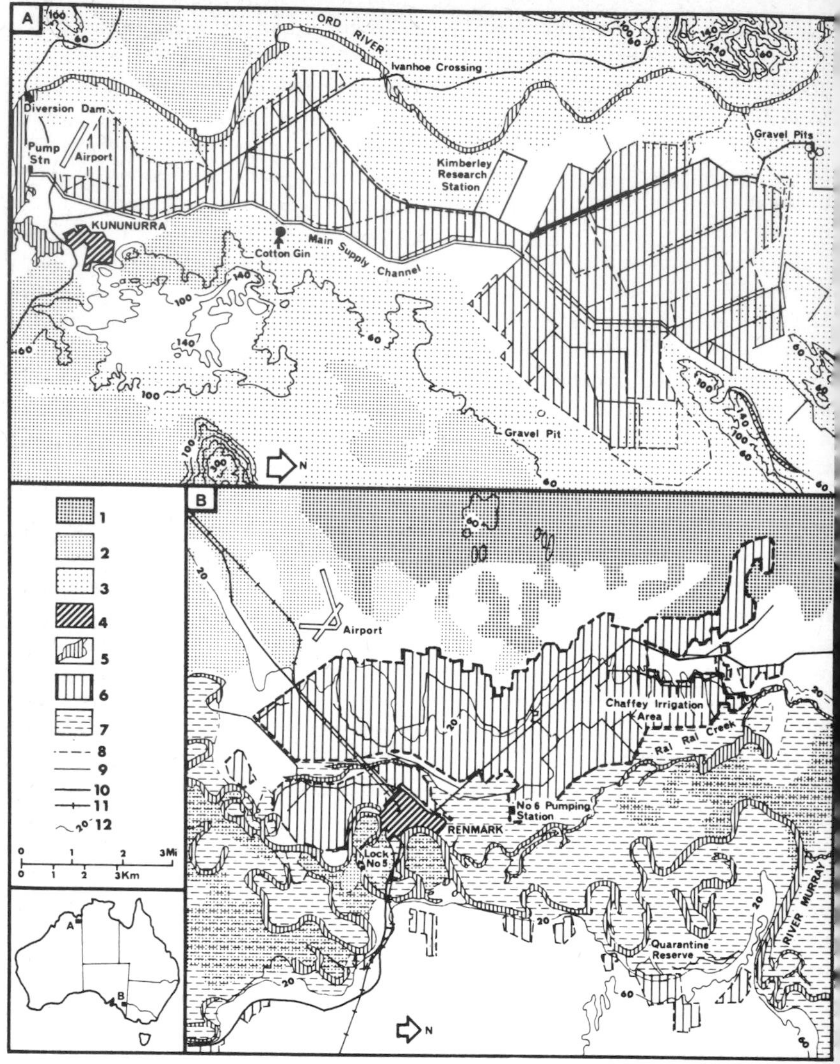

Fig. 9.8 Irrigation farmscapes
A. The Ord River Scheme, N.T.
B. The Renmark irrigation area, S.A.
1, Dense mallee scrub; **2**, Medium scrub; **3**, Open scrub; **4**, Urban area; **5**, Permanent watercourse; **6**, Irrigated area; **7**, Land liable to annual flooding; **8**, Drainage channels; **9**, Irrigation channels; **10**, Main roads; **11**, Railways; **12**, Contours (metres).

(*Sources:* A – Kununurra Sheet, 1 : 100 000, 1972; B – Renmark Sheet, 1 : 100 000, 1972)

of appearance which is not always met in other rural scenes. Fence lines, roads, channels have mathematical exactness, irregular edges whether of vegetation or farm are rare, the surveyor's lines are everywhere impressed upon the land. There is a richness too of colours – from black to deep red soils and from white cotton to orange and red fruits, and a richness of textures – from the rough masses of orchards to the horizontal geometries of the rice fields (Fig. 6.1). Here, most of all, the rural scenes are evidence of man's transformation of the plant and animal worlds.

To a traveller there can be no doubt, coming say on the Sydney–Adelaide highway from the treeless and waterless plains of the pastoral lands around Hay and Balranald into the lush growth of the irrigated lands of Mildura and Renmark, that irrigation has produced intensive and apparently successful land settlement in what otherwise would have been just more pastoral country. And yet the irrigated landscapes have their critics. Agricultural economists have argued that capital invested here has been less wisely invested than if it had been sunk into the grain landscapes. They have argued that Australia pays a high cost for its irrigation water because the variable rainfall requires twice the storage per area that is possible in the USA, for example; further that none of the schemes have ever paid for themselves, and that higher production could have been achieved from investment elsewhere. Their arguments have short-term economic force but ignore the social benefits of intensive settlement in these areas, the political climates of opinion which founded them, take no account of the integration of irrigated with non-irrigated land uses and ignore the aesthetic benefits of this rich landscape. The country towns which the irrigated landscapes support have an air of success and an aesthetic appeal not always found in their equivalents in the grain or pastoral landscapes.

The environmental impact of agriculture

Australia, alone of the continents, had had no significant disturbance of its soils by agriculture until the last decade of the eighteenth century and it is therefore not surprising that the ensuing process of land preparation for tillage was to have marked impact on the local environments.

Table 6.1 (p. 65) shows only the generalised impacts upon the biotic land cover but even this is an impressive account. Little if any of the original ecosystems have survived the onslaught of the plough. Locally, perhaps a third of the land retains some elements, much modified by timber felling and livestock grazing, but for the bulk of the land the original cover has long since been replaced – the forests and woodlands by exotic grasslands and croplands, the savannah woodlands and shrublands by croplands.

Not only those plants which were intended to grow now bloom in the agricultural landscapes. With the original grain seeds came weeds such as thistles (*Carduus* and *Cirsium* spp.) and plantains (*Plantago* spp.); out from the gardens spread the decorative soursobs (*Oxalis ceruna*), broom (*Cystis* spp.) and gorse (*Ulex* spp.), while blackberries (*Rubus* spp.) ran wild along the roadsides. Many thrived because they originally grew in similar climates elsewhere. Thus estimates suggest that over 400 of the 654 exotic species now found in South Australia came from Europe, particularly from similar winter-rain locations in the Mediterranean, while plants from South Africa, Chile and California were also well represented.

With the original seeds came also fungal diseases and pests. South American weevils thrived on introduced fruits and root crops, while aphids, fruit fly and codlin moth raided the orchards and phylloxera from Europe devastated the vineyards in the 1890s.

The replacement of tree growth over much of the agricultural landscapes by grasses or grain crops brought significant changes in soil moisture conditions. Clearance of the trees initially increased the surface water run-off from the area, but in certain conditions of low rolling relief, as on the interior plains, the replacement of the deep-rooted trees by shallow-rooted grasses and grains resulted in rising watertables in the soil since less was lost by transpiration. In the wetter areas this has led to water-logging and, in the drier 15–25 inches (380–630 mm) rainfall wheatlands, to the 'salting' from evaporation of surface soils some ten to twenty years after first clearance.

Of direct accelerated soil erosion from cropped lands there has been abundant evidence, particularly since the various state soil conservation services were organised in the late 1930s and 1940s. Most of the erosion has come from surface water run-off, but drought conditions always favour wind erosion and in 1944 dust from the eroding inland wheat fields of South Australia and New South Wales was settling on the snow fields of New Zealand, while between the paddocks men with horse-teams and scoops on Government relief tried to clear the blocked roads over the reactivated sand dunes.

Surveys of the Hunter Valley of New South Wales, one of the earliest cultivated areas of the continent, showed that by 1943 some 58 per cent of the valley was showing the effects of erosion, 38 per cent being moderate to severe gullying and 19 per cent being sheet erosion. By 1961, largely as the result of soil conservation measures, the area affected by gullying had been reduced slightly to 35 per cent, but the less spectacular sheet erosion had increased to 30 per cent of the area. Renewed conservation measures were claimed by 1970 to have reduced these figures to 20 per cent and 25 per cent respectively, leaving the remaining 55 per cent of the valley free of obvious soil erosion.

Such improvement of the erosion conditions, however, should not be assumed to be general, for the massive capital investment in flood control and soil conservation measures by the Hunter Valley Research Foundation in cooperation with the state Government from 1955 onwards make this a special 'show piece'. Elsewhere in the state a resurvey in 1967 of the areas surveyed in 1941–43 showed a massive increase of 3000 square miles (7800 km^2) of gully erosion, 70 per cent of which had taken place in the grain farming country. So significant has been the amount of soil removed in this way that claims have been made that the Gwydir River draining west to the Darling system has become blocked by a 'raft' of new sediments some 9 miles (15 km) long. The impact of the plough is likely to be felt for many years to come.

10
The mining landscapes

While pastoral settlement proved to be the pioneer method of land occupation over most of the continent, the development of mining often provided both a rapid sequel and in some cases even the pioneer method of resource use. Further, wherever mining took place, its impact on the original landscape was more striking visually and more farreaching economically than pastoral land-use. Such mining landscapes where the product of the application of capital, labour and technology to the mining of ores for either local or overseas use – what might be generally termed the mining system of resource use.

The nature and origins of the mining systems

Because of the variations in value for weight of the ores mined, and of the varying demands for them, and because of the wide variation in costs of mining those ores and shipping them to their markets, we need to recognise not one but a series of mining systems, each with its own landscape and functional organisation. Thus the low value-for-weight rocks which provided building materials (such as clay for bricks, sandstone and limestone for construction, lime as limestone or sea shells with sand and gravel for mortar), being found widely were mined as close to the market (the building sites) as possible. Each settlement of any size soon acquired its claypits and brickfields, its quarries and lime-kilns. Rocks with a higher value-for-weight ratio, such as the fossil fuels or metallic ores and fluxes for their refinement, tended to have more limited occurrences – at least in concentrations rich enough to be worth mining, and the mining systems included elaborate transport networks to link scattered mines with markets either concentrated in the main settlements or exported through them initially to overseas consumers. In fact one of the first stimuli for coastal trade in New South Wales was provided by the need to ship coal from Newcastle and the Illawarra coast to the main market in Sydney, and the most recent railways to be built in Australia (in the 1960s) have links between the iron ore mines in the Pilbara region of Western Australia and the wharves of Dampier and Port Hedland, and the black coal fields of central Queensland and the wharves of Rockhampton and Gladstone (Fig. 10.1). In each case the markets are the Japanese steel-mills. Finally, for the most precious rocks, the gemstones, precious metals and nuclear fuel base, uranium, widely scattered but individually much more valuable, the systems became even more spatially extensive, with linkages to markets around the world and with capital, technology and often labour drawn from almost as far afield.

To work the quarries and mines, first European, later American and most recently Japanese experts, expertise and capital have been imported. Cornish and Derbyshire lead miners came to work the copper mines in South Australia and Western Australia in the 1840s and 1860s; Northumberland miners came out to work the Newcastle coal pits of New South Wales in the 1880s and 1890s, while British, Irish, American, Chinese and many other nationalities joined the gold rushes to New South Wales and Victoria in the 1850s, through Queensland in the 1860s and 1870s, and on to Western Australia in the 1890s and the turn of the century. Massive steam engines were shipped around the world from Britain to pump out the deep shafts, to crush and grade the ores; diamond-tipped drills from the United States oil fields were brought out to continue the search in Australia in the 1880s and were finally successful in the 1960s; German chemists and mining engineers helped solve problems of refining gold chlorides in Western Australia in the early twentieth century, and Japanese geologists and capital helped open up the massive Pilbara iron ore fields in the 1960s.

The evolution of the mining systems

While the nature of the ore and its market, as noted above, was the basic influence differentiating between the various types of mining activity, the site for that activity was decided upon by a complex process of carefully accumulated knowledge laced with a fair proportion of chance. This accumulation of knowledge of the environment – a process to be found still occurring in all spheres of resource use and management in Australia, is most apparent in the mining industry and one example must suffice for the many which exist. In 1937, the iron ore reserves of Australia were estimated to be 522 million tons, of which only *260 million* tons were close enough to the coast (less than 100 miles (160 km) away) to be useful at the time. Those figures gave a future supply for only fifty years at the 1938 consumption rate and, with fears of a European war, export of ore was banned. By 1959, ores within 100 miles (160 km) of the coast were reassessed at *368 million* tons, and in 1960, the export ban was lifted. As a result of further geological exploration encouraged by the removal of this ban, by 1965 estimates put the total iron ore reserves at 16 000 million tons, of which *1254 million* tons were immediately useful.

On the world scale as well as in Australia, increased knowledge of basic geological formations seems automatically to increase the chances of further significant mineral finds. The Australian iron boom of the mid-1960s itself generated a boom in general mineral exploration (from the 1950s to the late 1960s capital outlays for example increased ten-fold) and part of the results were massive finds of nickel in Western Australia, where similarities of the

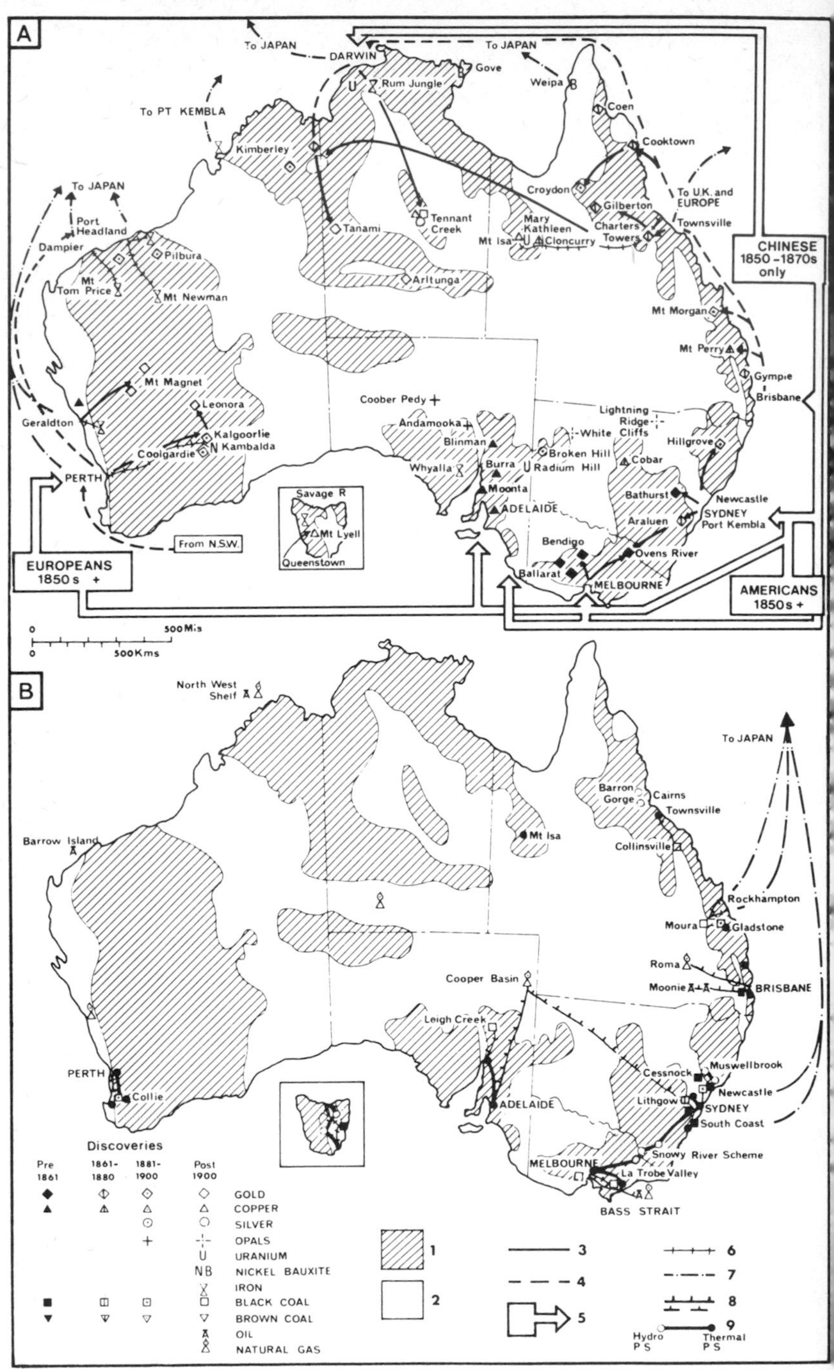
A
To JAPAN
DARWIN
To JAPAN
Gove
Weipa
Rum Jungle
To PT KEMBLA
Coen
Kimberley
Cooktown
To JAPAN
Croydon
To U.K. and EUROPE
Gilberton
Port Headland
Tennant Creek
Tanami
Mary Kathleen
Charters Towers
Townsville
Dampier
Mt Isa
Cloncurry
Pilbura
CHINESE 1850-1870s only
Mt Tom Price
Mt Newman
Arltunga
Mt Morgan
Mt Perry
Gympie
Mt Magnet
Brisbane
Coober Pedy
Lightning Ridge
Leonora
Andamooka
White Cliffs
Geraldton
Hillgrove
Blinman
Broken Hill
Kalgoorlie
Kambalda
Cobar
Coolgardie
Radium Hill
Whyalla
Burra
Savage R
Bathurst
Moonta
PERTH
Newcastle
ADELAIDE
SYDNEY
Port Kembla
Mt Lyell
Araluen
Bendigo
Queenstown
From N.S.W.
Ovens River
EUROPEANS 1850s +
Ballarat
MELBOURNE
AMERICANS 1850s +
0 500Mls
0 500Kms
B
North West Shelf
To JAPAN
Barron Gorge
Cairns
Townsville
Mt Isa
Barrow Island
Collinsville
Rockhampton
Moura
Gladstone
Roma
Moonie
BRISBANE
Cooper Basin
Leigh Creek
Muswellbrook
Cessnock
PERTH
Newcastle
Collie
Lithgow
SYDNEY
ADELAIDE
South Coast
Discoveries
Snowy River Scheme
Pre 1861
1861-1880
1881-1900
Post 1900
MELBOURNE
La Trobe Valley
GOLD
COPPER
BASS STRAIT
SILVER
OPALS
URANIUM
NICKEL BAUXITE
IRON
BLACK COAL
BROWN COAL
OIL
NATURAL GAS
1
2
3
4
5
6
7
8
9
Hydro PS
Thermal PS

Shield Zone with the already proven Canadian nickel-bearing shield rocks encouraged detailed prospecting. Phosphates in massive quantities were found in north-western Queensland by careful reexamination of old artesian bore and oil drill logs and renewed systematic search of potential sites.

The systematic, highly technical and generally impersonal nature of the current mineral exploration in the continent should not blind us, however, to the random and very personal origins of much of that knowledge. Many of the initial finds of semiprecious and precious ores had been made accidently by stockmen on pastoral properties. Copper was discovered at Burra (South Australia) in 1845 in this way (Fig. 10.2), as was copper again in 1860 at Moonta (South Australia), the silver and lead of Broken Hill in 1883 (New South Wales), and copper again at Mt Isa (Queensland) in 1927. The same may be said for most of the *first* gold discoveries, before the prospectors began to make systematic searches, encouraged by these random discoveries (Fig. 10.1A). Thus it might be argued that the pastoral system prepared the way for the mining system by providing, in the activities of its stations' musterers and boundary riders, increasing chance for accidental discovery of useful minerals.

Once discovered, there seems to have been a sequence of resource development common to most of the various types of precious and semi-precious mining activities. Initially, discoveries were of mineral outcrops which could be worked by individuals with nothing more complex than pick and shovel, wheelbarrow and windlass. As the outcrops were worked through and the shafts deepened, additional capital to pay for pumping machinery, drills, hoisting gear and possibly dynamite had to be raised – usually by syndicates of miners and later companies. What had been a one-man operation evolved through time into 100- or 1000-man operations involving thousands of pounds worth of steam-engines, cable hoists, water pumps, underground tramways and processing machinery, with an attendant wage-labour force of mine managers, engine drivers and firemen, pulleymen and winding house supervisors, as well as hierarchies of miners from 'face-men' directly mining the ore to 'tub-men' trundling it away to the hoists. Profits no longer found their way mostly into the local 'grog-shops', 'pubs' and dance halls, but began to flow across the world to relatives at home –

Fig. 10.1 Mining landscapes: evolution 1788–1970s
A. The search for precious and semiprecious minerals
B. The search for fuels
Key for both:
Geology: 1, Mineralised zones; 2, Non-mineralised, mainly sedimentary rock, zones.
Mining rushes (pre-1914): 3, Land routes; 4, Sea routes; 5, Origin of overseas miners.
Export of minerals (1970s): 6, Rail routes; 7, Sea routes; 8, Natural gas pipelines (actual and projected); 9, Main electric transmission lines, hydro-electric and thermal-electric power station complexes.

(*Sources:* Australia, 1962–73; Blainey, 1969)

Fig. 10.2 **Burra, S.A., 1968**
The spoil heaps of the copper workings begun in 1840s. Both open-cut and adit methods were used and the Cornish influence shows in the solidly built engine-house and chimney stacks. This scene by 1973 has been destroyed and replaced by further open-cuts as copper prices encouraged reworking of the old spoil heaps and low grade ones.

whether in Europe, America or China – and shareholders in London and New York. Such a story could be documented for most of the copper, silver-lead and gold mining operations which survived the exhaustion of the surface ores.

The changing application of technology in response to modified resource availability, which this sequence demonstrates, was paralleled by modification of the legal framework within which mining took place. Except for early land sales in South Australia, the Crown had retained ownership of all minerals and use was allowed only by licence. Initially, licences were for small areas (64 square feet (6 m^2)) in Victoria and obviously intended for individual miner's use, but as the need for cooperation or increased capital became obvious, provision was made for the amalgamation of licences and the granting of large areas for mineral prospecting. The iron ore and petroleum prospecting licences of the 1960s, for example, awarded sole rights of search and development over thousands of square miles of the continent to individual companies – many of them, as in the Copper Basin natural gas fields, overseas owned, although offering shares on the local stock markets.

The one main exception to this trend has been in the mining of opals, where small individual miner's licences are still used, apparently because of the general surface occurrence of these solution-derived gemstones (most shafts are still less than 50 ft (15 m) deep). Mining equipment is still rudimentary, although some miners at Coober Pedy and Andamooka (South Australia) have recently begun to use bulldozers to work their claims.

No matter how powerful the technology to win the ore from the ground, however, a major factor in the success of mining was the cost of transport to market. The stimulus of the coal discoveries at Newcastle to coastal trade with Sydney has been noted above and most of the major successful mining operations have had associated with them complex transport systems to bring the product to market. The low volatile brown coals of Victoria and black coals of South Australia, the Latrobe Valley (Muswellbrook) and Leigh Creek fields respectively, only could be exploited by a combination of rail transport (for compressed briquettes to Melbourne domestic fireplaces on the one hand and the coal to the Port Augusta power station on the other) and the innovations in electric power transmission technology, which allowed fossil fuel energy to be transported efficiently over 200 miles (320 km) to the major metropolitan consumers of Melbourne and Adelaide respectively (Fig. 10.1B). The rail links of the 1960s bringing iron ore from Western Australia and black coal from inland Queensland to the coasts for the shipment to Japan have used the most modern rail technology with individual trains of over $1\frac{1}{2}$ miles ($2\frac{1}{2}$ km) in length moving 20 000 tons of ore at a time. Construction of pipelines to bring natural gas from the Bass Strait fields to Melbourne, and from the Cooper Basin fields to Adelaide (and potentially in mid-1970s to Sydney) have further emphasised the importance of more efficient transport technology in opening up remote sources of minerals.

The spread of the mining systems

Given the characteristics of the ores and the evolution of systems for their discovery, the spread of the mining systems was a complex process scattered widely over space and time. The mining and quarrying of constructional materials were often unspectacular activities at the edge of the settlements whereas the mining of coal was a highly localised and, where transport allowed, a remote activity. By comparison, the high value-for-weight of the semiprecious and precious minerals could support the remotest of mines and it is the sequence of the discovery and exploration of these minerals which provides the widest extension, both in space and time, of the mining systems over the continent.

Copper was found in the hills inland from Adelaide within five years of the first European settlement; by 1848, the mine at Burra, 100 miles (160 km) to the north, was one of the world's leading copper producers, with the ore being partially refined at Adelaide before shipment to Welsh copper mills. At that time copper was providing most of the new colony's external income. Further discoveries in South Australia in the 1860s were followed by finds in Queensland, New South Wales and Tasmania and the most recent discoveries have come from reworking of old mines at Cobar (New South Wales) from 1969 and the Flinders Ranges (including Burra) of South Australia from 1972 (Fig. 10.2).

The most spectacular spatial shifts of the mining systems, however, were to the various gold and opal fields. Gold had been found on pastoral properties at least as early as the 1840s, but not until the Californian Gold Rush of 1849 stimulated local prospecting did the Australian finds become headline news. From 1851 when the first 'strikes' were made public until the worldwide economic depression of the 1930s, 'rushes' of miners to a succession of gold fields took place (Fig. 10.1A). Initially the finds were of alluvial gold washed from quartz exposures in the mineralised pre-Cambrian and Paleozoic rocks, but the origins of the gold-bearing gravels were soon traced and quartz mining soon followed. As had occurred with copper, individual colonies encouraged their own discoveries, partly to hold onto a population which threatened in the 1850s particularly to head off on the latest 'rush', and partly to encourage more immigration.

The first finds in New South Wales in 1851 were matched by strikes in Victoria, in Queensland from the 1860s onwards and Western Australia and Northern Territory relatively late – the 1880s and 1890s. Rushes to the opal fields of Lightning Ridge and White Cliffs (New South Wales) came at the same time and were renewed here and in South Australia in the 1930s, with minor flurries of activity subsequently.

Although the depression of the 1930s saw a general slump in mining activity the stimulus of the demand for uranium for atomic weapons and as an energy source post-1945, together with the successful iron ore discoveries and oil and natural gas finds of the 1960s, has been such that no part of the continent has been completely free of prospectors since approximately the 1880s. On foot or horseback, more recently by truck and aircraft, with geological hammer, quicksilver and acid, geiger-counter and seismic survey, the outcrops and buried reefs have been and still are being plotted and their contents analysed. In Western Australia, gold reefs worked out by the 1890s brought fortunes to nickel prospectors in 1969, the ochres used in corroborees in 1770 were being mined for Japanese steel-mills in 1970.

To cope with the problems technology was adapted and techniques modified. Where water was scarce, as on the Kalgoorlie gold fields of Western Australia, 'dry blowing' or winnowing of the powdered ore was developed; where the silver and gold was in the form of chlorides, special 'roasting' and chemical treatment processes had to be adopted. And behind all the processes at the minehead, the lines of transport and communication stretched off to the coast and the overseas markets.

The spread of the mining system over the continent has been a complex process both in time and place. The spread inland, initially following on the heels of the pastoralists, eventually outstripped them and found commercial ores in the remotest parts of the arid interior. The discovery of new ores in such locations continues but it is now paralleled by the careful reexamination of old mining areas, for the line between the useful and the useless fluctuates because of the demands for new raw materials and with increasing prices or reduced production costs for the old ones.

The environmental impact of mining

The impacts of the various mining systems have been and still are both direct (immediate and often shortlived) and indirect (less immediate but longer lasting). The systems produced some of the most impressive population shifts in the history of the continent. In less than a decade, after the first gold discoveries in 1851, almost half a million immigrants arrived in Australia, and Western Australia's late gold rushes increased its population by over 100 000 from 1885 to 1900.

Most of these immigrants stayed on in the continent, not necessarily as miners, after the rushes had faded away. A significant proportion of them were non-Europeans, especially Chinese, who numbered 24 000 in Victoria by 1861 and were to be the ancestors of some of the non-Europeans who remained in the Australian population long after the further entry of their countrymen was officially prohibited (1854 in Victoria, 1886 in the other colonies) by what became known as the 'White Australia Policy'.

After brief periods on the mineral fields, many miners tried other jobs, particularly when their initial capital ran out without a profitable return – which was the majority of the cases. Chinese ex-miners became market gardeners on the outback pastoral stations and on the edge of the larger towns. British miners, with a similar agricultural tradition of small-holdings (in their case as security for the traditionally inevitable slumps in the mining industry), joined the ranks of the new smallholders testing the provisions of the new agricultural settlement acts of the 1860s onwards. The overall population increase stimulated local demand for agricultural and pastoral produce – particularly beef and mutton – and a rural boom resulted.

The profits from the mines, particularly once the companies entered the scene, became a major prop to the colonial economies in addition to the indirect stimulus to rural production. Between 1852 and 1860, Australian gold production alone was worth £11.2 million per year and between 1898 and 1911 the figure was £13·.7 million per year. Some of this went directly into the local economy as payment for food, clothing and shelter, and a variety of legal and illegal entertainments. A large proportion of it found its way into the colonial banks from where it was relocated as loans for the development of new pastoral properties or farms. By the 1880s in Victoria, the richest colony, two-thirds of all bank loans were for the development of these new lands (Blainey, 1958). Capital from mining was a significant backup for the spread of rural settlement in the nineteenth century in Australia.

The impact on urban settlement was more immediate but usually less permanent. The tents, wooden shacks and dirt tracks of the first mining camp often faded away as quickly as the ores ran out – the only evidence being the regrowth of bushy shrubs, the uneven ground and the glint of

Fig. 10.3 Queenstown, Tas.
Dormitory (4000 population) for Mt Lyell copper mine, whose smelter fumes killed off most of native forest and the high rainfall (over 100 inches (2500 mm)) caused massive erosion on the bared slopes behind the town (1) which itself dates from the gold discoveries of 1881. Note the house styles, corrugated iron roofs, wooden walls and successive additions at rear (2). The only buildings over one storey are hotels or motels (3).

(*Source:* Don Stephens Pty. Ltd)

broken bottles in the disturbed soil. Other centres lingered on, then acquired a market or local government function if farms caught up with them – as Ballarat and Bendigo – or in the rare cases dug deeper, found more payable ores and became the Kalgoorlies, Broken Hills and Mt Isas – mining towns in their own right with over a third of their employees still in the mines.

The encouragement of the settlement of the continent to which the mining system contributed was achieved, however, at the expense of the specific environment in which mining took place. The environmental impact was rapid and in many cases long-lasting. Vegetation had to be removed to lay bare the rock outcrops, trees provided fuel for domestic fires as well as the steam engines and furnaces, timber for tent poles, stores and houses, and all edible animals, furred or feathered, tended to find their way into the cooking pot. Excavation destroyed the soil, heaped up new hills of waste rock, disoriented the natural drainage lines and realigned the local water

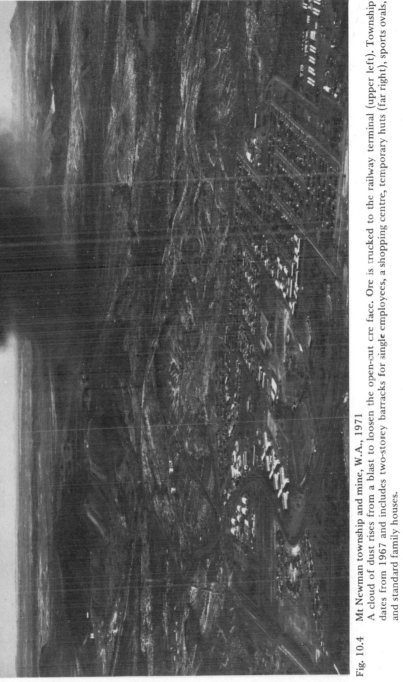

Fig. 10.4 Mt Newman township and mine, W.A., 1971
A cloud of dust rises from a blast to loosen the open-cut ore face. Ore is trucked to the railway terminal (upper left). Township dates from 1967 and includes two-storey barracks for single employees, a shopping centre, temporary huts (far right), sports ovals, and standard family houses.

(*Source:* Department of Development and Decentralisation, W.A.)

tables. The result, when the ores were exhausted, was impressive. The English writer Anthony Trollope described the deserted Gympie gold field of Queensland in 1874 as 'what one might suppose the earth would appear after the day of judgment has emptied all the graves'.

Such scars were slow to heal. In some cases, as with modern open cast mining of coal or beach sands, some reconstruction of the surface has been attempted, slopes regraded and some vegetation replanted. In others, particularly on the earlier gold fields, nothing was done and vegetation recolonised the sites only slowly and sometimes wildlife returned, but it was a much modified vegetation and a decimated wildlife (Fig. 10.3). Such potential scars are still being made – on the Queensland coastal sand dunes, on the Latrobe Valley brown coal fields of Victoria, the South Australian opal fields and the Pilbara iron fields of Western Australia (Fig. 10.4), while every large town still has its quarry and brick pits. As yet there has not been the demand to use them for recreational purposes that has arisen in the more crowded environments of Europe.

11
Urban landscapes – origins and evolution

Of the continental area in the 1970s, perhaps 1 per cent might be classed as urban land. Within this relatively minute area, however, are crowded the bulk (85%) of the population; without the demands for food and raw materials originating here, much of the remainder of the continent would be uninhabited; here are made most of the basic decisions (governmental and commercial) which lead to modifications of land use over the other 99 per cent of the continent, and it is through these entry points (particularly the six state capitals) that most visitors and migrants come and where they gain their first impressions of Australia. In fact not only people are crowded into this relatively minute area, but also an immense variety of the complex functions of a 'Westernised' society and the variety of land uses which are associated with them. Not merely are these urban landscapes interesting in their own right therefore, but an understanding of them provides a necessary insight into the landscapes of the remainder of the continent. From the smallest country centre, perhaps little more than a post office, a store and a few houses, to the sprawling grids of bitumen, bricks and concrete which mark the largest metropolitan centres, they hold the key to many of the explanations for the Australian landscape as a whole.

Definitions and dimensions in the 1970s

The urban landscapes of Australia however are easier to recognise visually than to define statistically. The continuously 'builtup' area of houses and gardens, streets, shops, offices and factories is immediately recognisable to the traveller flying into any of the major airports.

It is, however, only a unity in the visual sense, for the view encompasses a complex of land-uses and building structures, a variety of land ownerships, and a variety of administrative and statistical units. Also incorporated in the visual unit is a complex of separate historical evolutions – the spread of population, the growth of street patterns and land subdivision for houses and factories. Thus, while we will use the simple definition of the builtup area, we must recognise the difficulties in statistically documenting the characteristics of who lives there, how the whole functions (certainly, it will become obvious *not* as a whole) and how the various, often separate, patterns of buildings, streets and open spaces eventually merged to form the contemporary urban landscapes.

Censuses of population have been taken in Australia since 1851 and less comprehensive counts since first settlement, but even the current definitions of urban areas can be criticised. Two basic types are distinguished, 'metropolitan' (capital cities and their suburbs) and 'other urban' (the other legally defined urban areas down to unincorporated 'hamlets' of more than fifty population). Metropolitan census boundaries rarely keep up with the rapid spread of metropolitan suburbs so that each census tends to underestimate the people who would be part of a continuous builtup metropolitan unit. At the other end of the scale legal definitions of local government authority areas, upon which are based most of the census 'other urban' boundaries, vary between states because of different criteria used. At the lowest level we cannot be certain even that the population has truly an urban function, since unincorporated hamlets have no local government functions and may be little more than a few houses grouped together, inhabited by people who would hardly consider themselves urbanites.

The details of urban functions are still often hidden in the minute books of local councils, the ledgers of business houses and the accounts, held often only in their head, of the smaller shopkeepers. Further, patterns of building styles, the details of the evolution of Australian houses, shops, warehouses and town halls have been only examined in a preliminary manner. However, the last two decades have seen significant publications in both spheres, the first by urban geographers and economic historians, the second by historians of architecture, and these will be the main source of our comments. Even so, the pictures which emerge are by no means sharply defined and there is much scope for improvement.

Given, however, this albeit crude definition, and these indifferent sources, what is the spatial pattern of these urban landscape units? With the exception of the national capital, deliberately sited inland as a centre for continental Government, the state capital metropolitan centres are all coastal – reflecting the initial points of entry of European settlers, the importance of the first ports through which vital overseas supplies, people and equipment were transferred to inland destinations, and the surpluses and profits of settlement were exported (Fig. 6.3C, p. 62). Indeed, in the case of Sydney, Hobart and Brisbane the wharves of the port are within a few hundred metres of the present business heart of the city (Figs. 2.7, 2.8), in the case of Melbourne, Adelaide and Perth the present builtup area includes both original port and centre of the separate city – none more than 7 miles (11 km) away from each other.

The metropolitan centres are dominant, both in size of population and of builtup area, over the smaller, generally later developed centres. Thus, in 1971, the metropolitan state capitals contained 59 per cent of the total continental population. Each had between twice and thirty times the population of the next largest centre. In 1971, for example, the rounded census figures were for Tasmania, Hobart (130 000) over Launceston (62 000); New South Wales, Sydney (2 725 000) over Newcastle (250 000); Queensland, Brisbane (818 000) over Townsville (69 000); Victoria,

Melbourne (2 394 000) over Geelong (115 000); Western Australia, Perth (642 000) over Kalgoorlie (21 000); and South Australia, Adelaide (809 000) over Elizabeth (33 000).

In turn, these rivals to the metropolitan centres were considerably larger than the remaining centres. The 1971 Census showed that of the 516 urban centres in Australia, only 10 (including the 6 state capitals) had over 100 000 inhabitants, only 5 had from 50 000 to 100 000, only 63 had populations of 10 000 to 50 000, while the remainder (443) had less than 10 000 inhabitants. Although urban settlements had been widely founded over the continent from 1788 onwards and although by the 1970s most of these original centres remained as urban centres, they were often small with stagnant and ageing populations and physically decaying. In contrast, the favoured few – state capitals, industrial and manufacturing centres and regional market and administrative headquarters – were growing rapidly in population and physically expanding into the adjacent countryside. The explanation for the contrast lies in the history of European settlement, the patterns of resources and the various systems created to use them. The inherited colonial life styles, the dominance of commercial production, the effects of technological innovations especially in transport, communication and industrialisation, and the nature of the settlers themselves, all played significant roles in creating the urban landscapes of the 1970s.

The colonial inheritance

The creation of urban landscapes has been a rapid but, by world standards, a relatively recent event. Most of the structures are less than 100 years old, none of the ground plans are more than 200 years old (although many were copies of much older ground plans used in Europe before being adopted here). Not only are the landscapes recent, with relics of the first structures often still visible, but all were created on bare, roomy sites – no permanent settlement sites existed on the continent prior to the arrival of the Europeans – and there were few physical barriers to construction.

An urbanised society

An urbanised society came ashore with the first settlers, whether ex-pickpockets from the streets of London, their military gaolers, or the free labourers, artisans and capitalists. In Australia, from the late eighteenth century onwards, occupation of the land has always been from urban bases which were sited and established well before the full scope of continental resources was discovered. Whether as gaols, forts or transhipment points, the result was an 'instant' urban landscape, and by the time the colonial, dependent, nature of actual land settlement had become established early in the nineteenth century, the dominant role of the urban centres was complete.

British Imperial concepts of land administration, based upon control of rural areas from proclaimed urban centres, ensured that initially at least the decisions affecting control of land settlement should be urban based, and that such bases should be limited in number. Indeed the first settlers were, in more ways than one, not free agents. Both convicts and their gaolers brought ideas and attitudes to the resources which might vary considerably among them, but all were part of a global system – of administration – just as the sealers, and later the pastoralists, miners and farmers were part of another global system – of production, marketing and consumption. The full regalia of colonial administration existed before any of the colonists set foot on the continent and this affected not only the form but also the territorial organisation of the settlements.

Concentration of the settlers into urban centres was inevitable, given the contemporary attitude to the confinement of convicts in a central gaol. An urban form of settlement was further implicit in the strategic forts and their associated supply depots and barracks, and the shore depots and processing centres for the maritime activities. Once the process of inland settlement got under way, the official supervision and control of the settlement process further encouraged the multiplication of urban centres by providing the nucleus for urban growth around official services such as the police hut or court house, later post and telegraph office, as well as by laying out official townships within the official land survey system.

Initially, the number of centres were few, partly because of the small numbers of total European population, partly because of the lack of land-based industries, and partly because most centres were ports and the number of these was limited until 1813 by the East Indian Company's monopoly on trade in these southern waters. The end of this control and the expansion of free settlement into the interior (although delayed by official barriers until the 1820s) began an era of town founding associated with the division of the new lands for settlement.

Since settlement was officially supervised it is not surprising to find that the first areas to be allocated in the new sites were for official purposes. The first administrator, Governor Phillip, had instructions to lay out 'townships' which were to include reserves for barracks, town halls and public buildings, as well as reserves for a rector and school-master. These initial components were to be found in most of the first convict settlements in New South Wales and Queensland (Brisbane). Here the residence of the governor as a military commandant, the military barracks, the convict lines (and occasional female 'factory' for those women prisoners who were not sent out to work) were the standard units. Later, in the capitals of the free colonies of South Australia and Western Australia and in the post-convict days of the latter half of the nineteenth century in New South Wales, Queensland and Tasmania, the official residence, barracks and parade ground were joined by the Houses of Parliament and the Government offices – the official presence was reinforced by responsible Government (Figs. 11.1 and 11.2).

Perhaps the most obvious official components of the urban landscapes are the Government offices. Most of Australian land settlement was conceived of, planned in and still is administered from urban offices.

Fig. 11.1 Melbourne, Vic.
View southeast from city central business district, and railway station across Yarra River to Government House (residence of Governor of Victoria) and public parks (1) and War Memorial (2), along the wide avenue of St Kilda Road (3), designed for foot, vehicle and tram traffic, and now lined by new office and motel blocks to the suburbs expanding along the eastern shores of Port Phillip Bay (4).

(*Source:* Ministry of Tourism, State Government, Vic.)

Fig. 11.2 **Adelaide, S.A., the central business district**
1, Victoria Square, central one of five inner-city parks. Two others are shown top left and upper centre; **2,** Governor's residence; **3,** State Parliament House, with Government Printing Office to right; **4,** Central railway station, terminal for state rail network; **5,** Western section of parklands surrounding the city; **6,** Festival Theatre complex (in construction) with Torrens River to right. The complex of University, State Library and Museums is in bottom left corner.

(*Source:* Australian Information Service)

Initially these were the offices of the colonial secretaries, attempting to carry out British Imperial policies. Later, they were the offices of the local civil servants enforcing the decisions of the local urban state parliaments.

The offices themselves mushroomed in the latter half of the nineteenth century with representative state Governments. Each state created the various departments to cover aspects of resource use. Survey departments were created to delimit and allocate land, lands departments to control the disposal and administration of ownership, posts and telegraphs, main roads and railways departments controlled the spread of the communication networks so vital to global links of production and commerce, while departments of mines, agriculture and forests supervised the development of specific resources. Even the Commonwealth Government, as owner of the Commonwealth Territories, had to provide its own equivalents in Canberra.

Away from the capitals, officialdom was never *far* away – the gold commissioner's tent, surveyor's camp and police lines were among the first urban units on the gold fields; the surveyors' camp, police hut and post office among the first urban units in many of the country town sites. Even twentieth century land settlement schemes saw the future town sites graced first by the state Department of Works camp from where each day the mechanised equipment sallied forth to clear, or drain and level the land for the new farmers awaiting their chance at the ballot for new blocks. The country towns, once established, often came to contain the local administrative offices for the shires, or district councils or road districts, the emergency fire brigade headquarters, the offices of the pasture protection boards, the silo of the wheat board and railway station (Fig. 6.2).

Like all generalisations this picture can be disproved in detail, but the significance of the official areas, still central to most of the Australian urban landscapes, is immediately apparent to the visitor. In the state capitals the heavy 'Victorian' architecture housing the Government departments came to dominate the central areas until challenged on the skyline by the private office skyscrapers from the 1960s onwards. At the small town or suburban level the same dominance is found in the town hall, municipal, council or shire offices (Fig. 11.3). Even at the level of the smallest urban centre, the post office and sign advertising the local branch of the Commonwealth Savings Bank are mute reminders of the official presence.

Not all of the official land at the future city centre was occupied by buildings and part was often dedicated as public parkland. By the time urban areas were being laid out in Australia, the idea of *public* parks had become accepted as a requisite for urban areas and from the outset of settlement there had been provision for public grazing lands, to be set aside for town dwellers' livestock, which often later became public open spaces.

The importance of urban centres to the settlement process not only meant that they were the first form of settlement to appear, but also that most were officially established. In a study of New South Wales, Jeans (1965) found that fifty-three towns had been surveyed by the colonial government between 1829 and 1842. Powell's study of Victorian land settlement (1970) found eight-ninths of inland towns to have been official foundations, and Williams (1966*a*) found three-quarters of South Australian towns so originated. Private towns have been much fewer and limited to special group settlements by immigrants (e.g. Australind, W.A.), speculative private ventures (e.g. Boydtown, N.S.W.), and, by far the largest, mining settlements, whether unplanned spasmodic growths on the nineteenth-century mining fields, or privately planned company towns such as Mary Kathleen (Qld.) and Mt Tom Price (W.A.).

A centralised administration

The influence of governments upon urban landscapes has not been limited to the details of their foundation or initial planning. From the outset of European settlement the continent has been divided up (at least on paper) into convenient units for Government, and these systems of territorial organisation, together with the systems of land survey and disposal which

Fig. 11.3 Rockhampton, Qld.
Originating as a port of entry for gold miners in 1858, the railway link inland from 1867 brought pastoral exports, and gold from Mt Morgan. Processing of pastoral and agricultural products still dominates jobs for th 45 000 population – meatworks, cotton-ginning, fruit canning, but the rival port of Gladstone is now drawing off some of the regional services. The ornate clock-tower of the post office building hides the reflecting dish of the radio–telephone link to Brisbane.

(*Source:* Government Tourist Bureau, Qld.)

backed them up, have left a permanent and in many cases indelible imprin on the urban scene. In effect the first urban centres became immediately th hub of territorial Government, a function which they in their modern rol as the metropolitan centres have never shed.

From 1770 to 1836 the continent of Australia was progressively claime for the British Crown and apportioned between the emerging colonies, eac colonial territory being administered from the first major settlement centr to be established (Fig. 8.3). Despite an abortive attempt to create a ne state out of the southern half of the Northern Territory in 1926–31, an the agitations of the various New State movements, particularly in Ne South Wales and Queensland, the pattern of administrative areas ha remained basically stable since the Commonwealth took over the Norther Territory in 1911, the major exception being the relocation of th

Commonwealth administrative centre from Melbourne to Canberra in the Australian Capital Territory in 1927.

The boundaries for these administrative units have been lines of convenience, initially drawn across land unsettled or very sparsely settled by Europeans, often aligned arbitrarily to latitude and longitude, rarely in detail drawn in response to any local opinions. The one case where local settlers were vocal, on the Queensland–New South Wales border, their wishes were ignored and the disgruntled locals began the first agitation for a new state – 'New England' (Rose, 1955). Such arbitrary boundaries were to affect the development of urban centres later, were to divide the political allegiance of settlements on opposite banks of the Murray River and force state governments to economic subsidies on state railway freights to maintain links with remote border centres in the face of competition from other state capitals spatially more advantaged.

That the continent was so divided was a function of the sequence of separatist pressures resulting from different systems of colonisation, different methods of resource use and the problems of administering vast land areas before modern communication media were available. Thus an attempt in 1850 to maintain Sydney's administrative supervision of the newly independent colony of Victoria, as well as the colonies of Tasmania, South Australia and Western Australia, was abandoned in 1861 as unworkable because of the communication difficulties involved. Significantly, one of the first functions of the Federal Government was the construction of the transcontinental railway line to link, for the first time effectively by land, the western with the eastern half of the continent.

Local administration

The pattern of local administration in Britain prior to Australian settlement was organised on a three-tier hierarchy from the 'county' level, down to the 'hundreds', and finally to the base of the pyramid – the 'parishes'. The latter, prior to reforms in 1834, had control of finance, police and most civil functions (roads and poor law). With the opening of Australia to free settlement in the 1820s the previous purely military administration was modified and the British system introduced with only the definitions regularised. Thus, in 1825, Governor Brisbane was instructed to lay out the territory of the colony of New South Wales in the sequence of parishes (25 square miles or 63 km^2) forming hundreds (100 square miles or 250 km^2), which in turn formed counties of 1600 square miles or 4000 km^2. Implied here was not only a spatial organisation but a hierarchy of administrative centres, from the parish village to the county town, evenly scattered over the countryside.

While these units were surveyed at some time in all of the colonies, the units never functioned effectively for administrative purposes, although counties and hundreds have been used for collection of statistics, and in South Australia official surveyors attempted to survey a Government town in every hundred. The basic problem was that population densities were rarely sufficient to support this hierarchy of administration and associated urban centres which had been introduced from an environment where land-use and associated population patterns were much more intensive than Australia's. With parishes perhaps comprising a couple of paddocks of a pastoral property and perhaps two or three hundreds incorporated into a property in the early nineteenth century, it was not surprising that government was left to the colonial capital and administration of the local law and order left to the squatter Justices of the Peace. The units became useful only as a reference system for land survey and disposal and, as mentioned before, for the collection of data by the central statistical offices of the colonial, later state, capitals.

With 29 per cent of the continent in the 1960s offering no apparent economic return, and another 57 per cent offering very low return per unit area as extensive pastoral lands, with population densities of less than 1 per square mile (2.6 km^2) (Table 6.2), it is not surprising that local representative government is still absent from such areas. In fact government here is directly centralised on the state capital with all decisions made there and from whence finances are managed. Over 85 per cent of South Australia (containing 2 per cent of state population) has no local government; the Western Division (Western third) of New South Wales was governed directly from Sydney until 1955 when local shires began to be created, but one-third of the division (*c*. 12% of the state) still lacks local control of local affairs (McPhail, 1968). In such areas local urban centres have little if any regional administrative function, and even in the settled agricultural areas the basic problem of insufficient population and therefore insufficient tax support for local government has meant that very few of the smallest urban centres have any administrative function.

Urban land survey

Most Australian urban centres existed on paper before they were laid out on the ground. In some, e.g. Adelaide and Darwin, blocks were even bought and resold before the first survey peg was hammered in. This prior 'planning', together with the official origin of perhaps two-thirds of Australian urban centres and their short history, lies behind the remarkable uniformity of the urban landscapes. Most of the official urban settlements and many of the private foundations have in fact a common heritage of land survey and disposal.

Systems of urban survey developed particularly rapidly from 1830 onwards, with the combined foundations of new colonies in South and Western Australia, the settlements in what was to become Victoria and the action of the New South Wales Government in founding new towns after 1829. Despite the small numbers of qualified surveyors, approximately 15[illegible] new towns were laid out before mid-century in the various colonies and the systems which were to dominate future urban planning were already established by that date.

In principle both private and official surveys had much in common and tended to produce very similar urban patterns. Survey had to precede occupation – the 'squatter' was as great an anathema to the private speculator as the officialdom; the site had to be as easy to survey as possible, the flatter the better; the survey itself had to be simple and efficient in its use of the ground, i.e. a geometric grid of rectangular blocks and streets; public land was to be allocated beforehand and all land for private disposal had to be in attractively sized blocks to encourage sales.

The results have been remarkable. The first grid was laid out along Sydney Cove in 1788 and thereafter has only been seriously challenged in isolated architect-designed suburban subdivisions, and in the national capital Canberra. Elsewhere it is the ubiquitous frame within which all urban landscapes are set. Where private and official surveys lay alongside each other (as in West Maitland and Maitland, East Gosford and Gosford, N.S.W.) there *were* contrasts, but only in alignment of the grids! In part this dominance has been the result of suburban spread into rural lands which were themselves surveyed on grid lines, but it mainly represents the acceptance of the grid as the basic frame for the core of each urban area.

The similarity extends to the size of blocks within the urban areas. Governor Phillip had ordered Sydney blocks to be 60 ft by 150 ft (18 m by 45 m) and although often ignored in early years, Robin Boyd, the Australian architect, claims that the average size of urban blocks (in the 1960s) was 60 ft by 150 ft! In the period of extensive town foundation in New South Wales from 1829 to 1849 the favoured size block was half an acre (20 ares), and half-acre lots were surveyed in South Australia and the Northern Territory. There were exceptions Newcastle had quarter-acre (10 ares) blocks because survey came after settlement and structures already existed, while larger blocks (up to 2 acres (80 ares)) were allocated in some early New South Wales towns to 'persons of means and responsibility' (Jeans, 1965).

Exceptions to the rigid grid system were few but reflected again introduced ideas as much as any adaptation to local terrain or climatic conditions. Thus German immigrants to South Australia tended to lay out their houses along the main roads in a street-village (*strassendorf*) form with initially no grid of streets behind this line of houses, while the colonial Government town grid plans were bent and distorted to accommodate river frontages and lake or sea coast sites. Overall however the rectangular grid dominated, here the roads cramped and narrow to reduce the area lost to real estate speculation, there the roads broad, six lanes or more wide, to accommodate the tram and road ways and public reserves of the grandiose town planners, but all at right angles and as straight as the surveyors' lines.

Urban planning

Although few of the urban surveys made any attempt to plan the complete use of the urban lands, there was some evidence of intended uses for urban lands. The main examples were in the allocation of at least some parts of all urban areas to public use. Such areas were either isolated blocks strategically sited in the overall design, or peripheral areas of land reserved for special uses. 'Common land' had been a feature of all townships founded in New South Wales, whether deliberately laid out or by default of any other use within the square mile sections set aside for the Village Reserves. Similar reserves, basically for grazing townfolks' animals, were surveyed in all other colonies, but in South Australia and Darwin in Northern Territory (laid out by South Australian surveyors) they were merged into 'parklands' which surrounded the area surveyed for 'town lots', separating it from the 'suburban lots' beyond. In South Australia miniatures of Adelaide's basic plan, reproduced with minor adaptations to local sites, formed the main examples of new town plans, laid out throughout the state until the 1920s, when Reade the state planner suggested that this ubiquitous design had outlived its usefulness. Melbourne, surveyed in 1837, one year later than Adelaide, had a similar core of 'town lands' astride the Yarra, surrounded by a reserve, with 'suburban blocks' of 5 to 40 acres (2 to 16 ha) on the east (Richmond and Collingwood), and 'country lands' of 640 to 1200 acre (260 to 480 ha) lots beyond.

The planning of the use of urban space had been considered from the outset of settlement. Jeans (1965, p. 196) comments for New South Wales:

> In centres for which a regional importance was expected, public squares were considered appropriate, as architectural features to be fronted by the more monumental public buildings. . . . The squares were not to be confused with market places, for which separate provision was made, usually around a stream or pond to preserve public access to water, and often at the junction of roads crossing the site before the plan was made. . . . Planners excluded 'noxious industries' or restricted them to sites permitting easy effluent disposal. Waterfront land was generally reserved for wharves, watering places for travelling stock and for public recreation, to prevent private monopoly though more remote and waterless tracts were also set aside as parks.

Rudimentary land use planning of a similar type was evident in Victoria but there was often a marked gap between intention and achievement in all colonies.

Basically the problem was that there was no effective control of the use to which urban land was put, once title had been transferred from the Crown. Under the *laissez-faire* method of auction sales and in the absence of any but the most rudimentary constraints which often were not enforced anyhow, use of urban land went unnoticed and uncontrolled. Even where size of blocks was intended to encourage certain uses, inability to enforce the plans meant that the designed pattern of use was never realised. Thus in New South Wales Government town plans after 1829, 'cultivation allotments' of 2 to $2\frac{1}{2}$ acres (1 ha) were surveyed to encourage 'mechanics' to become part-time farmers, and 'suburban allotments' of from 10 to 140 acres (4 to 56 ha) were suggested to provide a local food supply for the towns. While the contemporary success of this scheme is hard to assess, the long-term effect seems merely to have provided somewhat larger units for real estate subdivision and speculation once the town began to physically expand in the late nineteenth century.

Local authorities were either disinterested in, or powerless to do anything about, the detailed control of land use for most of the nineteenth century. 'Town planning' as such came to the public eye at the time of deliberations on the future site of the nation's capital, Canberra, in the first two decades of the twentieth century, and was stimulated by the work of two planners – C. C. Reade, who arrived to be South Australia's State Planner at Adelaide in 1916, and J. Sulman, whose book, *Town Planning in Australia*, was published in 1921. Both men made a local impact (see Chapter 12) but the world depression of the 1930s killed general interest until the renewed urban expansions of the 1950s and 1960s.

One feature of the urban landscape, however, which was ubiquitously planned and which was occasionally even known before the actual site had been surveyed, was the name given to the place. One of the first Surveyor Generals of New South Wales, Sir Thomas Mitchell, complained that the Aboriginal names which his men were adopting in the 1840s for the inland localities were both difficult to pronounce and appeared to change from season to season. However once adopted they remained to dot the rural landscape.

Initially, however, British personal names dominated the urban landscapes with colonial secretaries (Perth), local governors (Brisbane), prime ministers (Melbourne, Palmerston later to be Darwin), royalty (Williamstown, Vic. and Adelaide). Transfer of settlers brought transfers of home place names, so that as an ex-hiker along the Cheshire–Derbyshire borders I find Australia's Buxton (N.S.W.), Macclesfield and Stockport (S.A.) particularly satisfying! These, however, are only a fraction of the total transfers. Non-British settlers brought their own home or familiar names, from the German settlements at Klemzig or Langdorf in South Australia to the Spanish monks at New Noria (W.A.), but the dominance of British names remains. Indeed, within the towns, street and subdivision names betray the history of the time of subdivision. From the battlefields of the Crimea, the Boer War and the First and Second World Wars have come the Balaklava and Mafeking Avenues, the Ypres and Tobruk roads; the Smuts, Haig and Churchill drives and crescents. Indeed, German place names were removed from several South Australian towns during the First World War and British titles substituted, e.g. Klemzig became Gaza (a battlefield in the Palestine Campaign) in 1916 until 1935 when it reverted back and Langdorf became Kaldukee (an Aboriginal name) thereafter. Of the Korean or Vietnam Wars, however, there is as yet scant evidence in the place names.

Aboriginal names have been adopted for urban centres and street names, particularly since 1945, although the trend was set earlier by the name of the national capital, Canberra, and by usage in the interior of the continent, e.g. Toowoomba, Wagga Wagga and Gundagai.

Architecture

Building styles and conventions came in with the first settlers and have continued to draw their inspiration from outside rather than from within the continent. Thus the visitor from Europe or North America would find little that he had not seen before. The public office buildings he will find have a familiar nineteenth-century 'Victorian' grandeur in stone, while new private office buildings, arising from the demolition sites of their Victorian predecessors, exhibit the steel and glass skyscrapers of international design (Figs. 2.7, 11.1). Only the ubiquitous detached single-storey house set in its individual garden will seem unusual, and that only by its dominance in numbers, for the designs and materials will be generally familiar.

There has been no Australian Frank Lloyd Wright to reverse the traditional inflow of ideas and styles from overseas. Complaints that preconceived plans were imported and erected without thought of local climatic differences or problems began early and have continued in all subsequent architectural surveys (Angas, 1847, p. 235):

> The conventional ideas of the old country have been carried out to the very letter as if they had been law; no allowance is made for the wide difference of climate, and consequently of habits, between the two countries; but here [in N.S.W.] in a latitude of 34° south, we have houses destitute of verandahs or screen-work built with great glaring windows and high roofs, as if to imbibe all the sun possible.

Later builders at least enclosed their houses with an encircling verandah but the general complaint of the mid-nineteenth century was echoed for example by the leading Australian architect, Robin Boyd, in his book *The Australian Ugliness* published in 1960.

Yet the urban landscape has several distinctive architectural features, the first being the dominance, even in the largest urban centres, of the detached single-storey house and garden. Boyd claims that this small house 'probably more than anything else that man has done has made the face of Australia' and certainly the urban view and the statistics bear him out. The number of one-family houses of four to six rooms comprised 79 per cent of all houses in Australia in 1971, while 84 per cent of all dwellings in the larger metropolitan areas were detached private houses. Of the total population at the same time, 84 per cent lived in unshared private houses. And still the aim of the newly-marrieds, inspecting the real estate agents' display boards, or the current weekend display home in the outer suburbs, is for a place of their own, which means the traditional detached house and its garden.

The designs of the house evolved, as Boyd has shown, from the simple British two-roomed country cottage of the eighteenth century through a sequence in time to the three bedroom, lounge, dining room–kitchen, bathroom–lavatory pattern of the 1970s (Fig. 11.4). The evolution was both by the adoption of new styles from overseas and by independent additions as families and standards of living grew. Thus any one house might become an amalgam of often homemade additions as soon as the

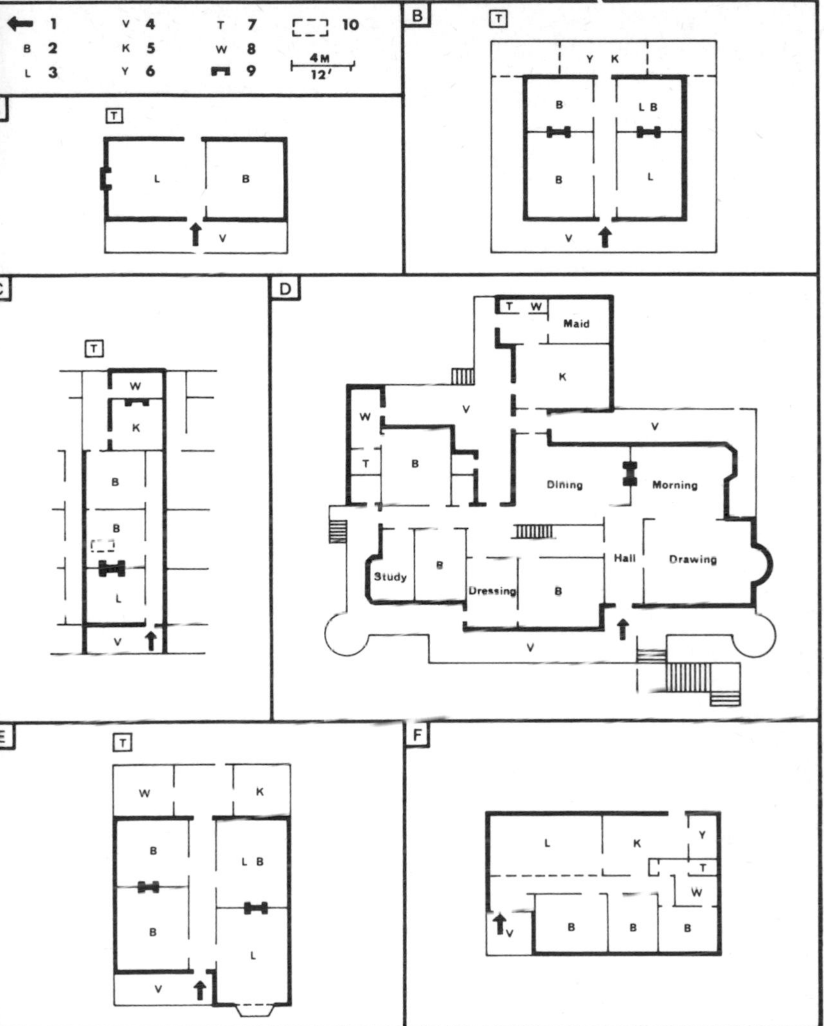

Fig. 11.4 House plans, 1788–1970
A, Primitive cottage, 1788–1850s; B, Bungalow, 1830s–60s; C, Terrace tenement for the workers, 1870s–90s; D, Opulence for the bosses, 1890s; E, Suburban style, 1880s–1920s (with modifications up to 1950s); F, Suburban style, 1960s–70s.
Key:
1, Main entrance; 2–8, Functions: B, Bedroom, K, Kitchen, L, Living room, T, Lavatory, V, Verandah, W, Bathroom, Y, Laundry; **9**, Fireplace; **10**, Skylight.

(*Source:* Boyd, 1961, and 1970 building plan)

original builder, who indeed may have been the owner himself, has finished his work (Spate, 1956, pp. 180–1):

> In one case . . . a two-roomed unlined dwelling of 1925 received a verandah in 1927, a bedroom under the verandah in 1929, a bathroom in 1930, two sleep-outs in 1933; the walls were lined in 1936 and the lounge enlarged in 1940.

Such examples have been common both in major urban centres and country towns (Fig. 10.3). A minimal amount of official interference, in safety and health standards, has enabled housing until the last two decades to be highly variable in form and quality of construction. Not that dominant styles and conventions were absent, but in detail home owners could and did modify the basic designs. Only since the 1950s, with the expansion of Government-sponsored cheap housing constructed by the various state housing trusts and the growth of nation-wide building firms with the ability to produce virtually entire suburban developments themselves from a limited number of 'model houses', have there been any marked trends towards reduction in the variety of detail in housing styles.

Perhaps the only concessions to the environment seen in the private homes have been the verandah – reduced from its enveloping function in earlier forms to the tiny porch in many modern houses, the use of structures on stilts in northern Australia (supposedly to avoid termites and give some added cooling effects), and the ubiquitous use of wire insect screens on all wall openings.

Larger mansions were a feature of nineteenth-century construction in Australia, either as homesteads for the pastoral properties, or as town houses for the successful commercial executives and Government officials. But the twentieth century has seen many of these sold to be subdivided into flats, or for institutions, or demolished and the sites re-used. Thus in the 1890s Victoria alone had over 1200 houses of twenty or more rooms, by mid-1930s there were only 515 in the whole of Australia.

The materials available for building were initially varied but came, partly by necessity and partly by convention, to be dominated by traditional media. The first, rapidly built, dwellings of mud and local timber were succeeded by a sequence of structures which Boyd (1961, p. 124) identified as:

> [the] first house was of wattle and dab, his second pisé [rammed earth], his third of bark sheets, his fourth a log cabin, his fifth of axed slabs. Then the nails and sheets of iron and glass began to arrive from England or from a previously settled colony. Fully prefabricated houses came for his leaders [of wood or iron]. Bricks were made, stone was quarried, cement, steel, pulp board and plastics followed each other from overseas. That was the white man's order of structural progress. As late as 1900 whenever he started a new town in the back blocks he followed the sequence through.

One of the first effective roofing materials was corrugated iron sheeting which was introduced at mid-nineteenth century and which by its cheapness, ease of transportation and efficiency in shedding rainfall into the galvanised iron rainwater tanks dominated not only country but also city housing until the early twentieth century. It lost its dominance to the prestigious tiles which added first a bright red and later a multicoloured roofscape to cities from the turn of the century onwards.

Walls may have begun as mud or earth but wood soon came to dominate and still does for over a third of all houses; in Victoria it is over half of all house walls, in Queensland and Tasmania over 70 per cent. The diffusion of brick – whether veneer (one course with wooden-plaster inner wall) or solid – has spread from the metropolitan centres outwards post the 1920s so that country towns still tend to have a higher proportion of wooden houses than the larger cities, where brick homes may be over half of the total. In the 1970s practically all new house construction is of the brick wall and tile roof type, the exceptions being some corrugated iron roofs on Housing Trust estates, and their prestressed concrete tower blocks of flats, together with the prefabricated wood and asbestos sheeting housing units designed for the newest mining towns of central and northern Australia. Historically the odd-man-out in building materials has been South Australia, where local stone dominated early construction and declined sharply in importance across the state borders to the east, a result apparently of an initial lack of good local timber producing a tradition of stone construction which applied even to remote frontier farms, as their ruins still show (Rose, 1962) (Fig. 9.2).

Land, until the crowding of the metropolitan centres of the 1950s and 1960s, had always been cheap and there had been no widespread financial incentive to build flats or multiple unit dwellings until pressures for housing were aggravated by the Second World War hiatus in house building and the influx of migrants post-1945. It is true that isolated blocks of multistorey flats began to appear after 1910, but the boom in their construction did not begin until the 1930s and was limited to Sydney and Melbourne where it was associated with demands for central residential space rather than overall pressure on land. Local council regulations kept most down to three or four storeys, but from the 1950s onwards regulations were relaxed and high-rise blocks, from the luxurious apartments with Sydney Harbour vistas to standardised home-units of the Victorian Housing Commission overlooking the slums of Melbourne's inner suburbs, began to dominate the residential skylines. In the one case architectural styles could be expensive, individualistic, featuristic and striking; in the other they were forced to be cheap, standardised and obtrusively functional.

Technological innovations and urban design

To the colonial inheritance of ideas, methods and attitudes was added a century and a half of technological innovations which enabled latent resources to be discovered and new patterns of rural and urban land use to emerge. Most innovations came from overseas, with the immigrants, but some and many of them significant were of local origin.

Transport systems: the external links

Paralleling the urbanisation of Europe and the 'western world', the evolution of transport systems in the nineteenth and twentieth centuries has been a major force for change in Australian urban landscapes. Such systems provided both improved efficiencies in the inter-urban and rural-urban flows of goods, people and ideas, linking Australian centres with world centres, and improved efficiencies within those centres, allowing through improved internal movements a more efficient functioning of the whole.

Basically three types of transport systems had relevance to urban landscapes. As centres for administration whether of official government or private commercial nature, a communication system between governors and governed, producer and merchant, merchant and customer was essential. As centres for the collection and despatch of goods, a system of freight transport was implicit, and as a habitation for a substantial residential work force, a passenger transport system for the journey to work became increasingly necessary with increasing size of the urban area.

The evolution of various communication systems reflects increasing efficiency in the speed by which information or orders could be transferred over greater and greater distances. It is perhaps significant that the development of commercial use of land resources in the 1820s was followed by the first postal services in New South Wales in 1828. Services were initially linked to each colonial capital and from there direct to Britain by a regular shipping service which began from Sydney in 1844. Inter-capital links came as a second stage in each case. Rapid expansion of the volume of mail followed the population inflows of the 1850s and for the next half-century each state saw the volume of mail as an index of commercial prosperity. The General Post Office buildings were in size and architectural grandeur among the most imposing of the cluster of official buildings in each capital city centre, with often miniatures in the larger regional centres (Fig. 11.3), its 'country cousin' as noted above still often the only Government 'office' in the smallest centres.

Almost exactly thirty years after the first inland mail service was established, in 1854, the first telegraph lines began to span the continent. In fact the first lines linked the capitals and their ports for news of the latest ship arrivals and departures, but again the sequence paralleled in time and supplemented the posts. First the line to the port, then a line to the next state capital and finally the whole continental network linked to the rest of the world, particularly (in the volume of messages) to Britain. From 1854 to 1877 the lines were being looped through desert, scrub and forest, to bring the producer and consumer even closer together.

With the combination of telegraph and post the international commercial firms began to emerge, the stock agents began to buy and sell before the vool was off the sheep's back, grocery stores and hardware merchants began o advertise in the newspapers circulating by post and to order direct from Britain if necessary.

Thus the local newspaper at Bourke 500 miles (800 km) inland from Sydney carried in the 1880s, as its front page advertisements, the latest ailing dates and cost of cabins on the steamers to Britain, anything from nedicinal cures to saddlery items to be mailed anywhere in the colony, official notices of lost and found livestock and private warnings to stock hieves and trespassing drovers. On the second page, printed in Sydney and ailed to Bourke before the local items were added, were the latest syndi-ated reports from London on the European political scene, city editorials on the New South Wales rabbit problem, the latest chapters from books by Dickens or his imitators and the latest in 'Irishmen, Scotsmen and Englishmen' jokes.

By comparison, the influence of the telephone and radio have been more ubtle. Although set up in most capitals by the 1890s, the telephone ystems appear to have expanded mainly in the 1920s and post the Second World War when initially business and more recently private subscribers ave sought the speeding up of internal urban communications. The social mplications in Australia, however, have never been adequately studied so he real impact is not known.

The expansion of domestic radio services had an immediate impact on ity skylines when the first clumsy aerials appeared but again its social mplications are difficult to assess. Its impact was possibly greater in the ommercial and public service fields where in combination with aircraft it ecame the backbone of the Royal Flying Doctor Service which from 1928 as provided centralised 'urban' hospital services as well as a social com-nunication network to the sparsely populated and remote interior.

More obvious in its impact on the patterns of urban entertainment has een the spread of television coverage, which, originating in Sydney in 956, by 1960 had covered all capitals and many regional centres. By nid-1960s the drop in attendance at communal entertainments, particularly he cinema, had caused widespread closures of suburban cinemas and, oinciding with the increased car mobility of the housewife, their conver-ion to shopping centres. As a feature of the skyline, the TV transmission owers had come to dominate both urban and the most densely settled uburban areas.

Evolving technology in freight transport systems has basically improved he capacity of the urban centres of Australia, as elsewhere in the world, to unction as nodes in which the links from the spatially diffuse production entres are drawn together and goods marshalled to and from their roducers and consumers.

The early importance of water transport was not only for external links, ut also for coastal and limited river navigation. Until the arrival of the ailway the south-eastern interior was at the mercy of the Murray–Darling teamer navigation and that was at the mercy of drought and snags. The railways, however, soon drew off the river trade in the 1880s, leaving Echuca, Wentworth, Morgan, Bourke and many other river towns with mouldering wharves and warehouses along the river bank, and paddle steamers and barges rotting quietly in forgotten backwaters until rediscovered and renovated by renewed tourist interests in the 1960s. In contrast, the coastal freight trade has continued its importance, not only as a feeder to the main ports for export, but as a source of supplies and provisions for settlements – especially in tropical Western Australia, Darwin and northern Queensland. As late as the 1920s for example, as noted by *The Australian* (8 July 1968):

> a commercial traveller making his rounds in northern parts of N.S.W. would put his car on a coastal steamer [at Sydney], have it landed at the Macleay River to cover the area back of Kempsey, ship it again to the Clarence to make his calls in the Grafton area, and then again by ship to the Richmond River to cover the area around Lismore.

The main land transport, however, was by the rail systems from *c*. 1870s to the 1950s (Fig. 6.3B). Not only did the state and later commonwealth systems service the inland production centres, they often created them. Some of the sidings spaced at 5 mile intervals along the lines in the wheat country might sometimes acquire a post office, school, hotel and – in the 1940s and 1950s – a silo to form the nucleus of an urban centre (Fig. 9.3). While most remained a siding, however, the importance of the railway as the link, with the telegraph, to the outside world cannot be overestimated. Although many sites with a railway may never have developed into towns, few towns without a railway survived very long after 1880. The exceptions would be mainly the small coastal ports.

While the railway station or siding often formed a focus for country towns, for the larger cities the mainline stations or, in the case of each state capital, the terminal building and yards of the state railway system became an integral part of the inner city. Located as close as possible to the central business district, the rail lines were laid out often on some of the public open space or parkland left from the original designs (as Melbourne and Adelaide). The main state marshalling yards, however, were usually more remote from the capital city and it was here that the country produce was organised for the final movement to the dockside and incoming overseas freight organised for the regular trains to the country centres.

By the 1970s, however, such locations are well within the builtup area and the air space over the terminal buildings and track complexes is coming under consideration as potential office and retail space by the urban planners.

In the 1950s, the competition from motor truck freight transport had begun to make inroads into the empire of the railways. Particularly in the pastoral areas, the flexibility and speed of motor trucking of livestock and wool has caused the closure of several of the remoter rail spurs, especially in Western Australia, and despite competitive rail freight charges the pastoralists seem to be preferring the road transport, so that the wool warehouses no longer need to be alongside the railyards.

In contrast, bulk handling of grain from the 1940s onwards seems to have favoured the railways, with Government-controlled silos sited to use the Government-controlled railway networks, and thus continue to support the small urban country centres. As yet the location of vast country or suburban container warehouses to avoid city traffic holdups has not taken place and all traffic tends to be channelled to and from the city centres – semitrailers (some 400 a day on the Sydney–Melbourne run alone) providing day and night services between the state capitals. Planning of road systems to cope with this increase in external freight movement into and out of the cities has paralleled attempts to cope with the rapid increases in private passenger car movements in the last decade, and the resultant direct-line freeway systems have begun to cut through the older grid pattern of streets.

External links were not limited to freight, and the expansion of public transport networks between urban centres both reduced the remoteness of the country areas and encouraged a mobility of population which was to culminate in the rural–urban movement of the twentieth century. Private horsedrawn 'stage coaches' operated between urban centres from the first in 1814 (between Sydney and Paramatta) to the last in 1924 (between two country towns in Queensland, Surat and Yeulba). The first major boom came with the gold rushes in the 1850s and the first sharp demand for passenger transport from the ports to the inland fields. Regular inter-city services began between Sydney, Melbourne and Adelaide at the same time, 1850–52, and with the expansion of the railway net the coaches extended their runs, serving as feeders to the expanding railheads as well as carrying the mail.

For the country cousin of western New South Wales to visit his Sydney relations in the 1880s might involve a horseback ride from his station to the nearest Cobb and Company staging post to catch the weekly coach into Bourke. From Bourke to Sydney was a relatively comfortable if tedious rail journey of two to three days, and once arrived in Sydney the final leg might be completed by steam tram or even a suburban rail trip. In the 1970s it would take less than twenty-four hours by private car door to door, perhaps five to six hours by commercial aircraft flight and Sydney taxi.

The last decade in fact has seen a doubling of annual air passenger movements within and to and from Australia to over 4.6 million (Fig. 6.3A). With the bulk of this movement between the state capitals, and specifically between Sydney and Melbourne, has come new international passenger facilities at Sydney's airport and a completely new international airport at Melbourne. From the most modern complexes of terminal buildings, maintenance hangars, offices, control towers and car parks linked by freeway to the adjacent city, to the grassed landing strips, ragged windsock and galvanised iron hangar-cum-airport office of the smallest of country towns, both formally and functionally the airports have acquired an increasingly significant place in the urban landscape. Apart from commercial passenger movements and air-freight, private aircraft now connect remote mining operations direct with metropolitan head offices, and provide the larger pastoral operations with their own direct links to the state capitals.

Transport systems: the internal links

For the centres which benefited most from the increasing efficiencies of external transport links, their success and the building expansion which it engendered posed separate problems of internal communication and transport. The systems adopted for the long-distance external links had some relevance, but for the relatively short-distance links within the urban centres special transport systems evolved and these in their turn unfluenced the pattern of urban expansion.

McCarty suggested in 1970 a three-fold classification of Australian capital cities 'defined by their size in relation to the available means of transport' which has a wider relevance. From their various foundation dates to approximately the 1870s and 1880s the capitals were 'walking cities' with the richer residents clustered at the core, and the workers around the port or inner suburban factories. From the 1880s to *c.* 1945 they became public transport oriented cities, with horse and cable-trams being replaced by steam and electric trams and the suburban railway network, all enabling a greater spread and a greater segregation of housing and workplace. Working class inner suburbs were now bounded on the margins by spreading middle-class areas, each with its particular architectural styles, and all could now be separated from the industrial areas of port or inner city. From 1945, the cities became oriented to the automobile both for private journeys to work and social activity and both inter- and intra-city freight movements.

The detailed influences on local landscapes were significantly different. Thus, in Melbourne the private cable and later electric trams operated in alternate parallel streets in the inner suburbs, stopping every 50 to 100 m to load passengers. The result was a linear pattern of shops along the route with a fairly complete infilling of terrace houses between the lines. By contrast, the suburban government railway stations attracted shops around them and created isolated nodes of shops and houses spaced out at 1–1½ mile intervals along the line and separated from each other initially by open countryside. Both, however, funnelled passengers into the centre of the city, to the government and private offices or the inner suburban factories.

Bus services began to replace trams as motor traffic increased in the 1950s, and only Melbourne retains a major tram network. Ballarat and Bendigo, the only two non-capital cities, have both lost their trams relatively recently (1970 and 1971 respectively). Although practically much more flexible than trams, so far the bus services have tended merely to run over the same centralising routes of the trams, movements between suburbs being relatively rare, except where centred on large shopping complexes.

For the housewife, the journey to shop has been transformed first by public transport, but particularly since the 1950s by the private car. Downtown shopping centres – the Elizabeth Street of Sydney, Collins Street of Melbourne, Rundle Street of Adelaide, have suffered from the congestion of on-street parking and have only survived by organising off-street car-parking in tower or underground sites, and the traditional trade of the office workers brought in by public transport. Some of the larger stores have joined the suburban shopping centres, where (mirrors of the American concept) the air-conditioned complexes of pedestrian malls and arcades lined by shops and restaurants rise from vast seas of bitumen car-parking areas (Fig. 11.5).

Industrialisation

The urbanised society which came ashore with the first settlers was clothed and equipped with products of the Industrial Revolution in Britain and Europe but they were to create demands for food, clothing and shelter which were to require industrial production from the new settlements. Thus it is not surprising to find the convicts providing the labour force for the first factories sited in the first settlements. The urban concentration of factory production began early and has continued to provide a significant segment of contemporary urban landscapes.

The need for shelter stimulated the first 'manufactories'. As soon as the convicts came ashore in 1788, they were put to work to saw timber and carve out wooden pegs, dig out brick pits, burn lime and quarry stone for the first urban structures. The needs of food and clothing were soon added, bread from the imported flour, woollen blankets in 1801 from the female convict factory at Paramatta.

The local demands and labour supply provided the stimulus for an array of what might be called basic industries which were to form the origins of the contemporary manufacturing patterns. Brickworks, saw mills, lime pits, breweries, cordial (aerated water) factories, flour mills, bakeries, dairies, creameries, abattoirs, tanneries, wheelwrights and blacksmiths shops took their places in the urban centres as each grew in size. By 1851, however, already the early lead of the first settlement at Sydney showed in the range of manufacturers, which, according to Walsh (1963, p. 50):

> included two distilleries, two breweries, two meat-preserving establishments, one woollen mill, five soap works, nine tanneries, three potteries, one copper-smelting works, eight ship and anchor works, and six rope walks. Over 3,700 tons of sugar were refined, 1,400 tons of soap, and 75,000 yards of cloth were manufactured.

By the turn of the century, although most of the inland towns had their own flour mills, bakeries, brewery, cordial factory, coach-builder and blacksmith, the spread of other types of industries had been much more restricted, for only about 28 per cent of Australian demands for all manufactured goods were being met locally. In some cases local demands were not sufficient to justify local production, in others the imported product

Fig. 11.5 Chadstone shopping centre, Melbourne
Opened in 1958, this was one of the first regional shopping centres (of which there are now over 100 in Australia). The central, partially enclosed, shopping area surrounded by car parks and bus parking bays, and adjacent to a major road (here National Route 1 to Sydney) are standard design features. The surrounding suburbs date from *c.* 1940s, predated by the Roman Catholic Convent left of the centre.

(*Source:* Australian Information Service)

was cheaper from economies of scale and despite transport around the world. Thus, from specialised and limited needs such as surveying instruments, to specialised but bulky items such as rails and railway equipment most was initially imported and that via the wharves of the state capitals.

Land settlement itself generated demands for some manufactured goods apart from the needs of the new urban communities. One of the major stimuli to local metal working was the mechanisation of agriculture from the 1830s onwards. The most obvious examples were found on the wheat farms. Australian grain harvesting machinery was invented, tested and mass produced independent of external influences or controls. Chaff cutters were being produced after 1837 in Adelaide, while Bull's wheat-stripper of 1843, after modifications by Ridley, was in production in many country towns of the wheatlands of South Australia and Victoria in the 1850s. McKay's harvester, combining stripping and winnowing, appeared in 1885 and manufacturing began in 1894, while the McKay–Taylor 'Sunshine Harvester', a combined header–harvester, began to appear in 1916.

Locally, manufacturing firms which owed their origins to machinery invented to cope with the pioneer stresses of agricultural settlement have continued as small engineering firms in country areas, supplying machinery and equipment from pumps to tractor tow-bar attachments, rain water tanks and on-farm silos. A large proportion of current supplies of tractors and harvesting machinery, however, now come from subsidiary firms of overseas companies located at state capitals (e.g. Massey Ferguson and International Harvester at Melbourne), and in the 1970s only one large independent firm remains (Horwood–Bagshaw in Adelaide).

In the larger urban centres, the demands for domestic power and light stimulated the creation of town gas plants after the 1880s and reached a peak in 1914, supplying centres even with populations as low as 1500–2000 persons. Dependence upon coal gas supplemented by hydro-electricity, until the petroleum and natural gas conversions of the 1960s, benefited coastal or railway locations, which were necessary to import the raw material mainly from New South Wales. The town gasometers still remain part of most of the larger town skylines although now holding natural gas from remote gas fields. Bottled petroleum gas has provided remoter centres with urban amenities by regular supplies from metropolitan refineries.

By mid-1950s, after an internal industrial revolution dating back to the 1920s, Australian manufacturers had begun to supply two-thirds of local demands and by 1970 approximately 75–80 per cent. A large proportion of this increased industrialisation accumulated around the largest urban centres as a result of several factors.

Expansion of local non-basic manufacturing was stimulated by wartime experiences of shortages of imported items and strategic policies aimed at selfsufficiency, and by traditional attitudes of local labour towards the encouragement of local job opportunities by tariffs against cheap imports. Labour, demand and power supplies were most usually available in the largest urban centres, and since these were usually also ports, they were the logical locale for new factories of overseas firms, assembling in Australia parts manufactured outside and which if imported whole would have paid the high tariffs. The protectionist policies dated mainly from Federation but Victoria and Queensland introduced them intermittently from the 1860s onwards, especially once unsuccessful gold miners began looking for urban jobs.

Concentration of industrial locations has also been a function of trends towards vertical integration of production, i.e. company control of the whole sequence of production from raw material to consumer item, and by the increasingly complex inter-relations of many industrial processes and the heavy reliance on component parts supplied by subcontractors. As examples of the first, the printing industry is dominated by the Australian Newsprint Mills of Tasmania, the sugar industry by the cane-mills and refineries of Colonial Sugar Refining Pty Ltd, the steel industry by the iron-ore fields, export and import wharves and blast furnaces of Broken Hill Proprietary Ltd, the glass industry by the sand pits and mills of the Australian Consolidated Industries. This vertical integration has led to the concentration of processing into few large plants around which urban centres have evolved, e.g. the paper-mill town of Boyer in Tasmania, the steel towns of Newcastle and Port Kembla in New South Wales and the sugar-mill towns such as Mosman, Bundaberg and Mackay along the Queensland coast.

Integration of production from many subcontracting firms has also tended to encourage the concentration of industrial plants, and in this case often the largest cities have had the greatest attraction. Hence the motor vehicle assembly plants at each of the mainland state capitals, each surrounded by small ancillary firms supplying parts for the main assembly line.

The urban space taken by industrial plants generally has been increasing rapidly in absolute terms since 1950 with the increasing demand for single storey plants with adjacent storage space and room for expansion. The spread of the urban areas over the same period has been so rapid however that relatively the industrial space has probably declined as a proportion of the total buildup area. Within the older multiple storey buildings of the inner city areas some industries such as dressmaking and provision of office supplies still flourish, but the old woollen-mills of east Melbourne for example are now subdivided for multiple small specialised industrial tenants.

The planning of industrial location by any authority other than the firm involved has been only a recent phenomenon in Australia. As a result, apart from a segregation of noxious industries such as tanneries, bonemeal factories and oil refineries, most of Australian urban areas are randomly sprinkled with industrial sites, which might vary from a backyard garage in which an enterprising mechanic is spending his evenings making roof-racks for private cars, to a several acre site dominated by the sprawl of a modern automated factory producing anything from bottled milk or 'Coca-Cola' to motor cars. Competition between suburbs for highly taxable industrial land use and rivalry between country town and capital city for factory employment tended to encourage the initial spread of industry in the nineteenth century before the economics of concentration and scale began to dominate locations in the twentieth century. The present pattern, a combination of the two, has recently had a further component added, in the form of industrial estates – areas zoned specifically for industrial use often peripheral to the main urban buildup area.

These industrial estates vary in design and ownership but basically aim to provide a uniform basic range of facilities, land, power, drainage and access for industrialists to adopt to their specific requirements. Some estates provided buildings ready made, others just the land for building. Some, the work of hopeful local councils, were isolated and only slowly occupied. Occasionally as in Elizabeth, South Australia, the estate was designed alongside a new residential unit, in this case a new town planned to ease the congestion of Adelaide, and some integration of jobs and homes could be attempted. Most were and still are starkly functional places, only rarely hidden by landscaping from the passing traffic (Fig. 7.3).

Overall planning of industrial location, however, had a stimulus from the Second World War when Japanese attacks on Darwin and Sydney brought home the coastal vulnerability of Australian industries and stimulated interest in relocation of industries away from the coastal urban centres – decentralisation as it became known. Although agreed on in principle in 1944 the attempts to reverse the twentieth-century trend and to attract industry away from particularly the metropolitan centres have been generally unsuccessful and the country towns have not greatly benefited.

Regional plans were drawn up in the late 1940s and 1950s but despite several financial inducements – free sites, reduced rail freight charges and cheaper power supplies – the relocation of existing factories has been minimal and only a few branch plants have been opened in the country towns. Towns closest to the largest centres have benefited most, e.g. towns within 50–60 miles (80–95 km) of the metropolitan centres gained 92 per cent of the national increase of workers in 1954–61. Concentration merely appears to have been spread rather than broken up into decentralised locations.

The major arguments against decentralisation seem to have been practical and economic. The economies of scale of the large, most modern factories, the labour they need and the markets they supply are not to be found in country towns. The trend in modern manufactories, e.g. chemicals, plastics, petroleum products and motor cars mentioned before, is for increasingly complex interrelations. The major employers, producing the largest volume of manufactures, occupying the largest areas are thus inexorably linked together and can only rationalise their production as close as possible to the largest urban centres – their main markets and often main sources of supplies.

The legacy of the concentration of land, sea and air routes upon the state capitals, their historical advantages over later settlements and the size of their populations have tended to favour them at the expense of all the other urban centres. As centres of state Government, the headquarters of industry and the site for most factories in the nation, they dominate the life of the continent. Yet that life is as varied as the people who live in those cities.

People

One of the main characteristics of Australian urban landscapes is change – for better or worse. The demolition sites of the city downtown areas, the new rows of brick veneer boxes in the suburbs, the overgrown empty lots and empty shops of the country towns are evidence of the changing demands and pressures of population.

Although increasing naturally by approximately 2 per cent per year, the national population is currently being supplemented by a deliberate policy of officially encouraged immigration which was revived in 1945 after a lapse in the 1930s depression years. Between 1947 and 1966 over 2 million immigrants arrived in Australia and in the latter year one in five of the Australian population was either a post-Second World War immigrant or the child of one. While the migrants still comprise a solid core of the traditional British stock, an increasing element from continental Europe has been apparent in the last twenty years, so that by 1966 approximately 3.6 per cent of the non-Aboriginal population was of European nationality. If we revert back to the definitions of the Introduction, the Australian population of 12.7 million by 1971 comprised approximately 106 000 Aborigines (of full or mixed blood), 10 070 000 Anglo–Australians, 2 196 000 Europeans and 302 000 other nationalities.

Movements

The increase of population has not been evenly spread throughout the settled areas. A basic shift of population from rural to urban areas began to occur from the First World War onwards, with the slowing down and, locally, the ending of new land settlement. Children of farming communities began to find less opportunities to either *become* farmers with the end of new land openings or *remain* farmers with economic trends towards amalgamation of holdings. With the economies of scale made possible by mechanisation and improved transport facilities, fewer local industries survived; beer began to come from city breweries, flour from city mills, vegetables from the metropolitan milk and vegetable zones and fruit from the Murray Valley, Queensland or Tasmanian specialist producers. Although some country towns benefited from the shift off the farm and began to accommodate 'town farmers' (Williams, 1969) most began to lose population – initially the natural increases as teenagers looked for jobs further afield, and eventually absolutely, as the population structure began to age and deaths outstripped births.

The beneficiaries of this shift were the largest towns, whether regional country centres or state capitals. Here pressure of population from rural–urban migration was heightened by immigration from abroad, as over three-quarters of the new settlers tended to stay in the larger cities. Overcrowding in the larger centres was thus paralleled by dereliction in the smaller towns.

The almost imperceptible change of birthrates over deathrates, and the movement of new settlers into and out of the towns and cities are hidden beneath the more obvious daily movements of urban populations to and from work, shops and entertainments. Each full working day, Monday to Friday, the major urban centres have a two-fold pulse of movements – the morning and evening 'rush hours' of the journey to and from work.

Three questions immediately come to mind, who moves, how far do they go and when? If we take the 1966 Census figures, 42 per cent of the population works and most of those, except possibly some of $3\frac{1}{2}$ per cent who were self employed, would be in the rush-hour crowds. They would be joined by the 22 per cent of the population which were school-children or students, so that some 60 per cent of the population would be on the move in the journey to and from work.

Distances moved vary from a few hundred metres in the case of school-children to up to 5–10 miles (8–16 km) for most of the workforce, while a few commuters may travel up to 20–30 miles (32–48 km) into the major centres.

The morning rush hour begins about 6.30 a.m. when labourers and semi-skilled workers begin their journeys to factories and new building sites. From about 8.00 a.m. to 9.00 or 9.30 a.m. the office workers, students and school-children are on the move and by 9.30 a.m. the movement of private cars and public transport has dropped to a trickle. Approximately 60 per cent of the journeys are made in the period 7.00 a.m. to 8.30 a.m. From 3.30 p.m. onwards the flow begins to reverse and by 6.30 p.m. most workers are back at home and the suburban streets and railway stations are again quiet.

The two peaks of movement are separated by the period of minimum traffic flow (overnight), but during the day minor increases in movement stem from the journey to shop of suburban housewives, the lunchtime movements usually of office workers on foot (but increasingly by car), and an increase in flows from *c.* 7.00 p.m. to 8.00 p.m. of journeys to evening entertainments, returning perhaps around midnight or later.

At weekends, the patterns of population movement change significantly. Only a portion of the workforce works Saturday mornings (retailers, construction workers and some of the factories on shifts), for the remainder of the population the movements are centred around further journeys to shop and the afternoon movements to popular seasonal outdoor entertainments, e.g. football and cricket at the various 'ovals', or to the beaches or parks for private swimming, walks and picnics.

While the majority (88%) of the population in 1966 claimed to be Christians and the scatter of churches, chapels or meeting halls reflected the pattern of denominations (33.6% Church of England, and 26.3% Roman Catholic to the 1.4% Baptists, 0.5% Salvation Army and 0.1% Brethren) the Sunday movements to these centres are only a fraction (perhaps a tenth) of the registered membership. Many more of the Sunday movements will be to beach, national park, sports oval or countryside.

Minorities

In detail, the urban landscapes of the 1970s showed the influence of certain minority groups, which in some cases appeared to be out of proportion to their total numbers. Two contrasting groups are worth examining as examples.

Since 1788 the Aborigines in Australia have tended to be the unseen and relatively insignificant element in Australian populations. As nomadic groups, it was not to be expected that they would make any major contribution to an urbanised intrusive society and those who did make contact and adopt urban ways were rapidly detribalised and decimated by introduced diseases, alcohol and conflicting policies of protection and assimilation. Initially a source of interest, then derision, the Aboriginal population rapidly disappeared from the main streets. In the 1970s they remained in remote interior reserves, peripheral camps around some country towns and in the poorer and older residential areas of the larger cities. Significantly the various denominational mission stations, located in areas of Aboriginal concentration, shifted from the coastal settlements first to successively more remote inland sites in the 1850s to 1880s to avoid the advancing tide of European settlement and to search for fresh unsullied tribes to convert as the first converts died out. Eventually, full circle, they had to return to the cities in 1950s where Aborigines had joined the Anglo–Australian in-migration.

The contemporary location of the Aboriginal population is, however, largely conjectural, as not until the 1971 Census were they included. All prior work therefore has been of limited value and based on local rather than general sources. The detailed picture which the census will show is likely to be of a marked contrast between the remote inland full blood population and the urban mixed-blood population, which is being constantly and increasingly added to by in-migration of country Aborigines. Hausfeld in 1965 suggested that of the 12 000 Aborigines in New South Wales who could be located (some 75% of the estimated total) half were in Sydney, a quarter on official reserves and a quarter working on pastoral properties. Gale's study of South Australia (1969) showed that the migration to urban centres was usually, but not always, the second stage of a shift from tribal areas, the first being to the nearest mission or Government station. Part of the movement was involuntary, the result of an increasing crime rate among Aborigines and their confinement in city gaols; but most has been deliberate choice, to obtain better medical care, visit relatives or seek work. By 1966 Gale estimated one-fifth of the state's Aboriginal population was in Adelaide. With such movement have come problems common to all such movements historically, lack of employment, breakdown of traditional ethical values with resultant exposure to crime and vice, but against these must be set the 'successes'(?), the 10 per cent of Gale's study group who by 1966 had become so assimilated with Anglo–Australian ways that they were no longer regarded by their relatives as Aborigines.

In contrast, a much more apparent minority group in Australian cities are the continental European immigrant groups. A study of Melbourne, whose immigrant population was one of the largest in the country, showed that in 1961 almost one-quarter of the metropolitan population was of direct overseas migrant origin, three-quarters of this having arrived since 1947. Migrants appeared to have moved into both the northern and western suburbs where most of the new housing and urban sprawl of Anglo–Australians was being carried out, and into the inner city eastern and southern suburbs which otherwise showed losses of Anglo–Australian populations. National minorities tended to be grouped together, with Maltese, Greek, Yugoslavian and Ukrainian groups most obvious, Italian, Russian, Polish, Czechoslovakian, Dutch, Hungarians, Austrians and Germans less so. Chain migration processes initially ensured continuity of concentrations of southern European groups such as Italians and Greeks and some of the refugee 'Displaced Persons' (post-1945) seem to have felt the need to stay close to fellow nationals. However, all groups showed the influence of the economic job-opportunities of industrial suburbs, sited to the east and southeast over the period. British migrants, as might be expected from a group with less cultural contrasts, showed least tendency to congregate in specific urban areas (Johnston, 1969).

In terms of the visible landscape the impact of continental Europeans has been most evident in the inner city areas, where they have taken over and renovated old residential properties – the narrow semidetached cottages dating back to 1870s and 1880s – and have opened delicatessen shops ('delis'), cafes for European foods, tailors and milliners shops to vary the patterns of retailing.

Summary

The complex origins and evolution of urban landscapes have created the great variety of Australian urban forms and functions. To describe and explain the resultant implied patterns and processes we need to look in the next chapter more closely at some possible theoretical explanations and the extent to which specific examples bear out these theories.

12
Urban landscapes - patterns and processes

Chapter 11 painted the origins and evolution of Australian urban landscapes with a broad brush; this chapter will attempt to pick out some of the finer details of the patterns both of, and within, the urban landscapes which have resulted. For convenience and to document the marked formal and functional differences between them, we shall distinguish between the federal and state capital cities and the other, generally smaller, towns when examining the patterns *within* these centres.

The patterns of towns and cities

Rose (1967) commented that 'the urban map of Australia is a picture of a series of highly diversified productive agglomerations, the capital cities, surrounded by far and thinly flung points of specialised production [the towns]'. Such a map justifies separate consideration of the two basic components but hides the fact that there are marked patterns in the spatial location of those centres of specialised production. For the cities those patterns can be described in regard to state boundaries and the ocean and the historical evolution has been already discussed in Chapter 11. For the towns those patterns can be described in regard to simpler geometry; in fact, two basic patterns of 'centrality' and 'linearity'.

Centrality might be defined as a pattern which suggests an even and regular spacing of towns of a similar population size over the whole area of study, where distances from towns are limited and where all areas are within reasonable reach of some of these 'central places'. *Linearity* might be defined as a pattern which suggests regular spacing of towns of equal population sizes along certain limited axes, which makes for uneven accessibility and long distances between towns of equal size if they are not in the same axes. Such patterns are not peculiar to Australia and various explanations for their occurrence have been offered which have relevance to their emergence here.

Explanations: central place theory

Christaller's central place theory attempted to explain a hierarchical mathematical relationship between the population, function and distribution of urban centres observed in southern Germany (Christaller, 1933, translation

Table 12.1 Central places in Tasmania

Type	Order of centre	Distance apart (km)			Mean population (000)		
		Tasmania	Germany	Theory (K = 3)	Tasmania	Germany	Theory (K = 3)
Provincial city	1	–	187	187	–	500.0	500.0
City	2	158	109	108	86.3	100.0	90.0
Major town	3	90	63	62	13.6	30.0	27.0
Town	4	43	36	36	3.3	10.0	9.0
Minor town	5	26	21	21	1.1	4.0	3.5
Village	6	9	13	12	0.3	2.0	1.5
Hamlet	7	6	7	7	0.1	1.2	0.8

Note
Orders same as Fig. 12.1.
Source: Christaller (1966); Scott (1964)

1966). After examination of the services provided and areas served by these centres, he demonstrated that a hierarchy of seven types of central places existed, from hamlets of *c.* 1200 people to provincial cities of 500 000 (Table 12.1), above which were the national capitals of 1–2 million or more. At each level of the hierarchy the areas served by each centre closely approximated the optimal honeycomb of hexagons (Fig. 12.1). The number of lower order places served by a higher order centre varied according to the services provided. Thus for optimal marketing access not affected by existing transport routes each centre served three others (including itself) i.e. a K = 3 network; where transport routes affected access each served four others, a K = 4 network; and finally where administrative functions were added, each centre served seven others, a K = 7 network. In effect the study demonstrated that there was a logical geometry in the spacing of the urban centres, whatever their size; a geometry that reflected a hierarchy of increasing services in the higher order centres evolved over a considerable period of time.

Explanations: mercantile theory

More recently, the limitations of the central place theory have been realised and a complementary *mercantile theory* has been offered (Vance, 1970). This theory lays greater emphasis on the fact that in the lands colonised by Europeans from the seventeenth century onwards, trade with the mother country was the dominant influence on the formation of urban centres. The emphasis is less on the customer–retailer relationship (implicit in central place theory), but rather on the retailer–wholesaler relationship, the argument being that 'trade spreads outwards from the city, or the mother country, leading to the complex flowering of the rural economy at home as well as in a distant plantation of staple-producing colonists' (Vance, 1970, p. 11).

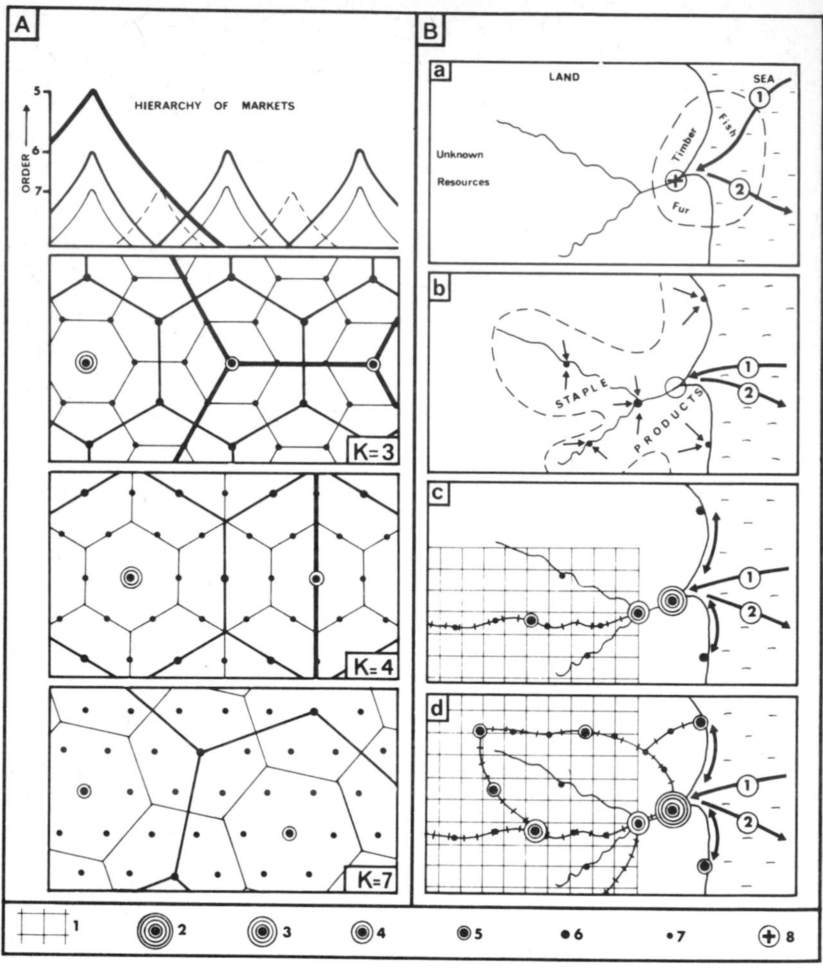

Fig. 12.1 Theories of urban patterns

A. Central place theory

Hypothetical layout of 'central places' resulting from only marketing access (K = 3), distorted by transport accessibility (K = 4), and by administrative functions (K = 7). See text for fuller explanation.

B. Mercantile theory

The four sequences (a–d) of the development of urban centres in a colonial location, with first river then railway transport; imports of manufactures from home country (1) and exports of raw materials and semifinished goods to home country (2).

Key to both:

1, Rural land subdivisional survey; **2–7**, Descending hierarchy of urban centres based upon decreasing scale and type of functional roles; **8**, Initial trading–entrepôt centre.

(*Sources:* Haggett, 1972; Vance, 1970)

That trade was essentially a process of wholesaling of goods – both manufactured items from the mother country and raw materials and foodstuffs from the colony, which itself encouraged the development of a special type of urban pattern tied together and delimited by the transport network. In this pattern there were fewer types of centres, perhaps two or three at most. Dominating the scene in range of functions and size of population were the *entrepôt cities* where the external links between colony and mother country were 'unravelled', from whence on major transport routes the distribution of imports was controlled, and whither back along the same routes the collection of exports was channelled. Apart from these few centres, the remaining towns formed either *workplace towns* 'where men harvested a wealth from untended resources' or *fundamental trading centres* where a limited number of doctors, dentists and lawyers provided sufficient essential services and the one or two general stores (through their mail order catalogues) were 'sufficiently flexible to offer the patient frontiersman the ultimate satisfaction of a great variety of wants' (Vance, 1970, p. 85). The location of both however was tied to transport routes to external centres, basically through the entrepôt cities to the home country markets and suppliers (Fig. 12.1B). The population differences between the two major types was considerable, the towns developing populations of over 5000 the cities qualifying when populations rose above 50 000.

The mercantile theory represents an open system where subsequent external influences may have effects on any prior patterns, and has therefore a dynamic component not found in the central place theory. Thus the model is seen to evolve in five stages through time, from an initial search and resource discovery period; to the exploitation by harvest of natural storage (marine, timber) resources; to the planting of settlers to raise 'staple' products for the home country and consume its manufactures; to the introduction of internal trade and manufacture in the colony with the setting up of depots for the collection of the local staples inland; and finally to the dominant position of internal trade and the beginnings of a central place hierarchy based upon increasing volumes of consumer–retailer trading.

Explanations: the Australian experience

Two studies have attempted to apply the central place theory to the patterns of Australian towns. A hierarchy of six types of central place was noted for Tasmania in the 1950s (Scott, 1964), and although population data were suspect, some comparison with the German patterns was possible (Table 12.1).

In Tasmania, Scott found the smallest centres (hamlets) to have at least a post office and telephone exchange with often a general store, primary school and community hall. Villages, next in size, always had the general store and a wider variety of functions but none dominant. Minor towns, the third rank, had a doctor, bank and various extra official services, while some had small processing plants. Towns had all these together with a greater variety of shops for the higher valued items and professional services, while two major towns were distinguished by their departmental stores. Two cities completed the ranking, with a full array of shopping and professional services together with extensive administration functions, one of them being the state capital, Hobart.

While this, the most comprehensive survey in Australia yet to appear, suggested a parallel to the hypothetical geometries of the Christaller model, the patterns and hierarchies were distorted. Population levels in Tasmania tended to be lower throughout the hierarchy, i.e. more functions were to be found in Tasmania centres than in German centres of equivalent rank, but there were more smaller centres in Tasmania than would have been predicted from the German model. One possible explanation was the uneven terrain in Tasmania, which posed barriers to transport and varied the density of population supported by the land. The history of land settlement also distorted the picture since the land was not all settled simultaneously, and the earliest centres to be established obtained a marked commercial advantage over later sites. A further problem was the changing technology of transport of goods, people and information. Scott's survey predated the changeover from manned to automatic telephone exchanges and this has reduced the functions of the lower order of centres. Extensive use of private cars has reduced the inconvenience of travel, hence customers are now prepared to travel further than before, especially as the quality of rural roads is being improved each year. Scott's survey also predated the arrival of television in Tasmania and the associated decline of rural cinemas – a further function lost by the towns and villages.

In New South Wales a further attempt to apply the central place theory found that while a definite hierarchy of market areas existed, the spatial pattern bore scant resemblance to the theoretical hexagons and the boundaries were themselves changing with changes in methods of retailing and the changes in numbers and ages of local populations (Daly and Brown, 1964). Terrain again distorted the theoretical patterns and the sequence of settlement from the east gave initial and lasting dominance to a few rather than many centres (Fig. 12.2).

Only one study so far has attempted explanations for both centrality and linearity in Australia. Smailes described both patterns in South Australia and provided an explanation which has wider relevance in Australia (Smailes, 1969). Briefly he found centrality in the oldest established, most evenly high quality farmlands north from Adelaide and linearity in the drier and later settled areas both west and east of this core. An even pattern of close land subdivision into 80–160 acre (32–64 ha) blocks, divided for administration into hundreds, each with a Government town laid out within it, had been provided for the core area, and over time a pattern of service centres had grown up which paralleled central place theory. Beyond this, however, and representing more careful Government land classification for settlement after substantial drought failures in the last decades of the nineteenth century, land was divided into larger blocks (640 acres (260 ha) and above) and towns were only located along the railway lines which were

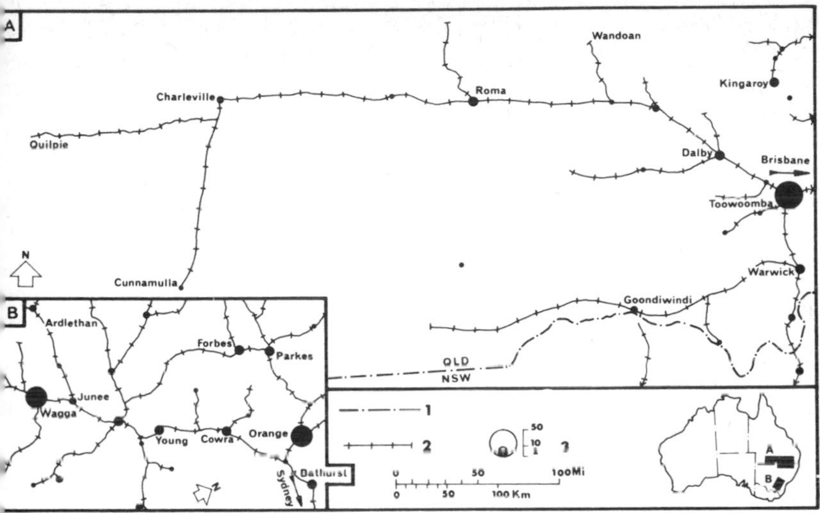

Fig. 12.2 Urban patterns, 1970s
A. Mercantile patterns? Southern Qld.
B. Central place patterns? Central N.S.W.
1, State border; 2, Railways; 3, Population of urban centres in thousands (1966 Census).

(*Source:* Maps accompanying census data for each state, 1969)

recognised as essential for the successful export of the wheat crops to be grown on the new lands. Such a pattern inevitably produced town plans at regular intervals along the railway rights-of-way and over time some of them prospered, but most never grew beyond a railway siding, general store and post office, with first a bag-grain shed and later the ubiquitous concrete silo.

This recognition of the role of the communication routes, as establishing the axes along which towns were spaced is fundamental to any explanation of the linear town patterns in Australia. Whether along the Murray–Darling navigation, or the 'wheat railways' of Victoria, South Australia and Western Australia, or the 'pastoral railways' of central and southern Queensland (Fig. 12.2A), the pattern was the result of a policy of provision of linear communication along which the depots for collection of produce of the mercantile theory were located at regular intervals.

The patterns of towns, however, as the mercantile theory recognised, are changing. Any process which reduces the number of customers must affect the pattern of both wholesaling and retailing. Mechanisation of agriculture, enlargement of holdings – whether from economic necessity or former preferences, easier personal communication by car over improved rural roads, lack of local job opportunities for non-farm labour, retirement, all have contributed to rural–urban migration, not to the smallest centres but to local regional centres, and the state capitals. The result has been the decline of the majority of smaller centres and the temporary growth of local regional centres (Williams, 1970), while only around the edge of the metropolitan centres do the towns appear to be generally increasing in population.

Patterns in towns

One fundamental question which might be posed of the Australian townscapes is to what extent do they reflect differences in town functions. If we can describe the rural landscape as the product of particular systems of resource use, can we say the same for the towns? We might expect so, since the development of the rural resource use systems has been by an urban oriented society as we have seen in the last chapter. But how true is this in fact? What are the functions of the towns and do their forms reflect them? The unifying forces have been illustrated in the last chapter; how successful have been the forces for differentiation and eccentricity? We need first to estimate the range of functions and then examine the range of forms.

The functions of Australian towns

A continent-wide study of the functions of Australian towns in 1954 suggested nine major types of towns could be distinguished, based upon the proportion of workers in each town in the various categories of employment (Table 12.2). In spite of the classification into the nine types, however, the author stressed that Australian towns did not fit into the traditional view of single function centres, as all had significant numbers of their workers in a variety of job categories. The mining towns came closest to being simple functional units in terms of the dominance of mining employment, but even here, employment in services and transport, etc., was still important.

Bearing this limitation in mind, analysis of Table 12.2 shows that most

Table 12.2 Australian town functions and populations in 1950s

Main functions of towns	*Number of towns*	*Population 1954 (000s)*	
		Max.	*Min.*
Manufacturing	78	1863.2	0.8
Service	178	19.2	0.8
Tourist resorts	35	23.1	1.0
Transport	23	7.4	0.5
Communications	15	4.4	0.8
Mining	25	31.4	1.2
Public utilities	15	9.0	1.1
Administration	34	40.5	1.5
Primary production	28	7.1	0.8
Total	442		

Source: Smith (1965)

Australian towns fell into the category of service centres, i.e. providing commercial and financial services for the production of primary, agricultural and manufactured goods. This dominance is to be expected in a society so geared to commercial production of foodstuffs and raw materials for overseas markets, and tends to reinforce the mercantile theory. The number of manufacturing centres might also be expected, particularly those processing agricultural products or mineral ores. The variety of other functions reflects in part the importance of communications and transport in the commercial economy, the specialised mining and primary production centres, and the network of territorial administration and provision of power and water supplies needed in a complex 'western' society.

One feature which is immediately apparent from the table, however, is that functions do not seem to be limited by size nor vice versa. This reflects the earlier point that there are virtually no single function Australian towns. Thus a 'town' of less than 1000 population in 1954 could be a manufacturing, or service, or transport, or communication, or a primary production centre. The larger the town, however, the greater the chance of it being classified as a manufacturing centre.

Form: function in Australian towns

Given such a possible division of functions, was this division paralleled by the form of the towns? No equivalent continental-wide study exists but a survey of Queensland towns in the early 1960s enables some comparisons to be made (Table 12.3).

Despite the varying size of populations (from less than 1000 to almost 20 000) and equivalent variation in size of urban area, the variations in land use do seem to bear out the variation in functions but in a subtle rather than an obvious way. The exception is the newest and smallest town – Theodore, in 1961 just being developed as a centre for an irrigation scheme and showing over half the urban area then still in vacant lots. For the other towns however the overwhelming impression is of a basically similar pattern of land-use within the urban areas. In each there was a high proportion of land in both residential (reflecting single house lots) and transport uses (reflecting a ubiquitous but under-used road grid) with never less than 10 per cent (and in the case of the old mining centre of Charters Towers almost a third) of the area in vacant lots.

Apart from these three dominant land uses, the links between form and function show in the subtler variations in the commercial, industrial and public utility/professional uses. Thus the main manufacturing centres, Bundaberg and Ingham, do have the highest proportion of their areas in industrial and storage uses, and the service and administrative centres have the highest proportions in public utilities and professional uses. The variation in recreational and social land uses also shows some association with the regional centres, whatever their size.

Not all forms can be tied to present functions, however, for change through time has left relics in the urban as well as the rural landscapes. A

Table 12.3 Urban land use, Qld., 1960s

		Land use of urban area (%) (a) 1961 (b)								
Town and function	*Population 1966*	*Resi-dential*	*Com-mercial*	*Indus-trial*	*Trans-port*	*Utility and pro-fessional*	*Recre-ation*	*Vacant*	*Urban area (b) (acres)*	*Urban density 1966 (pop./acre)*
Theodore (*b*) Irrigation project centre.	640	6	1	<1	28	4	7	54	323	0.9
Atherton (*b*) Centre dairy region. (*c*) Service centre.	2871	30	4	1	30	7	18	10	399	7.2
Ingham (*b*) Sugar milling. (*c*) Service (manufacturing).	5358	29	4	2	30	4	12	20	749	7.1
Roma (*b*) Centre wheat and sheep region. (*c*) Service (primary production).	5996	32	2	1	21	9	7	17	819	7.3
Charters Towers (*b*) Mining (declining). (*c*) Administration.	7602	27	2	1	30	9	3	28	1843	4.0
Bundaberg (*b*) Centre sugar region. (*c*) Manufacturing.	25 404	37	1	3	21	6	12	21	3618	7.0
Average land use (*b*)		30	2	3	30	11	10	14		

Notes

tudy of seven small country towns in northern Tasmania showed that by he 1960s the numbers and architectural styles of remaining buildings howed a positive correlation between the broad pattern of social and conomic change and the periods of building activity (Solomon and Goodhand, 1965). Prosperity in agriculture, especially after the boom in demand following the Victorian gold discoveries in the 1850s until soil xhaustion in the 1870s and as a result of improvements in husbandry after he Second World War, was reflected in increased local building which was till evident at mid-1960s. At that time on the average over a third of the buildings dated from the first and 42 per cent from the latter period of prosperity.

In the extreme cases, present form may have no relation to present unction, mainly because there *is no* present function. Farwell (1965), in a urvey of the *Ghost Towns of Australia*, lists twenty-three towns. They are, however, only a minute fraction of the many whose distribution outlines he main mining areas of the continent, especially the alluvial gold fields, where wealth was found and exhausted often within months. Most of the ites would not now be recognisable – the exceptions are where stone was used, or heavy machinery was too bulky to drag away, or where the enovators have reconstructed the buildings as a tourist attraction – as at Hill End (N.S.W.).

Problems of survival: the small towns

As suggested earlier, changes in patterns of demand for services and goods have affected the small towns in Australia and most are struggling to survive. Two examples must serve to illustrate the difficulties many towns are acing.

The first example is drawn from pastoral lands in south–central Queensland where a survey of five small towns was made in the 1950s (Dick, 1960) Table 12.4). Goondiwindi, the largest centre, was established in 1869 as a police post on the Queensland–New South Wales border and became a distribution point for the local cattle and sheep stations and a border control point for fat cattle moving south for slaughter. Population increased lowly and was *c*. 500 when the town council was formed in 1888. Thereafter it increased until to *c*. 3000 at the time of survey. In 1958 it was providing retail services to approximately 7400 people in a 7600 square mile 19 760 km^2) area and had a neat well-kept appearance with 95 per cent of ts residential lots having gardens and lawns. Almost a third of its streets were sealed with bitumen although less than 5 per cent of the footpaths had a bitumen surface.

In contrast, Wandoan, founded in 1902 at the end of a spur railway line, was hit by the depression and rural production losses from prickly pear nfestations of the 1930s, during which it lost population. The late start and close proximity of other equivalent centres appear to have further held back ts development, so that local government continued to be administered from a shire centre *c*. 40 miles (65 km) away; streets remained unsealed, the

Table 12.4 Small town form and function, Qld., 1958

	Towns			
Item	*Goondiwindi*		*Wandoan*	
Population 1958	2984		322	
Workforce (%)	37		36	
Population of trade service area (inc. town itself) 1954	7390		710	
Trade area (sq. ml.)	7650		1325	
Houses 1958				
Total	685		87	
Built pre-1945 (%)	61		69	
Rectangular plan (%)	95		96	
Corrugated iron roofs (%)	96		95	
Wooden walls (%)	95		92	
Verandahs (%)	70		57	
House lots without lawn or garden (%)	25		53	
Functions 1958				
	No.	*Units*	*No.*	*Uni*
Commercial and business	34	116	17	27
Professional	10	20	4	4
Industries	10	16	3	5
Others	26	57	10	15

Source: Dick (1960)

town unsewered and the appearance as a result was unkempt and the overa impression one of neglect and decay.

In the 1960s Goondiwindi managed to maintain a slow absolute popul: tion increase, whereas Wandoan declined. However, in a situation wher already in the 1950s 50–60 per cent of rural landowners traded direct wit Brisbane for most non-perishable items, the future for such centres withou some incentive for local population increase was bleak and Goondiwindi ha lost population by 1971.

Problems of survival: the mining towns

The largest mining towns as defined by Smith's 1965 survey of tow functions was Broken Hill (Fig. 12.3). In 1954 it was a thriving town an regional centre with a population of 31 351, in 1972 it was a troubled tow of *c.* 29 800 with one of its two major mines about to close down.

Discovered by a pastoral station hand in 1883, the organisation of company to mine the silver chlorides took two years and production bega in 1885 with a rush of miners to peg claims on the east–west ridge covere by short grasses and acacia scrub. A maze of trails to the ridge was soo replaced by a surveyed official grid with street names as appropriate a Sulphide, Bromide, Cobalt, Beryl, Oxide and Argent.

Fig. 12.3 **Broken Hill, N.S.W.**
View northeast along the line of lode and mining area (1-2), over the western regeneration reserve (3-1-4), to the central business district (5). The grid pattern of residential streets contrasts with the stark semi-arid plains of the grassland ecosystem.

(*Source:* Australian News and Information Service)

Companies took over the deep mining when shallow holes were worked out, and costly lifting gear and pit props had to be imported. Experiments with smelting began in 1886 but it proved cheaper to move the ore by the special railway built to Port Pirie after 1889.

Population of the town reached a peak of 35 000 in 1915 with wartime demands for lead and zinc. This was achieved despite early problems of an adequate water supply – only solved in 1952 with construction of a pipeline from storages on the Darling River, and the severe environmental stresses of the arid environment in summer, when temperatures over 100°F (38°C) were often accompanied by high winds and dust storms. The latter problem was partly eased by reestablishment of natural vegetation (with some exotics) in a peripheral shelter belt begun in 1937, and the mining companies, while financing the shelter belts, also encouraged street tree-planting.

Housing began with tents and progressed through box-like shanties of wood and hessian with corrugated iron roofs, through rectangular or L-shaped board or iron-walled structures in the 1880s to 1920s with separate kitchen (to reduce heat and fire risk) and earth closet at the rear, to bungalow style houses from 1920s to 1950s, with iron walls, porticoes and ubiquitous iron roofs. Some mining company housing estates have been built since the 1950s, with brick, fibro-asbestos and cement block walls under the traditional corrugated iron roof. Individual houses set on their own lots – originally dry and dusty wildernesses, now irrigated tree-lined gardens – dominate the scene.

The city itself however is dominated by both the central corridor of mining leases, where excavation, winding engine houses, processing plants and offices are packed together, and the central business district immediately to the north, with its gothic brick town hall, post office, trades hall and technical college.

The strength of the labour unions since a major successful strike in 1919 has restricted immigration of new miners, limited the employment of non-residents and married women and brought union controls over newspapers and retail trading hours, as well as encouraging provision of special camps on Adelaide's beaches for annual mine holidays.

The old isolation which initially threatened the success of any mining has been broken by sealed highways – to Adelaide and Melbourne completed, to Sydney almost so, and the first unbroken trans-continental 'Indian-Pacific' train service (Sydney to Perth) which began in 1970.

Although estimates of the life of the mines have always varied, the future of the town was not really in doubt until mid-1972, when the management of the second largest mine announced that it would close in several weeks time because of unprofitable operations. An attempt to revitalise the mine with union support has an uncertain future. If the mine does close the town's population must fall rapidly for miners and their families are over half the population and as a regional centre estimates have suggested there would be support for only *c*. 5000 population.

Problems of success: the industrial towns

The largest industrial centre in Australia outside the state capitals in 1971 was Newcastle, N.S.W., with a population of 250 000 (Fig. 12.4). Right from its foundation in 1801 the settlement at the mouth of the Hunter River was intended to provide industrial raw materials – coal, lime and timber – for the other settlements. First worked by convicts, the adit coal mines were taken over by the Australian Agricultural Company in 1831 and with the exhaustion of shallower ores, shafts of this and competing companies spread inland, following the deeper seams, with particular success in the 1880s and 1890s when what came to be internationally recognised as excellent steam (bunker) coal was in great demand for the world's spreading steam-ship routes and gas coal for Australian suburban lighting and heating systems. By the 1890s, new coalmining villages such as Cessnock, Abermain, Stanford Merthy and Pelaw Main indicated by their names the origins of the imported miners, but Newcastle remained as the entrepôt centre, exporting both its coal and wheat from the expanding wheatlands and importing manufactured goods for local consumption.

Fig. 12.4 Newcastle, N.S.W.
View from ocean over main city beaches across central business district to Hunter Valley estuary with smoke from Broken Hill Proprietary iron-smelter complex in centre, and docks at left. Hunter Valley stretches off into distance.

(*Source:* Department of Tourism, N.S.W.)

Newcastle's dominance as an industrial centre was considerably enhanced by the siting of the first major iron and steel plant of the Broken Hill Proprietary Company in 1915 on low estuary lands close to the town, alongside a state dockyard opened a year earlier. This was to become the largest iron and steel complex in Australia until surpassed by Port Kembla–Wollongong by 1950, and the employment it offered was a significant complement to the port and general wholesale function of the town.

Until 1940 the builtup area clustered around the central business district, and the ironworks and dockyards along the river bank, but the 1950s and 1960s saw the expansion of housing southwards onto a higher ridge dividing the Hunter Valley from the drowned valleys which formed Lake Macquarie. This expansion absorbed some of the isolated original mining villages which remained as revitalised retail centres in the new suburbs.

The spread of the suburbs, together with a massive decline in mining employment opportunities from decreased demand for gas coal in the 1950s, forced commuters to travel further to their riverside jobs. By the mid-1960s 30 per cent of male workers in the coalmining towns (which had boomed in the 1880s and 1890s) had to travel over 13 miles (21 km) to their new jobs in Newcastle by bus or private car, and journey times could be up to four hours per day. At the same time 22 per cent of the resident workforce of Maitland – a regional service centre *c*. 18 miles (29 km) away – also were commuting to Newcastle (Holmes, 1965; and Daly, 1970).

Apart from a commuter problem, success in industrial development generated a rapid increase in demand for water. As early as 1942 Newcastle's daily *per capita* consumption (73 gallons (329 litres)) was almost double Sydney's 43 gallons (196 litres). The problem was compounded by increasing industrial demand for water; at the turn of the century it averaged just over 20 gallons (90 litres) but by mid-1960s was up to 130 gallons (585 litres) *per capita* per day. Demand has been met in an unusual pattern of supply, first from wells and water-trains, then direct post-1885 from the Hunter River, then a mountain storage programme from 1924, then (as an emergency measure) by pumping from underground sand acquifers in 1930, and finally an increase in storage capacity in 1964. In each case the future demand curve was thought to have been topped but demand increased at a faster rate and Tweedie reported in 1967 that once more the water authorities were looking for additional supplies.

Ironically, part of the concern in the late 1960s stems from proposed new industrial developments – on land reclaimed in the estuary – including an aluminium smelter and paper-pulp complex, both high water consumers and polluters. Such locations are in part the result of the state's decentralisation schemes to aid so-called 'depression areas' and in 1958 Newcastle was included in the coalmining areas which were suffering massive unemployment for the reasons noted above. Newcastle gained new industries, new commuters and reopened the old problem of its water supply.

Patterns in cities

Ideally, each of the state capitals should be considered separately here, since each has its particular history and character. Space would prevent anything but a thumbnail sketch of each, however, and so as a compromise an attempt has been made to cover three of the seven to illustrate the range of patterns and factors which seem to have influenced them. No survey could omit the largest centre, Sydney, nor the national capital, Canberra, while Adelaide was chosen as representing the compromise between the speculators' dream of the one, Sydney, and the planners' dream of the other, Canberra.

Sydney: the speculators' dream?

That the first permanent European settlement in the continent should still dominate by size of population and commercial activity all other settlements in the continent almost 200 years later is a remarkable tribute to the processes of resource exploitation and land settlement in Australia (Fig. 2.7). In the story of its growth Sydney encompasses most of the influences upon urban development noted in Chapter 11, but above all it reflects the *laissez-faire* policies which enable speculation in land development. As the contributor on 'Town Planning' in the *Australian Encyclopaedia* (Jose and Carter, 1925) noted sadly: 'Sydney grew, as most of its suburbs have grown since, by the uncoordinated and often conflicting efforts of private landowners and speculators.'

The result by the 1970s was a sprawling builtup area stretching some 30 miles (48 km) south-westwards and 20 miles (32 km) northwards. To illustrate the sequence of growth and the resultant problems which will have to be faced in the 1970s, comments will be made upon two figures which summarise the spatial and temporary patterns of Sydney's development (Figs. 12.5 and 12.6).

The expansion of Sydney's builtup area has reflected the way in which the various impetuses for growth have been channelled and distorted by both the physical site and the available technology. The firm ground close to the deep harbour and good water of the Tank Stream were the bases for the initial siting in 1788, while the broken plateau surfaces (carrying infertile acid soils) to the immediate north and south of the Port Jackson harbour contrasting with the lower smoother terrains on the clay shales to the west leading to the Hawkesbury River, were the constraints initially channelling growth to the west and southwest (Fig. 12.5A). The cliffed coast with sandy embayments drew the leisured masses once the provision of public holidays was established in the late-nineteenth century.

The actual spread of the builtup area shows a close parallel to a model of what might have been expected, given the initial site on the south bank of the harbour (Fig. 12.5). From the first landing point which might be expected to develop into a port, construction of new buildings whether for residence or employment could spread out evenly given equal transport facilities or along linear lobes if transport provision (say by railway) was uneven. Trans-harbour communication (ferries or a bridge) would be needed for any large development on the north shore, but terrain and inconvenience of access would militate against large industrial comples here. Expansion of area would reflect stimuli of demands from growing population, the availability of land to be built on and the availability and inclination of capitalists to risk their funds in real estate development.

The graph of population growth and the accompanying diagram of percentage growth of population and builtup area (Fig. 12.5B) provides a crude yardstick against which to measure the evolution of the 1970s cityscape. If the rates of increase of population had been paralleled by an equivalent rate of increase of the builtup area, we might have expected that looking back from 1961 (when data were available) that periodic growth rates of population and area should be equal. In fact they are very much

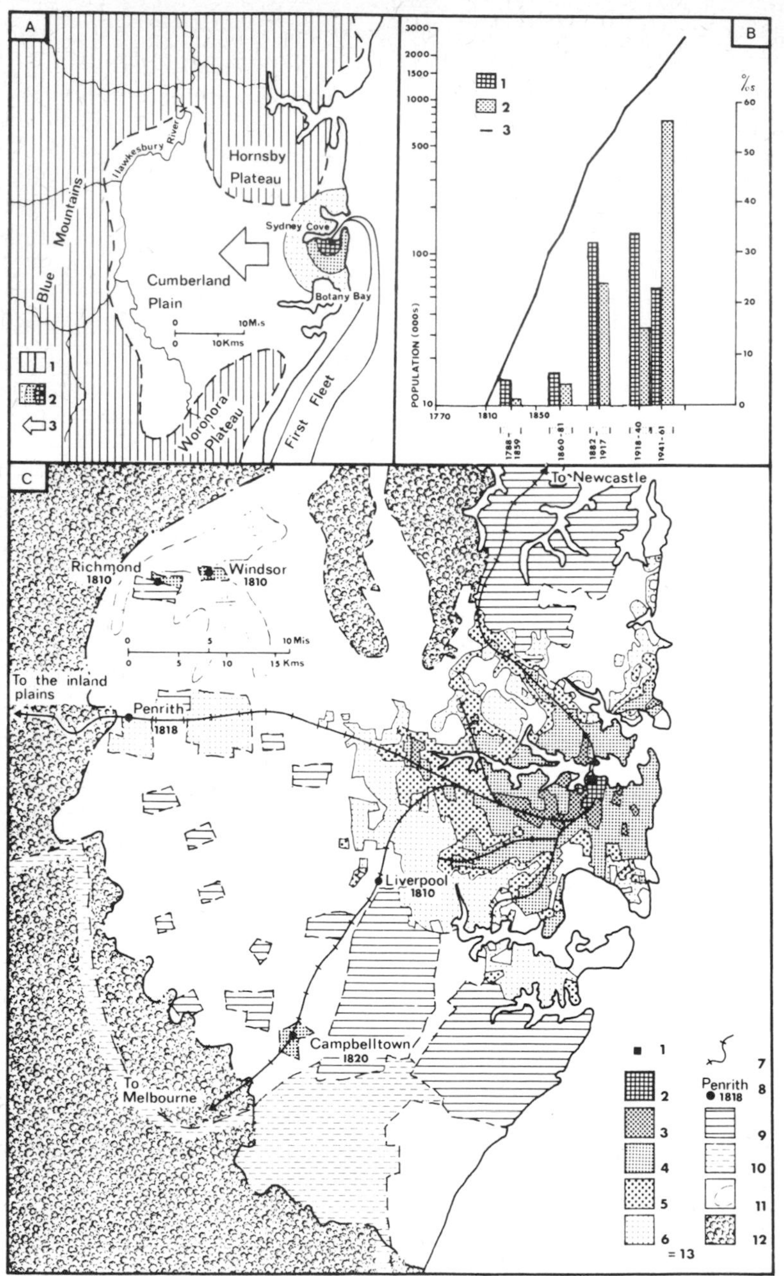

Fig. 12.5 Sydney's expansion, 1788–1960s

A. The site

1, Mountains and plateaus over 500 ft (150 m); 2, Hypothetical sequence

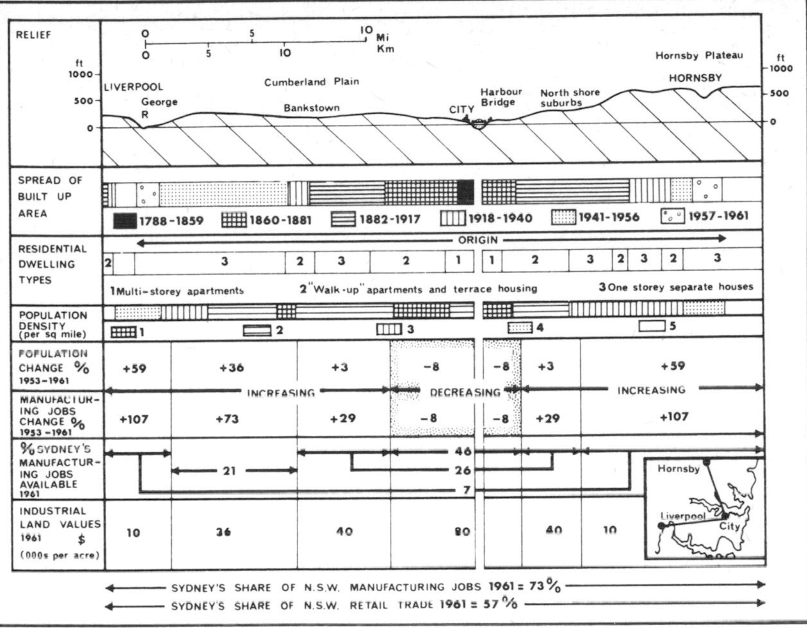

Fig. 12.6 Urban patterns in Sydney
Patterns of the spread of the builtup area, 1788–1961, the types of dwellings, population densities and trends, and trends in job opportunities and land values in the 1960s are shown along a line from Liverpool through the city centre to Hornsby (inset map).
Population densities: 1, >11 000 per square mile; 2, 7000 to 11 000; 3, 3000 to 7000; 4, 500 to 3000; 5, <500.

(*Sources:* See text)

Caption to Fig. 12.5 – continued

of expansion from Sydney Cove, with undistorted land access; 3, Main line of possible expansion of city.

B. Growth of population and builtup area
1, Percentage of total 1961 population added to total during period indicated for each bar graph; 2, Percentage of total 1961 builtup area added to total during period indicated; 3, Population numbers. Inclination shows relative rates of increase over periods.

C. Expansion of builtup area
1, City central business district
Areas builtup by: 2, 1860; 3, 1881; 4, 1917; 5, 1940; 6, 1960s;
7, Railways built by 1890; 8, Country settlements with date of founding;
9, Parks and Reserves, 1970s; 10, Major water catchments; 11, Land remaining for urban expansion, area liable to flooding indicated;
12, Rugged terrain – mainly native forest and woodland; 13, Sydney Harbour Bridge.

(*Sources:* Jeans, 1972; Winston, 1957)

unequal, suggesting that urban population densities have changed significantly over time, both as the result of time lags between demand (from population increase) and supply (new home constructions).

By 1859, some seventy years after the first settlement, only 1 per cent of the future 1961 area of Sydney was occupied and that by only 5 per cent of the future population total. The next twenty years saw an additional 6 per cent of the 1961 population accommodated on an additional 4 per cent of the area. By almost the end of the First World War the Sydney population had reached 43 per cent of the 1961 total, living on only 29 per cent of the 1961 area. By 1940 a further population expansion had brought the percentage up to 77 per cent but cramped into 44 per cent of the 1961 area. Between 1940 and 1961 an increase of 23 per cent of the 1961 population was paralleled by a remarkable doubling of the area of the city (reflecting an increase of 56 per cent of the 1961 area over the period).

Some explanation of these sequences can be given by a brief review of development of the city's functions and internal patterns over the periods in question. From the first settlement of 1788 to mid-nineteenth century, the administration and gaol function dominated the early years, and not until the 1820s did commercial activity begin to make its mark upon the town, with whalers and timber carriers tied up at the quays and an entrepôt function both for inland settlements and the Pacific Islands developing. By 1859, after the steady immigration of free colonists from the 1830s and initial flush of the gold discoveries, a contemporary commentator was already describing the overcrowded terraces of the poorer working class (where cholera had raged in 1856) as 'The social cesspools of Sydney' – with unmade, unlit, unsewered streets and structures in danger of imminent collapse.

From 1860 to 1887 was a period of initial slackening then increasing rate of population growth. Net immigration increased gradually through the period and the capital from gold began to be invested in dockyards, factories for the local market and the railway network which was both to link Sydney with the inland (to Bathurst by 1880) and to allow the spread of 'Sydneysiders' into the surrounding countryside. The full effects of the change in land transport media were to be felt in the next period but expansion of the builtup area westwards along the railway to Paramatta (completed 1855) and the beginning of the residential use of the north shore and recreational area of Manly following the introduction of steam ferries in the late 1850s were significant expansions.

The thirty-five years 1882–1917 saw a six-fold expansion of the builtup area despite the fact that population only showed a four-fold increase. For the first time expansion of area overtook relative expansion of population. Why? The answer lies in the multiplicity of intra-urban transport media which became available in this period, enabling the journey to work to be lengthened. Railways were extended to the south and even to the north shore; harbour ferry services increased six-fold 1880–1913; and trams began to shuttle workers to and from the inner suburbs. Horse trams, steam trams and then from 1893 the electric trams in fact carried most of the workers using public transport – by 1905 130 million passengers a year, by 1922 almost 300 million a year.

The expansion of the builtup area was mainly by construction of terrace houses (often with each unit only 16 ft 6 inches (5 m) wide) and speculative subdivisions, as in Paddington, Darlinghurst and Annandale (Fig. 11.4C). At least, however, these were serviced by the newly-fledged metropolitan water scheme.

This boom period reflected booms in agricultural and pastoral production, en route through Sydney for overseas export, avoidance of a speculative crash of land prices which ruined many of the capitalists from rival Melbourne, and the creation of a commercial complex of merchant traders and manufacturers who began to realise the potential of the local market.

The end of the First World War began a period of population growth not paralleled by equivalent suburban expansion. Electrification of the railways to Paramatta and other western suburbs seems to have encouraged speculative expansion there. The motor bus began to replace tram services, and motor transport as well as railways benefited from the completion of the harbour bridge in 1932, after over 100 years of debate on its merits. Significantly, the bridge when opened could accommodate foot, motor, tram and railway commuters and the north shore real estate speculators got to work. In the south the Georges River bridge had been completed in 1929 but this served rather to extend the links of the city and did not encourage subdivisions until post-1945 and the increased use of private motor cars. On the shore of Botany Bay, polluted already by the noxious effluent of tanneries and metal factories, the first international airport was opened in 1935. A new dimension was being added to the city's functions.

Very little construction took place during the Second World War, but from the late-1940s onwards a massive expansion of the builtup area began. Initially it was hoped that the 'post-war reconstruction' would be a planned operation. In 1945 a Cumberland County Council was set up and in 1957 an overall development plan for the city and country was accepted, planning for a population of 2.5 million in 1972. Intended to consolidate the builtup area by filling in gaps left by indiscriminate speculation, a 'green belt' constriction was placed on the only possible zone of expansion in the west, and factories were to be encouraged (by cheap land) to move from the old inner suburbs to more spacious sites in outer suburbs and thus reduce the congestion of vehicular traffic resulting from the heritage of centralised commuter ferry, train and tram services. The multiplicity of independent local urban governments within the Sydney metropolitan area hindered centralised controls, however, and the speculators were always two steps ahead of the planners. Thus, despite some local government schemes – usually walk-up two to four storey apartment or six to ten storey apartment blocks – most of the housing has been provided by speculative builders and real estate companies as separate single-storey houses set in a standard 50–60 ft by 150 ft (15–18 m by 45 m) lot with minimal provision of schools, shopping centres or recreation facilities, and often no sewerage systems.

The results by the 1970s are illustrated in Fig. 12.6 above. Within the 1961 builtup area population was still densest close to the city centre but was beginning to increase most rapidly on the fringes of the city, where the greatest increase in jobs in manufacturing was occurring. In the 1960s Penrith (30 miles (48 km) from city centre but benefiting from suburban sprawl and fast commuter trains) had increased its 1961 population by 182 per cent, and the outer limits of the city had grown at a rate of 10 per cent compound interest over the same period. In contrast the suburbs adjacent to the city centre had lost up to 5 per cent of their population while the city centre had lost 9 per cent. This pattern was virtually identical with the other major Australian cities (excluding Canberra, as will be seen below), and has been standard in most western cities since the 1950s.

Despite high industrial land values, however, almost half the city's manufacturing employment was still in the city centres in the 1960s – requiring daily commuter movements of often 20 miles (32 km) or more. A commentator on the Cumberland Plan's effects by 1962 noted that some decrease in the concentration of industry in the city centre had been achieved, but integration between commercial, industrial and residential activity had been worsened, not improved, because relocation of industry had not been paralleled by relocation of the other two components – the result was more traffic movements, not less! Thus one firm examined in detail (earth moving equipment) had links with fourteen other firms within the urban area, only half of which were within 1 mile (1.6 km) radius, the others being up to 12 miles (19 km) away (Logan, 1964).

Despite an overall plan forty separate local governments still administer the various urban areas of Sydney. Legally speaking, the city is but 5 square miles (13 km^2) surrounded by 927 square miles (2410 km^2) of municipal suburbs and 590 square miles (1530 km^2) in four shires, a total urban area of 1522 square miles (3953 km^2). It is this division of interests, mirroring at the official level, the division and conflict of interests between rival speculators found at the private business level, which has bedevilled any attempts at overall planning – attempts which date back at least to 1895 and the proposals then for a Greater Sydney Council on the lines of the London County Council of the day.

A further attempt at planning by the State Planning Authority in 1967 forecast that by AD 2000 the city's population, by that time 5 million, would have occupied all the available building land and the problems then will be where to find the next space for building. By then also the advancing tide of suburban housing from the two next largest towns in the state, Newcastle in the north and Port Kembla–Wollongong in the south, may well have occupied the prime sites and a megalopolis of 7–8 million people may stretch 130 miles (208 km) along the coast, broken only by the rugged plateaus – resources for recreation or water catchments.

To these specific Sydney problems of the 1960s need to be added the ubiquitous problems of the western cities – increasing crime rates, increasing traffic accidents and increasing environmental pollution, particularly smog and water pollution. At least a night curfew keeps air traffic out of the international airport and a research project in the 1970s is to investigate the other pollution problems of Botany Bay. Solutions to the other questions, however, seem more remote.

The contributor to the second *Australian Encyclopaedia* (Australia, 1958) quoted a visiting English architect's reaction to Sydney in 1947:

> When I consider the period in which Sydney grew up, I am amazed that you have come out of it so well. After all, the only city we have in England that is a contemporary of Sydney's is Middlesbrough – and Middlesbrough is like the wrath of God.

There seems to be time yet, however.

Canberra: the planners' dream?

Not until 1909, eight years after the creation of the Australian Commonwealth, was a site for the national capital decided upon; not until 1916 was work effectively begun on that site, and not until 1927 did the Commonwealth Parliament actually meet in the capital city. In part the delay was the result of the fairly specific constitutional site requirements for the city, in part the result of political manoeuvring by interested bodies, and in part the result of the opening up of the design of the city to international competition in 1911, the date of the laying of the foundation stone on Capital Hill.

From its inception Canberra was a planned city. The constitutional requirements for the site agreed to in 1899 were that it should be within a commonwealth territory of at least 100 square miles (260 km^2), in New South Wales but at least 100 miles (160 km) from Sydney. The site itself, so the final surveyor was instructed, should enable the design to be laid out in accord with principles of hygiene, picturesqueness and the practical possibility of expansion as well as beautification. The choice of the Limestone Plains between Black Mountain and Mt Ainslie has proved an apt one (Fig. 12.7).

Comparing the successful design by Walter Burley Griffin, a Chicago architect, and the 1970 reality, it is immediately apparent that the main design has been retained although significant modifications of details have taken place (Fig. 12.8). Most of the original road plans have been retained, and the Government centre, water and land axes are where Griffin intended them to be. The main change has been the extension of the Government office space into the area originally planned as the market centre, and the convertion of the original municipal centre into the main retail centre (civic). Industrial development has not yet occupied the original site, although future development will be channelled there and the railway route has never developed beyond the terminal in the southeast of the city.

Griffin was told to plan for a city of 25 000 to grow proportionately

Fig. 12.7 Canberra, A.C.T.
View along Griffin's Land Axis from Mt Ainslie, with War Memorial (left foreground) at opposite end of Anzac Parade to Commonwealth Parliament House (centre across lake) with Capital Hill behind. Suburb of Reid (right foreground) shows early grid design with central open space while Campbell (left foreground) shows the more recent curved street layouts of the Radburn Plan.

(*Source:* Australian News and Information Service)

with Australia's population. As the modern patterns show (Fig. 12.8B), planning in the 1970s is for a population ten times that figure, for the city already accommodates 142 000 (1971). Initial development after 1911 was hit by wartime economies, the depression of the 1930s and further wartime economies in the early 1940s. Provision of architectural decoration often predated provision of services for the inhabitants, trees predated people along most of the avenues (Fig. 0.1, p. 2), and no alcoholic beverages could be sold within the territory until the late 1920s! Styles of housing were limited to a few acceptable designs, land development was controlled and land ownership allowed only on a long lease system with controls on use and minimum values of building required.

Population grew slowly. In the depression years of the 1930s growth was

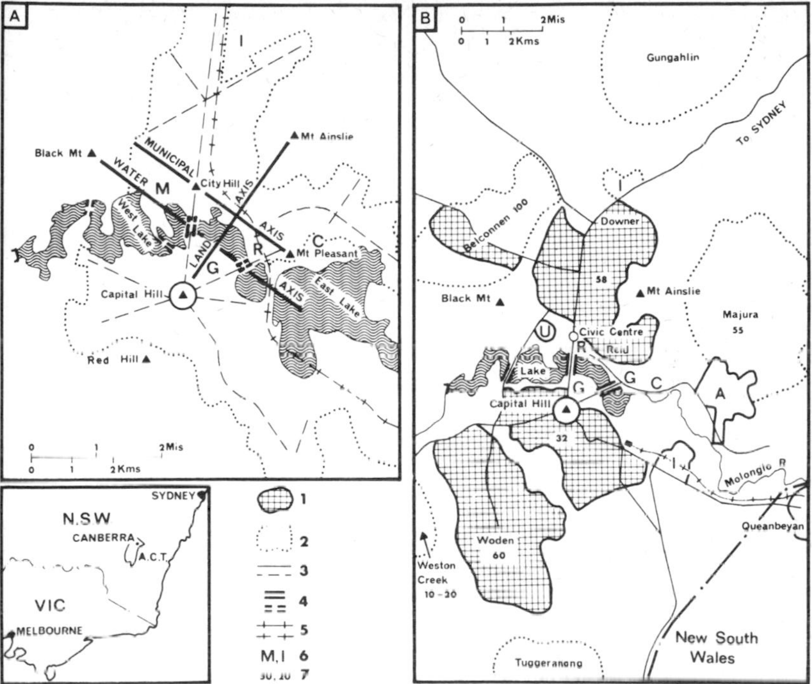

Fig. 12.8 Canberra, 1916 and 1970
A. W. B. Griffin's original plan, 1916
B. Canberra 1970
Key for both maps:
Builtup area. 1, Actual; 2, Projected; 3, Avenues and main roads, actual and projected; 4, Bridges, actual and projected; 5, Railways, actual and projected; 6, Land-use zones. A, Airport; C, Military College; G, Government; I, Industrial Area; M, Municipal; R, Commercial; U, University. 7, Population of suburbs in thousands, actual or projected.

(*Source:* Linge, 1961, National Capital Development Commission)

from 2 to 7 per cent per year, but the 1950s saw the beginning of the boom rates of 10 per cent (with forecasts for 1970s of 7–8%). This boom came as a result first of the effective transfer of all Commonwealth Government headquarters to Canberra by 1963, bringing with them the civil servants and their families. This in turn generated a demand for housing which the National Capital Development Commission (NCDC – replacing the Federal Capital Commission in 1958) met by laying out new suburbs on the Radburn Plan (i.e. each as a self-contained residential, retail, primary and secondary education unit bypassed by through heavy traffic) along with some high-rise single and family apartment blocks. Controls upon housing styles have been loosened but minimum values still apply and for example the fencing of front gardens abutting onto the pavement 'nature strips' is

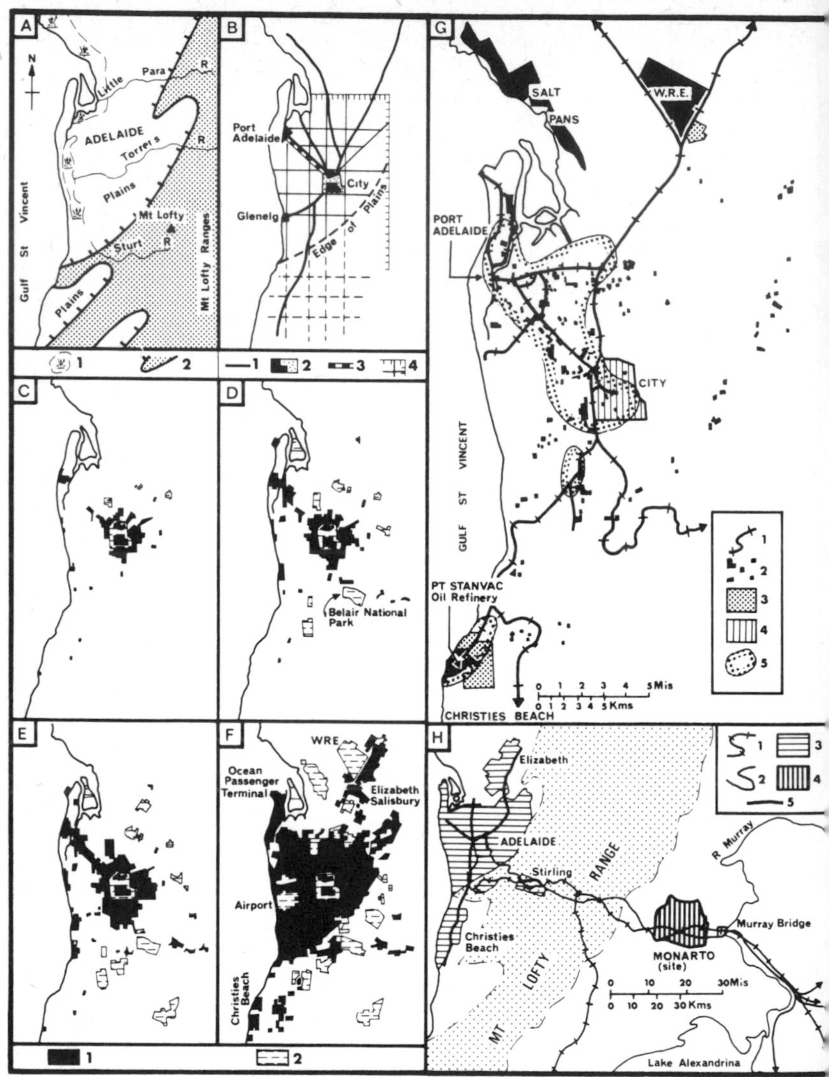

Fig. 12.9 Adelaide's expansion 1836–1970s

A. Site
1, Swamps; 2, Mt Lofty Ranges with northwest-facing scarps indicated.

B. Settlement design, 1836
1, Actual line of first main roads; 2, City urban lots and surrounding park-land as surveyed; 3, Proposed canal; 4, Edge of first area surveyed with main grid of roads indicated on and beyond the edge of the plains.

C. Urban area 1880

D. Urban area 1919

E. Urban area 1939

F. Urban area 1965

carefully controlled and house owners in each new subdivision are encouraged to beautify their gardens by free gifts of trees and shrubs.

Problems, however, can be found even in this planners' dream. The work force is still heavily weighted towards white-collar office jobs with little provision for the more mechanically minded school-leavers. The inhabitants complain of non-representation on the city's government (the NCDC), and the planners wonder about the enormous areas required for the low density suburbs (*c*. 5160 people per square mile or 8 persons per acre (20 per ha)), traffic congestion at 8.30 a.m. and 5.00 p.m. and the winter smog potentials of the inversion-prone basins into which the city has spread, and which already cause delays to early morning aircraft arrivals. At least in Canberra, however, there is abundant evidence that some thought is being given to the problems and that measures to attempt solutions could be both legislated and enforced. The function of the city as a capital is assured, and as a centre for national scientific and cultural leadership the foundations have been well-laid in the national university and national library. Whether there will be a planned ceiling on growth however remains to be seen but some alternatives have already been worked out (Fig. 12.8B).

Adelaide: the planner versus the speculator

While the other two cities show definite imprints of either planner or speculator, Adelaide's landscape has the marks of both. Laid out in 1836 by Colonel William Light it occupied with its revolutionary surrounding park lands or 'green belt' slightly higher ground close to the best freshwater site along the Torrens River in the centre of the Adelaide Plain (Figs. 12.9 and 11.2). Although some 6 miles (9 km) from its port, a road and proposed canal were to link the two (Fig. 12.9) and access to the northern interior was excellent. Beyond the parklands a mile wide road grid oriented to the then magnetic north was laid out in the surrounding countryside. The stage appeared to be set for an orderly growth of a prosperous city.

Arguments among colonists – in what one historian called a 'Paradise of Dissent' (Pike, 1957) – together with indifferent success of agriculture in the early years and only copper to attract mining immigrants saw the city

---

Caption to Fig. 12.9 – continued

Key for C–F:
1, Builtup area; 2, Reserves; WRE, Weapons Research Establishment.

G. Industrial Adelaide *c*. 1970
1, Railways; 2, Industrial sites (quarries to factories); 3, Zoned for industrial development; 4, City and surrounding parklands; 5, Air pollution zones (>16 tons of solids per square mile per month).

H. Adelaide's New Town for the 1970s–80s
1, Railways; 2, Planned motorway to Melbourne; 3, Urban area *c*. 1970; 4, New town site for Monarto; 5, Planned motorways (freeways) within existing urban area (revised MATS plan).

(*Source: The Environment of South Australia*, Government Printer, 1972; Williams, 1966*b*)

grow indiscriminately and sporadically. By 1860 the city was still basically within the parklands with isolated agricultural villages dotting the plains beyond. Agricultural and further copper mining booms in the 1870s and 1880s brought extra capital and immigrants, a population growth rate of 6 per cent per year and the initiation of a horse-tram system in 1878 (aligned along the rural road grid) saw the expansion of the builtup area beyond the parklands to begin to engulf the nearest villages (Fig. 2.7C–E). Speculators subdivided with an eye to the expanding tram network, which in 1909 began to be converted to an electric system. Independent town councils were created in these new suburbs and standards of land use zoning, building design and public works varied accordingly between them. Because of the high income from rates on industrial land most suburban 'city' councils encouraged industry to locate almost indiscriminately within their boundaries – a partial reason for the wide scatter of industrial land within the metropolitan area (Fig. 12.9G). Forced economies in suburban council budgets, because of the low density of single housing on quarter acre (10 ares) blocks, were met by non-provision of underground street drainage and as a result winter storm-water run-off still surges westwards (downslope) to the sea, carrying a brown tide of sediment from unsealed footpaths and uncurbed gutters in many suburbs.

A brief flirtation with the English planner C. C. Reade, 1916 to 1920, produced a Town Planning and Development Act in 1920 but the only major contribution to the Adelaide cityscape was the laying out of a new suburb, appropriately named Colonel Light Gardens, in 1929. Here a 'thousand homes' for ex-servicemen were to be built at controlled prices in an environment designed to provide tree-shaded streets and abundant recreation reserves, with all service lines (electricity power and water) aligned along common lanes behind the houses. The repeal of the Act later in 1929 left this an island of planned suburbia to be engulfed by speculative subdivisions later.

The distress of the 1930s Depression saw the creation of a Government house-building agency – the South Australian Housing Trust – designed to provide cheap rented housing (semidetached to save costs) for lower-paid workers. From 1946 the trust has built some detached houses for sale, and since 1952 two- and three-storey apartments including old-people's homes. This provided official competition for the speculators and may have kept some land prices down.

Expanding population, however, post-1945 saw proposals for new town developments and in 1954, 17 miles (27 km) north of the city, a 'new town' on the contemporary English models of Harlow and Stevenage was opened at Elizabeth (Fig. 12.9F). A large military production and research complex (the Weapons Research Establishment (WRE)), derived from the United Kingdom atomic energy and rocket research programme and located alongside, helped provide jobs as did expansion of a motor car assembly plant from the city. Both here and in a smaller industrial development at Christies Beach, begun in 1961, the Housing Trust provided most of the housing, reproducing the semidetached or detached homes on quarter-acre blocks within a landscaped Radburn framework of associated schools and shopping areas with sealed roads, curbing and footpaths. Elsewhere in the city and on its expanding fringe indiscriminate subdivision continued.

The first comprehensive plan for the metropolitan area appeared in 1962 from a Town Planning Committee set up in 1955 (Adelaide, 1962). Looking ahead from the 1961 population of 734 000 to a possible 1.3 million in 1991, the report foresaw the expansion of the urban area with needs for greater suburban shopping centres and improved public rail and road transport – mainly by provision of a network of freeways to be used by both private cars and express buses. Their exact location was decided by a later Metropolitan Adelaide Transportation Study (MATS plan) in 1968. Road traffic was increasing at about 7 per cent per year, which would double the volume within ten years, and the proposed pattern of freeways was thought necessary to channel particularly the north–south movement through the urban area. The bulk of the cost of the plan ($436 million of the total $574 million) was the freeway system. A change of Government, plus public protest at the potential destruction of property and general character of the city required by the 79 miles (126 km) of freeways, brought modifications to the scheme and the proposal to site a further new town (Monarto) to siphon off the next 100 000 population increase (Fig. 12.9H). The details of this have yet to be decided, but the Canberra experience is likely to be considered.

Meanwhile the speculative expansion had leapfrogged over the protected 'Hills Face Zone' to the broad basins lying to the south. In the city centre, within the ring of the still present but reduced parklands, the office blocks continue to rise higher and higher, alongside the department stores which dominate city and even country shopping as far as 90–125 miles (144–200 km) away. From the tree-studded blocks in the hills the view westward over the city to the gulf is still magnificent in its breadth and sunset colourings, although marred more often each year by the grey murk of a smog (Fig. 12.9G) only partly controlled by 'air pollution potential' alerts banning the incineration of household refuse in the city's backyards.

13
The relict landscapes

Not all the original ecosystems of 1770 and their associated landscapes had been drastically modified by the 1970s. Crude estimates (Tables 6.1, p. 65 and 13.1) indicate that about 31–33 per cent of the continental area has remained relatively unchanged by human activity over the two centuries and both the location and possible rationale for the survival of these 'relict landscapes' needs some comment.

The concentration of these relict landscapes in the central and western areas of the continent is immediately apparent from Fig. 6.4 and Table 13.1.

Table 13.1 The relict ecosystems *c.* 1970

	Percentage of continental area		*Percentage reduction*
Ecosystem	*1770 (a)*	*1970 (b)*	*1770–1970 (c)*
Desert	12.0	12.0	0
Desert and grassland	0.8	0.8	0
Grassland	23.0	3.0	87
Grassland and shrubland	4.0	0.4	90
Grassland and woodland	25.2	6.3	75
Shrublands	8.0	5.0	37
Shrubland and woodland	3.0	1.5	50
Woodlands	17.0	2.0	88
Alpine	0.1	0.1	0?
Forest			
Sclerophyll	5.0	1.5	70
Rain	1.8	0.2	90
Marsh	0.1	0.1	0?
Total as % of Continent	100.0	32.9	67.1

Notes
a. From Fig. 4.1.
b. Comparison of Fig. 4.1 and Fig. 6.3.
c. Calculated as $a - b/a \times 100$.

Bearing in mind the original patterns of the 1770 ecosystems (Fig. 4.1), the extent to which modification had taken place by the 1970s is indicated in Table 13.1.

At the continental scale the greatest survival of ecosystems and their associated landscapes appears to be at either end of the environmental spectrum, that is both the hot arid interior lands and the much smaller areas of cool and wet humid alpine lands of the southeast and coastal marshlands of the north. The greatest modifications appear to have occurred in those ecosystems found between these extremes. Thus the grasslands, the shrublands, the woodlands and the forestlands all seem to have suffered major reduction in their original area. From 80 to 90 per cent of the forests have been clear-felled or so thinned as to change their species composition; the same process has affected 88 per cent of the woodlands. For the areas of mixed grassland, woodland and shrubland, a combination of tree-felling for timber and to clear land for agriculture, the ploughing up of natural grassland for agriculture and the selective impact on grassland and shrubland species composition of prolonged intensive grazing by domestic livestock has resulted in modifications of 50 to 90 per cent of the original areas of these ecosystems.

At the arid fringes of intensive land use in the interior, in the impassable marshlands of the northern coasts and in the high alpine lands of the southeast the impact of man over the last two centuries is less obvious. Major modification of the ecosystems at the continental scale seems absent although locally, particularly where the original ecosystems were of small extent, as the alpine lands, there has been some modification by grazing of livestock, the impacts of recreational land use and, specifically, constructions for the Snowy Mountains hydroelectric power scheme.

In one sense, these relict landscapes represent those areas of the continent which have remained up to the present time relatively unattractive to the Anglo–Australians. In another sense, however, they include areas which have been deliberately preserved from modification by the innovatory resource use systems. The relict landscapes in fact are of two types – vacant lands and reserved lands.

The vacant lands

Legally, some 20 per cent of the continent is still owned directly by the Crown and neither use by special governmental agency nor private use of the land is permitted. This represents in effect the area of the continent for which no use, official or private, has *yet* been found. The bulk of this is land which has never been owned by anyone except the Crown and which has not been greatly modified, either legally or illegally, by human activity. With the exception of small bands of pure blood Aborigines, perhaps 200 in number, wandering over parts of the central arid areas in traditional fashion, these lands are still uninhabited. These are the quiet 'timeless' lands of the continent.

In detail, especially in the arid interior, however, the peace of such lands will be broken by the passage of a small convoy of vehicles carrying a tourist 'outback safari' group, or a mineral exploration party; the clear skies above may be lined by the vapour trails of the international air routes or the fleeting passage of experimental rockets from the Woomera Research Station.

That these lands have not yet been considered useful is a function of their appraisal as resources. They are lands in the arid interior whose grazing capacity is either so low as to be economically useless at the moment or which is severely limited by lack of surface or subterranean water supplies. They are lands on the humid fringes of the continent where the natural vegetation has not yet been cleared for agriculture, because the economic incentives to expand the existing agricultural area are not yet sufficiently attractive. They are lands where the miners have not yet found payable ores. The emphasis throughout, is on their lack of attraction *as yet*; by implication they possess latent resources for the future. Their 'vacant' character is generally seen as only a temporary phenomenon.

The reserved lands

In contrast, the other type of relict landscapes are legally under the control of various governmental agencies as reserved lands for public or special uses (*c*. 12% of continent). In some cases this land was originally in private ownership and has been given or bequeathed to the Government for public use, but in most cases the land has been reserved from the vacant lands for the various governmental or public uses.

Aboriginal reserves

By far the largest area of reserved lands are the Aboriginal Reserves (*c*. 7% of continent in 1970) and probably 90 per cent of this area comprises relict landscapes (Fig. 6.4). The evolution of the present pattern of reserves needs explanation, particularly since it bears no relation to the original pattern of the *c*. 300 000 Indigenes in 1770.

Over the period 1788 to 1970s the Aboriginal population has been reduced in numbers and removed from traditional lands by contact and conflict with the invading Europeans and Anglo–Australians. The detailed documentation of that process of reduction and removal is only now being established (Rowley, 1972*a*, *b*, *c*) but the general patterns have been clear for some time.

The collapse of Aboriginal society in the face of stresses from the invading society was paralleled by, on the one hand, a retreat of the survivors inland in the face of the invasion from the coasts, and on the other a movement of inlanders to the invaders' settlements where they rapidly lost traditional culture and often their lives. From the 1830s onwards officialdom and missionaries became concerned that since the Aborigines did not appear able to survive intimate contact with European society, they should be protected in 'reserves' – that is land set aside for their sole use under official protection.

Because the first successful beachheads of European settlement were on the south and east coasts, the first of such reserves were here, but as the invaders pushed inland the Aboriginal population was rapidly reduced, these reserves emptied, became defunct and were replaced by new reserves further inland where food rations and blankets were dispensed. Eventually however, by the 1970s, a division of the reserves had become apparent. On the remote arid land reserves of the interior, mainly dating from the 1930s, traditional life could, in theory, still be carried on under official protection, with Anglo–Australian access officially controlled. From such reserves, an increasing number of Aborigines were moving to the main centres of Anglo–Australian population, where Government-run hostels and camping reserves provided the bases from which the Aborigines were beginning to mount their own 'urban' invasion, as we have seen in Chapter 11.

The pattern of Aboriginal reserves in the 1970s therefore reflects this interior, rural, concentration of the largest units in contrast to the peripheral, urban-oriented, much smaller reserves. Apart from the access roads to the official reserve headquarters, where a nucleus of buildings and perhaps an airstrip house the administrator, his staff, service facilities and living quarters for the semipermanent Aboriginal population, the landscape of these larger units is probably relatively unchanged from that of 1770. A similar pattern is to be found on the larger religious mission reserves, although here in the endeavour to introduce agriculture or pastoral operations the area cleared or affected by grazing animals may be considerable.

It is extremely doubtful whether these Aboriginal reserves will remain 'relict landscapes' for many more years. The minerals boom of the 1960s proved to the Australian public and not least the Aboriginal inhabitants themselves that the Aborigines did not have sole legal rights to the large reserves in central and northern Australia. Mining leases were obtained by Anglo–Australian and foreign companies in central Australia and exploitation of mineral ores literally cut the land from under the traditional hunting–gathering groups. Protests did not prevent mining commencing but forced commonwealth and state Governments to consider what became known as 'Aboriginal Land Rights'. In South Australia an Aboriginal Lands Trust was set up to develop the lands for the inhabitants in 1966 and the new Commonwealth Government, elected in December 1972, has promised to restore full rights of legal title to Aboriginal inhabitants in the reserves of the Northern Territory, which it controls. The restoration of such rights may mean the retention of existing traditional land-uses which have only minimal impact on these relict landscapes: they may, however, through external pressures or an increasing awareness of economic opportunities, result in Aboriginal development of Anglo–Australian land-use systems such as grazing, mining, agriculture or tourism, which will have immediate and obvious impacts on the landscape. I suspect the latter may be most popular and the question then will arise as to whether the Aborigines will make the same mistakes in land-use management, with the same impacts on the environment, as the Anglo–Australians have done in similar environments.

Recreation and scientific reserves

Some of the largest reserves have been created for recreation and for scientific purposes and are usually termed National Parks (Fig. 4.3), despite the fact that most have been created by the separate states and not the commonwealth Government. National Parks as evolved in Australia incorporate usually both land reserved for public access and recreation as well as land reserved for purposes of scientific study of its ecology. Where land is only reserved for the latter purpose it is usually known as a Wildlife Reserve or Flora and Fauna Reserve.

Reserves of Crown lands for these purposes began in the second half of the nineteenth century when scenic locations were set aside for public use. Some were areas much larger than could be foreseen from contemporary needs (e.g. the Royal National Park south of Sydney, founded in 1879 and comprising 18 000 acres (7200 ha); Wilson's Promontory National Park in Victoria of 102 000 acres (40 800 ha) founded in 1908), and have grown in value and public use over the years. Most of the areas, however, have been created within the last twenty years, in response to public demands for recreation areas which were increasing with standards of living and leisure-time. Thus in 1967 approximately 23 million acres (9 200 000 ha) were reserved in this way, by 1969 this had risen to 28 million acres (11 200 000 ha) and the trend is continuing into the 1970s.

It is difficult to generalise on the extent to which these reserves are preserving relict landscapes. The scientific reserves by their very definition are intended to preserve the indigenous ecology as unmodified as possible, by excluding all but the trained scientific observer. The National Parks in contrast encourage access by the general public, although that access may be limited in time, for example to daylight use, or in space as where portions of the parks are labelled 'wilderness areas' and public access may only be on foot. The range of types, and by implication the extent of the remaining relict landscapes, is illustrated by the National Parks of South Australia where at one end of the scale is the most recently created portion of the Simpson Desert National Park – 1.7 million acres (680 000 ha) of trackless and virtually unmodified relict landscape of linear desert sand dunes on the Queensland border, and at the other end of the scale the Belair Recreational Park – 2000 acres (800 ha) of woodland and forest 8 miles (13 km) from Adelaide, set up as a National Park in 1891 and frequented at weekends by city picnickers, cricket, football, tennis and golf enthusiasts. In this latter case the original grass ground cover has been replaced by exotic grasses and weeds, and the original timber stands have been thinned and added to by exotic tree plantings, while sporting ovals, tennis courts, barbecue areas, a Government nursery and the main-line railway from Adelaide to Melbourne may be found within its borders (Fig. 13.1)!

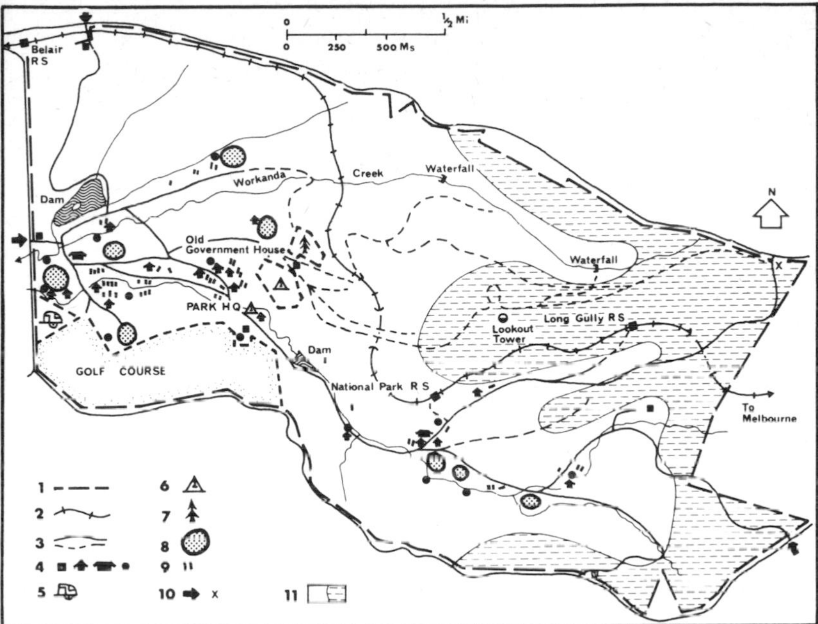

Fig. 13.1 Belair Recreation Park
1, Park boundary; 2, Adelaide–Melbourne railway; 3, Vehicle roads and foot-tracks; 4, Staff houses, public changing rooms, restaurant–kiosks, toilets; 5, Caravan park; 6, Playground; 7, State Forest Nursery; 8, Sports oval; 9, Tennis courts; 10, Vehicle entrances open, closed; 11, Original vegetation: Savannah woodland (blue gum); Sclerophyll forest (stringybark).

(*Source:* S.A. National Parks and Wildlife Service)

Other reserves

Of much less significance both in terms of their area and the amount of relict landscapes which they contain, are two other types of official reserves. Some lands have been reserved to preserve their resources for future use while others have been reserved for specific official purposes. Forest reserves are the most significant example of the first and in 1971 represented some 38 million acres (15 200 000 ha) of land where the timber supplies have been preserved for future use. The extent to which these represent relict landscapes is difficult to say, since grazing use may be permitted in some and human control of burning – both induced 'controlled burning' as practised in Western Australia since the 1960s to reduce dangers of *major* bush fire damage, and the bush-fire control itself, may have had significant effects on the original ecology.

Reserves for military purposes, usually as training grounds for men and equipment, include some remnants of relict landscapes, although most by the 1970s were significantly modified from their roles as 'battlefields'.

Summary

Despite virtually two centuries of European and Anglo–Australian occupation there remains almost one-third of the continent whose visual landscape is not markedly different from what it must have been in 1770. That such an area is so *small* is a tribute, however cynically the modern ecologist might view it, to the activities of a population which even in the 1970s has not yet risen over 14 million. That such an area is so *large* by comparison with *other* continents, is a remarkable illustration of the relative unattractiveness of the arid continental interior.

Part three

Visions of Australia 1770-1970

14
Sources and problems of interpretation of the visions of Australia 1770-1970

The Australian landscape of the 1970s is the product of several thousand years of interactions between man and the continental environment. These interactions have been motivated in part by man's basic needs of food, clothing and shelter, and particularly his changing ideas as to how those basic needs could be met in the environment. In part also, however, the interactions have been motivated by an array of attitudes and beliefs which have coloured man's actions according to his spiritual as well as his materialistic outlook. Over the years the attitudes and beliefs have changed and with them the human assessment or 'vision' of the environment. Put crudely, the Aboriginal hunter evaluated the environment of the Hamersley Ranges in 1770 differently than did the Japanese steel magnates in the 1970s, and their impact on the environment differed commensurately.

Particularly in the last 200 years, the human 'visions' have shown a variety of themes as a result of the superimposition of European and Anglo–Australian ideas onto those of the indigenous folk. The resources of the continental environment have been seen through many different eyes and we need to understand this variety to explain the complexities of the present-day vision, for the present seems to include most of the elements of past themes, just as the landscape itself contains many relics of past actions.

At any one time the contemporary vision might be expressed in various ways. Letters from settlers, books of reminiscences and travel, newspaper articles, official reports or policy statements, and the legislation which went with them, all provide *literary* evidence, while contemporary paintings and photographs by their subject matter and technique would provide further *graphic* clues. The facts of settlement themselves, the areas developed and the reasons given, down to the details of urban patterns and architecture, are further sources. Since we have already examined these latter sources in Part two, we shall stress here rather the evidence from literary and graphic sources. We shall first examine in this chapter the mechanics by which the visions were created in men's minds, and in Chapter 15 consider the character of the visions themselves.

The visions appear to have been the result of the interplay of three elements. First was the nature of the continental environment; second was the nature of the various men and women who made the assessments; and third were the means by which the assessments were made – the media of description and communication.

The problem of the environment

The global location of the Australian continent was a major cause of the lateness of European contact and seems to have reduced indigenous contacts with all but the peoples of the islands to the immediate north. Thus the indigenous assessment of landscape had been independently established long before the European invasion. The invaders themselves were remote from home, initially short even of food and raw materials and always short of capital (money and human) by comparison with the alternative and closer colonial opportunities of North and South America. Only twice in the two centuries since 1770, namely in the 1880s and 1960s, did the flow of outside wealth encourage dreams of continentalwide resource development. For the rest of the time decision-makers had to pinch and make do with less than the best and their attitudes to the land reflected this. They had plans but not the means to put them into force.

One of the major difficulties was the size of the continent and the cost of land transport (Blainey's *Tyranny of Distance*). Further, the basic ecological pattern of a thin fertile rim around an arid infertile core not only limited hopes of cheap water navigation, but forced all settlements to be peripheral and isolated rather than central and consolidated. The experience and problems of deteriorating environmental conditions inland so discouraged land exploration that considerable delays resulted in establishing the basic facts. Grenfell Price (1957, p. 188) commented:

> The European invaders discovered Lake Eyre with horses in 1840; they examined its northern shores with camels in 1874–75, but it was not until 1951 that they solved (by the use of motor trucks, motor boats, and aircraft) the extent of its filling and evaporation.

Not only was the continent less attractive the further inland one went, but the condition of the environment itself changed significantly not only from season to season, but from year to year as we have seen.

The impression gained by the explorers, therefore, varied according to the seasons and on the inland plains the result could be an impenetrable clay swamp with lush grasses in one month or a dusty cracked bare plain in another. The exploring accounts, not surprisingly therefore, were full of conflicting reports of country seen at different times, 'plains of promise' were 'barren deserts' depending upon whom you read and when, or even whether, they had been there.

To these problems of a changeable environment we must add a flora and fauna unfamiliar to European eyes and whose resource potential could only be appraised by slow and often painful experiences. In addition, the indigenous people appeared to be living at a much simpler level of material culture and their detailed knowledge of the natural resources seems to have been generally ignored as irrelevant to European life-styles and only of value to explorers searching for elusive water holes and river systems.

The various viewpoints

From 1788 onwards, the bulk of new knowledge about the continent was being absorbed by Europeans and their descendants in the new settlements. For the Aborigines, their knowledge began in like proportion to disappear as their numbers began to dwindle, through conflict with the European intruders, from epidemics, and as members of their group acquired European habits, customs and social values.

The European knowledge itself in part created, and at the same time formed part of, a vision of the continent and its resources. It was not one but a variety of visions depending upon the people involved. We can distinguish at least nine categories of attitudes, from the officials in Europe – mainly of course in Britain, but not forgetting their French, Spanish, Russian and German counterparts, through the local officials and politicians, the convicts, the free settlers (from capitalists to labourers), and the religious and political refugees, to the emigrant scientists and technicians (from geologists to miners, and botanists to 'gentlemen' farmers).

Briefly, the motives which influenced the various visions seem to have been as varied as the people concerned. The British officials in particular were concerned with establishing daughter settlements to fulfil specific roles. Thus, as we have seen, settlements could be strategic, to 'show the flag' against European rivals; social, to dispose of convicts; military, to establish bases of supply for stores and equipment for the Bitish Navy; and commercial, to provide raw materials and a trade outlet for British industry. Local officials had the immediate practical problems of settlement to face and saw the resources as positive or negative in so far as they aided or hindered the occupation of the land by first traditional and later, modified, systems of land use and resource development. Politicians seem to have had varying attitudes to the continental environment, but all, from the optimists to the pessimists, from far right to far left, saw the resources of the land as the basis on which the particular society they had in mind was to be founded. For many of the convicts the land was merely a gaol – a hell from which release came in an intermediate alcoholic, and then the final, oblivion; for some – artists and philosophers in their own right – the landscape had a fascination which never dimmed. The free settlers brought ideas as varied as the size of their purse. For some the land was merely a new locale for employment, with opportunities perhaps improved on those at home; for others, often the men with larger means, the land was a place to make their fortunes – to invest hard-won capital either in staid traditional ventures transplanted merely to a new locale, or chance a speculation on some new 'line'. The refugees from religious or political persecution brought traditional, or at least preconceived, ideas of how their society should be reconstructed in the new land, and the land's resources fitted into that econstruction. They transferred not merely people but their visible and piritual 'environment' from one side of the world to the other. Finally, the cientists and technicians brought an interest oriented more directly to the ınd itself, its form and content and the range of living things which moved .pon it – an interest in what was there for its own sake on the one hand, nd how it might prove useful on the other.

'he limitations of the 'media'

3etween the 'place' and the 'people' themselves, however, lay the 'media' by vhich the so-called facts of the one were made available to the audience of he other. The means by which information about the environment was uiltup had a significant influence upon the picture of the environment vhich emerged and the extent of this influence can be assessed by xamining the nature of the information available about the continent – articularly the written descriptions and the graphic illustrations.

'he sources

n the literary sources it is possible to distinguish two types of evidence. 'irst are the descriptions of the people who saw for themselves and ublished their experiences. These form the published writings of the fficial and private explorers and the travel books and reminiscences of the ocal pioneer settlers or world travellers such as Anthony Trollope in the 870s and J. A. Froude in the 1880s. Second are the larger group of descrip-ions at secondhand – the compendia of collected descriptions and inter-retations of the armchair geographers, the handbooks and guides for rospective migrants and the official papers published in the parliaments or utside for the information of the general public.

For the graphic sources, similarly, two basic types can be distinguished. irst and earliest to appear were the published lithographs, copper plate ngravings and paintings of Australian landscapes. Most explorers were iemselves trained topographic draughtsmen or had among their parties rtists and surveyors whose pencil sketches later appeared to the reading ublic as line engravings, lithographs or paintings in watercolours or oils. ıdividual artists provided a wealth of such illustrations – some produced ındscapes which still grace the world art galleries today, others had their ketches redrawn as illustrations for books of travel and exploration – just s Froude used the sketches of his travelling companion, Lord Elphinstone, ı his book *Oceana* (Froude, 1886).

Second, and gaining rapidly in importance in the latter half of the nine-eenth century, were the photographs of people and places. Officialdom in articular seems to have made use of photographs both in official reports to ie parliaments and in materials provided for overseas distribution. Thus in 871 the Queensland Government used Richard Daintree's photographs of 'pical settlements in different parts of the state as part of their official contribution to the London Exhibition of Art and Industry. From 1872 t 1876, as their agent general, Daintree used this collection as part of th official immigration propaganda. Apparently in the 1920s the same stat government was supplying 3¼ x 3¼ inches (8 x 8 cm) glass slides t overseas educational institutions, and the official handbooks and privat glossy 'coffee table' volumes still make extensive use of photographi materials.

The interpretation of the sources

To have this array of data is one thing, but to interpret it is another. Th image conveyed might not be that intended by the artist or writer and th image, even if conveyed as intended, might be itself warped or biased i some way by the writer himself or the tools available to him. In general, th process of observing the landscape was inhibited by the limitations of th observers' faculties. The human eye tends to find the broad panoramic vie unattractive 'unless it also has a vertical depth which allows the observer t dominate the landscape at one glance' (Gentilli, 1969, p. 105). Persona fears of claustrophobia in the forests or loneliness on the open plain together with the survival problems facing the explorers must hav influenced the observations recorded for posterity.

Not all the official observations were accepted as common knowledge The gap between the knowledge to be found in the *Government Gazette* and that held by local settlers could be wide indeed, as the New South Wale Surveyor General Mitchell found in 1846. In that year he retraced his line o march along the Namoi River Valley which he had officially opened up i 1836 and to whose natural features he had awarded official place names. Hi party discovered, however, that these official names were unknown to th local stockmen, who had provided their own place names for the feature

The written word was itself a source of confusion and errors and, a Mitchell's experience showed, not always an accurate indication of th actual knowledge in all men's minds. How many people could and did rea about the Australian landscape before they saw it themselves? Raymon Williams made various estimates of the increase of the reading public i England from the seventeenth to nineteenth centuries and suggested finall a figure of about 20 per cent of the adult public who *could* read (William 1961). How many *did* read about Australia is almost impossible to say bu would be worth trying to find out. At least some clues indicate that th literature *was* used, e.g. the successive editions of handbooks and guide and occasionally there is direct evidence, but for the most part we can onl guess how many read for themselves and how many heard from someon else.

Just what they heard was itself confusing and often conflicting. Part c the problem lay in semantics – for the words used in descriptions did nc always mean what the reader could be expected to think that they mean English observers gave traditional names to things which were not in fact th same, thus plants, birds and fishes were often called by the English names c the species they most resembled. Terms such as 'river' and 'stream' gave a false sense of permanence to what were often seasonally dry watercourses, while other names had their meanings modified to suit new circumstances, e.g. *creek* from 'tidal inlet' to 'dry watercourse'. The open woodland of the southeast inland plains was usually and enthusiastically described as 'parkland' – implying a 'cultivated' pattern of trees and grass, but in fact representing a vegetation community apparently mainly maintained by natural or Aboriginal fires which burned off the tree seedlings. Some Aboriginal words were adopted, especially for the peculiar water features of the inland (*billabong, tallywalka* and *warrambool*) and even new words were coined (as *anabranch* for a distributary of a river which rejoins it lower down its course), but up to mid-nineteenth century the descriptions were set in a terminology often much less than precisely depicting for the reader what the observer had seen.

Place names themselves, even when supposedly Aboriginal in origin, told little about the character of the site, since transliteration was rarely standardised, misunderstandings of what was being named were frequent and the Aboriginal names themselves apparently could change with seasonal conditions.

A second problem in the literary descriptions was the use of the method of analogy. Authors who were uncertain of the facts tended to fall back upon analogy to make forecasts of what reality ought to be. The device had been used before the first European settlement was established to forecast the resources of the environment. Jean Pierre Purry, a Swiss geographer who had worked in Batavia for the Dutch East India Company from 1713 to 1717, had made a study of the world climatic belts, of which he thought the most productive regions were those between the thirtieth and thirty-sixth parallels and especially about the thirty-third parallel. Within those latitudes in other as yet unsettled continents he argued, by analogy, similar successful resource development could be expected. One such latitude suggested by him to the Dutch in 1718 was Nuyts Land at the head of the Australian Bight; another more successful suggestion was to the British Government in 1724 for the settlement of South Carolina. Later, analogy was used to forecast a Mississippi-like inland river system and then a Great Lakes system for inland Australia similar to that in North America, and a future Australian population of 171 million was forecast in 1838 by dividing the continent into nine convenient units and awarding each the population of the European nation nearest in size, assuming of course an analogous land productivity potential.

The avenues of information

The information about Australia took not only various distinct and recognisable forms, but found its way to an audience by various avenues. Some were fortunate enough to have personal contacts who in their letters provided information of the new country. Such personal contacts were, however, for the fortunate few; the majority had to rely on the publications available and hearsay, the reliability of which varied enormously. By mid-nineteenth century authors were beginning to realise the conflicting nature of their accounts and were beginning to claim particular merit in their own publications. Each *Emigrant Journal* or *Handbook for Migrants* thus began to warn its readers against the false information provided by its competitors and authors generally began to document their impressions more carefully. At an average of a shilling (5p) per copy the journals and handbooks were not cheap, but presumably were within the means of the lower middle class to whom they seem to have been directed.

Independent organisations were formed to try to sift out and pass on to a wider public the more reliable of the accumulating information. The Society for the Diffusion of Useful Knowledge issued maps of parts of Australia from 1829 to 1831 as portions of a *Family Atlas* which was reissued *in toto* by Stanford in London in 1857. In addition the Society for Promoting Christian Knowledge produced a map of Australia in 1845, and there may have been many others.

In the latter half of the nineteenth century part of the functions of such societies was taken over by the official guides and handbooks prepared for the various international exhibitions held in Australia and elsewhere. As early as 1854, the New South Wales and Victorian Governments were preparing and exhibiting locally information intended for the Paris exhibition of 1855. Thereafter Australian exhibits of handbooks, photographs and produce were to be found at most of the international exhibitions (e.g. at London, 1862 and 1873; Philadelphia, 1876; Chicago, 1893; and Paris, 1908). Within Australia, intercolonial exhibitions offered similar channels for the diffusion of information on the environment, e.g. the Melbourne exhibition in 1866; Sydney, 1870, 1873 and 1875; and Brisbane, 1876. International exhibitions began in Australia in 1879 at Sydney, at Melbourne in 1880 and 1888, and at Adelaide in 1881, with several others later. Although the number and character of these exhibitions changed after the turn of the century, the Australian Commonwealth Government has maintained the practice of disseminating information, as witness the Australian Pavilion at the Expo '70 in Japan.

In all of the media, literary or graphic, however, the problem of bias and censorship, deliberate or accidental, remained. All authors and observers were themselves subject to the influence of contemporary philosophies or 'climates of opinion'. Many of these as we shall see were taken for granted at the time, but in assessing the various images from hindsight we must be aware of their influence. Not only private observers presented accounts which showed personal biases and contemporary ideals, but in Australia the colonial Governments themselves — rivals in Europe for immigrants and capital and virtually forced to take over the role of 'development' of the land for settlement in the absence of any other private enterprises large enough to tackle the job — took to the market place to tout their wares. Derogatory reports of continental resources tended to be overlooked or suppressed, while favourable comments were given wide publicity. As 'ecently as 1963 the Premier of Queensland could object – as a libel on the state – to a comment in the Commonwealth *Year Book* for 1962 that Cape York and Burketown were 'not suitable for continuous Caucasian habitation', and the controversy over the development of northern Australia still provides examples of biased reporting.

Out of this ever-changing pot-pourri of places, people and ideas, what can be said of the visions of Australia from 1770 to 1970? Five types of vision may be identified and are examined in the next chapter.

15
The five visions of Australia 1770-1970

Bearing in mind the problems of sources and interpretations illustrated in the previous chapter, five major types of vision of Australia seem to have emerged – visions reflecting the dominant perception of the various sources available. The images so created were not mutually exclusive, often they merged into each other, but occasionally they could be seen to dominate a period of time in splendid isolation.

A scientific vision

The initial vision of the continental landscape was derived from the European scientific expeditions in the southern Pacific from the late-eighteenth century. While it is easy to overlook the work of the Dutch explorers and Dampier's voyages of the seventeenth century, not until Cook's voyages and their French, Spanish and Russian equivalents was a body of knowledge assembled which was to stimulate interest in the continent and its landscapes. That interest from the outset was scientifically oriented.

The scientific vision which developed over the years from these first expeditions produced evidence of a spirit of inquiry into the natural phenomena of the continent for their own sake, as objects of novelty and curiosity to European eyes. We cannot understand the impact of this vision, however, without an explanation of the European climate of opinion which produced it. It would appear that the eighteenth-century European philosophers were attempting to replace Christian philosophy by rationalism and a concern for nature and the study of natural sciences. One of the largest areas of 'nature' unmodified by European man was considered to be the *Terra Australis Incognita* which the marine explorers were discovering in the late-eighteenth century. As a result great interest was focused on these areas and information on their inhabitants, their flora and fauna was carefully collected and tabulated. Vessels returning to Europe were 'literally crowded', reminisced one passenger in 1819 'so as to resemble Noah's Ark. There were kangaroos, black swans, a noble emu, cockatoos, parrots and smaller birds without number'. In Europe it was the great age for collectors, of butterflies, of strange sea shells, flowers, birds and animals of all types. Even royalty was infected by the enthusiasm. The results were the beginning of a 200 year sequence of landscape descriptions and analysis in a scientific manner, wherein the items of geology, flora and fauna were carefully described in literary and graphic form.

This general interest, particularly in Australia's unique flora and fauna, has never disappeared entirely and remains the basis for arguments in favour of nature reserves and wildlife sanctuaries, set up as much for their own sake as to preserve objects of scientific curiosity.

A parallel interest in the broader patterns of the environment seems to have been behind the concern for the particular problems which the continental environment posed for European settlement. Thus the aridity of the continental interior was the source of much speculation and argument on its origin and rationale. Rainfalls began to be registered at Adelaide in 1839 and Sydney in 1858, and were soon recognised to be the most important environmental data. Individual rainfalls, as we have seen in Chapter 8, had international relevance through their effects on grazing resources on foreign-owned pastoral properties in the 1880s. Speculation about the lack of surface drainage in the interiors despite effective rainfalls in the coastal watersheds led to forecasts of the existence of the artesian basins before they were actually discovered in the 1870s. In fact, the success of the artesian bores was a considerable boost to scientific investigations and there were early hopes of scientific solutions to the uncertainties of Australia's climate. From J. W. Gregory's concern for weather forecasting in 1904, through the pseudo-scientific rainmakers such as Charles Wragge's 'Vortex Guns' in western Queensland in the 1890s and J. C. Bradfield's plan to flood the Lake Eyre Basin in the 1940s, to the CSIRO's cloud-seeding experiments in the 1960s, the theme has been basically the same; that is, the attempt to control the weather of the continental environment.

Allied, apparently, to the problem of aridity were the contradictory characteristics of the continental soils. The general contradictions of the Australian landscape for the European observer were soon identified, that is the reversed seasons and daily northern path of the sun, but the soils came in for special mention (Sidney, 1853, p. 247):

> The soil of Australia presents as many anomalies as its configuration and animal and vegetable productions. In other parts of the world the most fertile tracts are generally found near the mouths of rivers; in Australia the greatest fertility usually commences where the navigation ceases. In Europe the valleys will generally be found full of rich soil; in Australia some of the richest mould is to be found on the top of the hills.

This 'contrariness' led, in the twentieth century, to research into soil fertility by the CSIRO and the discovery of unique trace element deficiencies in many soils as noted in Chapter 9.

In all the scientific interest and descriptions there seems to have been, and still is, a dichotomy of view. On the one hand there is what might be called the 'pure science' view of data for their own sake, seen as part of the world patterns and to provide clues for those general patterns, while on the other hand there is the 'applied science' view, which sees data in the light of their contribution to man's well being – as potential resources. Thus since the 1770s there have been attempts to classify and list phenomena as an inventory of the Australian landscape, alongside considered rankings of that inventory in terms of the resources so represented or the number of people which might be supported by them. Classification of the land was implicit in all early explorations by sea or land. It became explicit usually in the summary accounts written after several explorations and the experience of actual settlement had provided more ubiquitous data. Thus Atkinson's account of New South Wales in 1826 recognised as separate natural landscapes 'barren scrubs, bushes, forest lands, plains and alluvial lands'. Early classifications in fact were based upon vegetational variations with which land quality in an agricultural sense was often equated. Thus claims were made that the species of timber were the clues to agricultural potentials, e.g. in the words of a settler in 1827, 'the apple tree marking the good, and the spotted gum and stringy-bark the bad'. Despite proposals in 1914 by the father of Australian geography, Griffith Taylor, a national atlas to show the continental patterns did not appear until the 1950s, but in concept it dated back at least 100 years.

The patterns and descriptions themselves even in the scientific literature are still being revised. In 1946, estimates put the annual run-off of surface water from the continent at 60 million acre feet, in 1965 that figure was increased to 280 million acre feet as the result of continued scientific investigation. Indeed the rate of the scientific collection of data is increasing, particularly through the use of space photography. A recent comment (*Search*, July 1970, p. 10) was that:

> Australia will stand to receive every twenty days, repeat days, three times as much aerial or space photographic data on the whole of the continent [from the Earth Resources Technology Satellite orbited in 1972] as has been collected in the entire history of aerial photo-reconnaissance in this country.

The scientific view is likely to remain an important component of the vision of the Australian landscape for many decades to come.

The romantic vision

Alongside the scientific view of the landscape there seems to have been a parallel romantic vision. This expressed itself as a sympathetic response to the Aborigines, and a delight in the 'uncivilised' nature of the landscape leading to an almost Arcadian attitude to the countryside or 'bush'.

Not all the elements have been retained equally throughout the two centuries. Thus the initial sympathetic attitude to the Aborigines, derived in part from scientific curiosity, but also from a regard for a people closer to nature than the European invaders, was soon modified by experience of the deterioration of Aboriginal life in contact with European. Cook's sympathetic view that 'in reality they are far more happier than we Europeans . . . they live in Tranquility which is not disturbed by the Inequality of Condition: The Earth and the Sea of their own accord furnishes them with all things necessary for life' (Beaglehole, 1955, p. 399) was soon replaced by a more jaundiced attitude.

The major romantic appeal of the Australian landscape rested on the lack of evidence of human intrusion – it was a wilderness apparently unmodified by the hand of man. Many pioneer settlers found this wilderness had a 'wonderful charm' and it attracted artists such as George French Angas who claimed in the preface to his *Savage Life and Scenes in Australia and New Zealand* in 1847 that he 'went to the Antipodes activated by an ardent admiration of the grandeur and loveliness of Nature in her wildest aspect'.

From such a viewpoint, the onward march of civilisation was an intrusion, unwanted, but apparently inevitable. A Victorian pioneer (Bride, 1898, p. 239) commented:

> It has often been a source of regret to me that all the charms attending the traversing of a new country must give way to the march of civilisation; the camp on the grassy sward is now superseded by the noisy roadside inn; the quart-pot of tea by the bottle of ale. All the quiet serenity of an Australian bush, as we have known it, has yielded to the demands of population; and this, though a necessary change, is not the less to be regretted.

Such comments would have sympathetic hearing in many current Australian bush-walking clubs and nature preservation societies, and we can perhaps see the continuity of attitudes in the retreat to the bush for the picnic of the nineteenth century and the barbecue of the twentieth. True, the retreat is to a much modified bush and rather battered nature, encumbered by all the portable gear – the folding chairs and tables and bottled-gas stoves – of civilisation, but nonetheless it *is* a retreat, an escape to an environment recognised as having the particular attraction of contrasts with the 'civilised' everyday environment.

A subsidiary component of the romantic vision was the regard for strong vertical contrasts in the landscape. Initially only in the fringing eastern highlands was there sufficient relative relief to bring favourable comments, often then showing evidence of transfers of European preconceptions of what a romantic scene should be. 'In the Australian Alps', noted a visiting English physician in 1863, 'the scenery takes the character of a thoroughly Highland district.' He went on to contrast the 'parched plains of the lowland' with 'the lofty open heights, and the pure light atmosphere' of the summits. On the interior plains, the vertical theme was rare, but when found often exaggerated in the sketches of the first European explorers.

With increasing contact and experience in the nineteenth century the attraction of the landscape had other bases as we shall see. Nonetheless it is interesting to note that even in 1969 an anonymous writer on nature conservation in Australia could still illustrate an implicit bias by the comment 'that it is perhaps Australia's misfortune that her landscape does not possess the compelling grandeur of young mountain ranges and large native coniferous forests' (Anon, 1969, p. 73).

The colonial vision

Indifference to the scientific interest and romantic aura surrounding the landscapes had been evident in early European settlers, but it was not until two decades after the first permanent settlement that a definite reaction against the early enthusiasm for the landscape became widely evident. Commercial interests as we have seen had initially been limited to the marine resources of whaling and sealing, but by the 1820s an increasing concern for the potential resources of the land had led to the emergence of a new 'colonial' vision.

This new vision was not impressed by the natural scene. Commercially, neither the flora nor fauna seemed to offer much scope for exploitation. The animals were unattractive to European palates, land transport without extensive navigable rivers would be ruinously expensive and the Aborigines appeared indifferent or unwilling to become a subservient labour force.

In aesthetics also some opinions saw gross deficiencies in the landscape. By way of contrast to Humboldt's glowing accounts of the newly discovered American landscapes, it was claimed that 'there is not a single scene . . . [in New South Wales] of which a painter could make a landscape' (Smith, 1960, p. 421).

There seemed to be two main problems. One was the apparent monotony of the views and Anthony Trollope (1874, p. 128) put the case quite clearly:

> The fault of Australian scenery is its monotony. The eye after a while becomes fatigued with a landscape which at first charmed with its park-like aspect. One never gets out of the trees, and then it rarely happens that water lends its aid to improve the view . . . unceasing trees . . . become a bore, and the traveller begins to remember with regret the open charms of some cultivated plain.

The second problem was hinted at by Trollope, in that while the 'uncivilised' landscape might appeal to the romantics, to others it was, as a surveyor of the salt bush plains of the interior put it, nothing less than a veritable desolation. A visual wilderness was made even more unattractive to some by what was termed a 'blank past' with no visible legacy from past civilisations to diversify the land surface.

The only compensation in such circumstances was to turn from 'the silence and solitude that reign in these wide-spreading untenanted wastes' where nothing but emus 'enliven the monotony of the dreary expanse' to 'anticipate some future and not distant period, when these vast and in many cases fertile plains, shall be covered by productive flocks and herds, and enlivened by the presence and industry of civilized men' (Atkinson, 1826, p. 7).

In fact a strong body of opinion developed which saw the landscape as attractive only in so far as it was 'improved' by European man and his works. Where the landscape could offer little of value, it must be replaced or added to, whether by the animals and crops of the settlers under the promotions of the agricultural societies, or by the singing birds, game animals and fish of the various Acclimatisation Societies, both of which began to flourish in the mid-nineteenth century. In the twentieth century the process was effectively taken over by Government Departments of Agriculture and the CSIRO, the latter alone for example claiming to have introduced more than 3000 grass species into the country.

As early as 1789, the *vision of hope*, as Erasmus Darwin put it in his panegyric on the future of the new settlement at Botany Bay, was a combination of *peace, art* and *labour* which provided a remarkably close forecast of the future Sydney harbour scene (Phillip, 1789, frontispiece) (Fig. 2.7):

> *There* shall broad streets their stately walls extend,
> The circus widen, and the crescent bend;
> *There*, ray'd from cities o'e the cultur'd land,
> Shall bright canals, and solid roads expand. –
> *There* the proud arch, Colossus-like, bestride
> Yon glittering streams, and bound the chasing tide;
> Embellish'd villas crown the landscape-scene,
> Farms wave with gold, and orchards blush between. –
> *There* shall tall spires, and dome-capt towers ascend,
> And piers and quays their massy structures blend;
> While with each breeze approaching vessels glide,
> And northern treasures dance on every tide.

However, from the 1820s, the vision was portrayed with increasing regularity as a reality. An artist in 1821 attempted to 'show and convince from what slender beginnings and in how few years, the primeval forest . . . [may] be changed from a mournful and desolate wilderness, into the cheerful village, the busy town, and the crowded city'. The transition from Australian to European, or specifically British, landscape was already evident to the Polish explorer Strzelecki in 1845, and in 1885 the British historian Froude found the country between Melbourne and Ballarat impressively settled and transformed. Perhaps one of the best graphic illustrations was Glover's painting in the 1830s of his house and garden in Tasmania (Fig. 15.1). The line of division between the foreground (English) garden and the background of bush is a remarkable commentary on the contemporary attitudes.

Possibly deriving from this desire to improve on nature, was the indifferent regard for the natural landscape itself. The scale of the land was so large that there was no need of care in its use. If the aim was to transform it, then the quicker the better. Land clearance was widespread and often

ndiscriminate, fire and ring barking left gaunt skeletons to dot the paddocks and from rain forest to open woodland, from brigalow to mallee, the vision was the same – reduction to tilled fields or wide grazing paddocks. Tidiness was a feature only of the longer and more intensively settled lands. Elsewhere the first sign of civilisation was the litter of broken bottles – champagne bottles along the overlander's track from Sydney to Melbourne in the 1840s, according to Governor Gipps, mere beer bottles ('dead marines') along the Wilcannia to Bourke track in the 1880s.

In such a climate of opinion it is not surprising to find that one of the few kinds of landscape which was found attractive was the open woodland which resembled the manicured private parklands of England. The simile of the park was probably one of the widest used descriptive methods applied to the landscapes of south-eastern Australia. Elizabeth Macarthur was one of the first to use it in 1795 and it became a stock description and source of satisfaction often when other prospects failed to please. And if nature failed to provide it, man could soon remedy the omission. Froude (1886, p. 105) described a property – 'Ercildoun' – in western Victoria in 1885 as approached through three gates, the last giving onto:

> high trimmed hedges of evergreen, catching a sight at intervals of a sheet of water overhung with weeping willows; a moment more, and we were at the door of what might have been an ancient Scotch manor house, solidly built of rough-hewn granite, the walls overrun with ivy, climbing roses, and other multitudinous creepers, which formed a border to the diamond-paned, old-fashioned windows. On the north side was a clean-mown and carefully-watered lawn, with tennis-ground and croquet-ground, flower-beds bright with scarlet geraniums, heliotropes, verbenas, fuschias – we had arrived, in fact, at an English aristocrat's country house reproduced in another hemisphere, and shone upon at night by other constellations.

The vision had not only aesthetic but social implications.

A national vision

The second half of the nineteenth century saw the realisation of many of the hopes of the colonial developers and out of the success of land settlement and the wealth so accumulated, from mine, field and paddock, came a

---

Fig. 15.1 'Glover's House and Garden', Patterdale, Tas. (John Glover, 1835)
A transplanted English garden set down amid the endless eucalyptus. The house survives but after being derelict then used as a wheat store in the Second World War, it partly collapsed and was rebuilt with concrete and now painted white. The shape of the hills in the background was 'faked' but the real hills, much bulkier and less 'picturesque', are still covered in eucalyptus. The garden has disappeared.

(*Source:* Collection: the Art Gallery of South Australia)

confidence in and new attitudes to the continent and its landscape. From the conflict between man and nature had come the glorious union of Darwin's art and labour – a union which by late-nineteenth century was claimed to have produced a unique, Australian, landscape.

When the British Association for the Advancement of Science met for the first time in Australia in 1914, the President, Professor William Bateson, reminded his audience that their presence in Australia reflected 'those advances in science which have given man a control of the forces of Nature' and the President of Section E: Geography invited his audience to consider the Australian landscape as an example of man as a geographical agency (BA, 1915, p. 437):

> Set yourselves to write a geography of Australia as Australia was when first made known to Europe, and compare it with a geography now. . . . How much waste land, how many fringes of desert have been reclaimed? The wilderness has become pasture land, the pasture land is being converted into arable. The Blue Mountains, which barred the way into the interior, are now a health resort.

By 1914, man had transformed the original patterns and there was already evidence of considerable pride in the landscapes newly created.

Land settlement itself was being successfully extended in the latter half of the nineteenth century and by 1900 most of the areas which were eventually to be settled permanently had already had their first white occupants. From the golden fleece and the golden grain, the profits accumulated, bark huts became brick and stone homesteads, dirt tracks became highways and rail routes, and the river-steamers crunched their way over the snags and sand bars of the Murray–Darling with supplies and produce. The pioneers began to acquire an aura of their own.

'The Anglo–Saxon' wrote a journalist in 1893, 'has perished or is absorbed in the Interior much more rapidly than on the sea-slope and in the towns.' The new breed which had replaced him, according to such contemporary journalists and politicians, was to inherit this new arcady and create a new and unified nation with federation in 1901.

Significantly, it was in the cities and specifically in Melbourne which benefited most immediately from the gold rushes and land booms of the 1850s to 1880s, where the first evidence of the new attitudes became evident. It was in the cities where the early intercolonial exhibitions of Australia's economic development were mounted, and it was in Melbourne, the commercial capital of Australia, that the Centennial Exhibition of 1888 was housed in the monumental exhibition building – a 'Crystal Palace' but in enduring stone and marble and likely to be still available for the *next* centennial. Professor Asa Briggs (1963, p. 302) included Melbourne as the only overseas example in his study of *Victorian Cities*, not only because its rapid growth outstripped its rivals in the rest of the British Empire, but because it provided evidence in its buildings and society of an urban nationalism already evident by the 1880s:

> Melbourne in the 1880s was proud of its increasing 'urbanity'. . . . The feeling that there was a distinctive Australian future was nurtured in the cities: culture not nature was to make it. At a time when the Australian landscape was felt to be greatly inferior to that of Britain, the cities were already believed to have a superiority of their own. Their inhabitants were far better off . . . than the men and women of London. . . . They were relatively free too of a 'snob class'. At their best they felt that they were making history.

Certainly even in the 1970s, as we have seen, the central area of the Australian metropolises still owed many of their public buildings and private offices to this period of rapid investment in stone and brick, galvanised iron roofs and ironwork balconies. Even private house owners embellished roofs and cornices with elegant plaster and ironwork motifs as further evidence of confidence in the country's future, and even in the small towns and hamlets picture postcards implied a civic pride for even the humblest main street.

Professor Briggs goes on to suggest, however, that particularly after the financial crashes and collapse of the real estate land booms in the early 1890s, the cities lost their attraction as national identities and the emphasis of the patriots reverted to the countryside, which alone was thought to embody the true Australian spirit. Whether this was a sudden shift or the culmination of a trend is difficult to say. Certainly the peculiarities of the interior landscapes had been noted much earlier. Even Ernest Giles, exploring the waterless sands and ranges of central Australia in 1873, could point to the beauties of the fantastically shaped rock formations, and to the plains carpeted with flowers and trees, and echoing with bird songs. This beauty, or charm, of the relatively unsettled areas had an attraction reflecting the romantic vision, but specifically from the 1880s onwards a truly Australian School of Art can be distinguished, which built onto the romantic attitudes almost a patriotic concern to depict the true Australian countryside. Retiring from the cities to their rural suburbs, or camping in the bush itself, the painters began to produce the landscapes which were to parallel graphically the literary revolution of opinions being carried on via the columns of the Sydney newspaper *The Bulletin* and the pens of Henry Lawson, Banjo Paterson, William Ogilvie and Bernard O'Dowd. In print and on canvas the Australian Legend, as Russell Ward has called it, began to dominate the vision of the bush – the subjects were rural, the landscapes distinctly and unmistakably Australian in colour and realistic detail (Fig. 15.2).

Pride in the landscape was manifest in various ways. Besides the popular Press and the paintings noted above, a spate of new publications with titles such as *The Picturesque Atlas of Australasia* and *The New Atlas of Australia* began to appear in the 1880s. With maps, line drawings and engravings they depicted the Australian scenery, rural and urban. In part they reflected the growing external interest stemming from the increasing economic wealth, but also a response to complaints that the facts of local landscapes and

Fig. 15.2 'The Breakaway' (Tom Roberts, 1891)
A mob of sheep, being driven along a stock route in a period of drought, stampedes to the water hole (bottom right) past a sun-baked paddock where hawks hover over the carcases of livestock and a dust-devil whirls on the horizon.

(*Source:* Collection: The Art Gallery of South Australia)

geography were not available to even the local population. Thus in 1881, the Melbourne journalist and politician, David Blair, published his *Cyclopaedia of Australasia* in order to correct the 'ignorant misconceptions' and 'gross errors' of the geography of this part of the world. He complained that the Australian child in adult life had to unlearn all his school geography as this was taught from English texts and with only English examples: 'He has to learn that he was *not* born, and does not live, in a little Island in the Northern Sea; that June is *not* the month of bright and flowery Summer, and December the month of chilling ice and snow.' (Blair, 1881, p. viii.) With knowledge of conditions as they really were would come an understanding of the real 'home country' – Australia, and a fostering of a patriotic view of the land.

There were patriots even among the sober scientists in the late-nineteenth and early-twentieth centuries. At the British Association meeting in 1914, the Commonwealth Meteorologist claimed that 'the preconceived notion that Australia is the particularly drought-stricken and precarious area of the earth's surface' had been emphatically contradicted by the climate of the preceding decade. He admitted that seasonally dry periods were liable to be experienced, but were not to 'be regarded as drought, and an evil, but rather as Nature's wise provision for resting the soil' (BA, 1915, p. 442). Drought, as typifying the environmental challenge to land settlement, became no longer the threat to successful occupation but instead a peculiarity of the environment which might even have a beneficial as well as detrimental impact – and this in spite of accumulating evidence of substantial drought losses.

One major national task which faced the pioneers and scientists after federation was the settlement of the tropical north of the continent. The history of the various attempts (Grenfell Price, 1939; and Davidson, 1966) shows virtually unlimited and continuous optimism in the land resources for settlement, an optimism not borne out by the success of actual settlement. Despite setbacks and substantial economic losses, as late as 1954 the nineteenth-century optimism was still present, joined then by a moral argument for the 'development of the north'. At a national symposium on the problem in 1954, the former chairman of the Australian Institute of Political Science noted the general opinion that: 'Australia could not justify her retention of it [northern Australia] unless she exploited to the full its mineral resources and its capacity for food production. Our failure in this part of our continent seemed a national reproach which we should do our utmost to remove.' (AIPS, 1954, p. xiii.) At stake was not only the reputation of science but of the nation as a whole.

This apparently unlimited faith in national development, reflected in the many schemes for intensification of land settlement by purchase and subdivision of large estates for returned soldiers and others, has had to face increasing opposition in the last few decades. This opposition has been derived from a totally different image of the landscape – the ecological vision.

The ecological vision

While the optimists have tended to see the Australian landscape through rose-coloured spectacles, there have always been if not pessimists, at least some commentators who had reservations about the landscapes which they saw around them. Two questions seem to have troubled them and, in the twentieth century in particular, these have been brought to the forefront of public attention. The first was that nature was not necessarily as benevolent as the optimists would claim; she had a remarkable ability to inflict damage on man and his works whether by brief but savage catastrophes – such as the cyclones which have destroyed pearling fleets and towns around the northern coasts, and the massive floods which have swept the eastern coasts, or by the more insidious, but equally devastating droughts, which have continued to periodically disrupt rural and, more recently, even urban water supplies. Basically it is indeed water, either too much or too little, which concerned these commentators. In spite of increasing knowledge and technical knowhow, they suggested, nature has still to be treated with respect. Mere occupation of the land did not guarantee successful settlement as even the painters recognised (Fig. 15.3).

Fig. 15.3 'Angry Harrison's Store' (Sir Russell Drysdale, 1950)
One of the most impressive graphic comments on the problems of land settlement and the fate of the country towns in locations both environmentally and economically marginal.

(*Source:* Collection of Mr J. O. Fairfax)

A second question troubling commentators as early as mid-nineteenth century, but which has become a dominant theme only in the last few years, is the concern for the impact of man upon the Australian environment. Briefly, there seemed to be two basically opposing versions of that impact. The optimists claimed that conditions improved as the result of land clearance and stocking with domestic animals – the patter of tiny hooves consolidated the naturally loose soil, improved the rainfall run-off, and filled the reservoirs. The pessimists agreed but added riders that the hooves were cleft – thus, while the soil was consolidated it formed impervious hardpan, improved run-off meant greater soil erosion, and the reservoirs were indeed filled, but with silt. Massive stock losses and soil erosion in New South Wales and western Queensland at the turn of the century, and soil erosion in South Australia, Victoria, New South Wales and the channel country of Queensland in the late 1930s and early 1940s, resulted in official inquiries which expressed fears that even existing intensities of land settlement could not be maintained and let to official encouragement to reduce livestock densities and the setting up of Soil Conservation Services in most states.

Concern for the impact of land occupation in terms of long-term productivity has been paralleled in the last decade by an increasing concern for the broader non-economic ecological impacts of land clearance upon indigenous ecosystems of flora and fauna. A range of publications together with the work of the Australian Conservation Foundation since its foundation in 1965, not only have documented our impact on the continent but have produced a new ecological vision.

In this new vision are contained many components of three of the previous four visions. Thus the concern to preserve unique flora and fauna reflects both the scientific view and the hope that the majority of people might be thus enabled to satisfy their curiosity and see the rare items for themselves before they might be destroyed. Also implied is a concern to educate the public to appreciate the non-material aesthetic resources of the relatively unmodified natural landscape – a nurturing of the romantic view, of a 'natural environment' to which man can retreat from his 'built environment'. And finally there are national overtones, the preservation of a national heritage of uniquely Australian flora and fauna in which all citizens might have a pride and interest. There is no place here, however, for the colonial view, nature according to this vision cannot be improved upon. A test case for the clearance of mallee scrubs of the 'Little Desert' in Victoria in 1972 showed, in its resolution in favour of conservation, that perhaps for the first time in a direct confrontation, the ecological view had triumphed over the colonial view, the 'desert' was of more value in its state of nature than under the plough!

Prospect

Change has been a dominant characteristic of the Australian landscape over the last 200 years, and the pace of that change, particularly in attitudes to the landscape, has increased significantly in the last decade. As yet it is too early to make accurate predictions of the impact of these changes upon the overall landscape of Australia, but some suggestions can be made as to how the various component landscapes identified in this book might be affected in the next decade to the Orwellian 1984.

There seems no reason, short of warfare, to predict a significant modification of the current 1–2 per cent annual growth of Australian population. The potential for controlled population growth, which the combination of a low natural increase and a balancing immigration policy provides, seems to have been accepted by both major political parties and the Australian public. This slow but sure population increase will continue to put pressure directly upon the urban landscapes for residential and work space, and particularly upon the maritime and relict landscapes for recreation space. Improving efficiencies in transport, particularly air services, both public and private, will work to reduce Australia's tyranny of distance and expose remoter locations to more frequent access. Already the real-estate men are busily subdividing the north Queensland coast and soon here, as currently within a day's drive of the major cities, most 'ocean views' will be from 60 x 150 ft (18 x 46 m) lots.

The expansion of the urban landscapes which this population pressure will entail is likely to be mainly by suburban sprawl from the existing major cities, but some twenty new centres are planned – as Monarto (S.A.) and Albury–Wodonga (N.S.W.–Vic.). Given effective planning of the expansion, which is promised in these centres, there may be scope for Australian initiative to combine the best and eradicate the worst features of the much maligned 'suburban boxes', to curb both the speculative exploitation of unscrupulous 'developers' and the inhuman arrogance of remote planners. None of this expansion, however, is likely to shift the centre of gravity of population from the southeast of the continent (Fig. 6.3C, p. 62).

Inland, the pastoral and agricultural landscapes will continue to reflect both technological innovations, particularly in labour-saving devices, and the vacillations of the world marketplace. The natural and, increasingly, the improved grazing lands will continue to support some of the world's largest attle and sheep herds although species will reflect further genetic nnovation and changing management preferences. Diversification within gricultural production will be a slow process as long as world demand for nimal protein and wheat continues at its current high level, but the trend owards larger, more economic, production units will continue, and here as n the pastoral landscape, on remote farms and stations it will become ncreasingly difficult to obtain and provide acceptable amenities for the vork-force. One type of rural land settlement which is unlikely to be epeated in the next decade is the Government-sponsored irrigation scheme, ecause of the experience of the high cost of these ventures. Even the learance of 'bush' for new farms is likely to be looked at more carefully by fficialdom in the face of the outcry by the conservationists.

Mining activities will continue to provide significant foreign income from ale of increasingly scarce raw materials and provide a 'frontier' for dventuresome settlers in remote locations. The demonstrated vulnerability f the European nations and particularly Japan, Australia's most important ading partner, to Middle Eastern oil politics will encourage further foreign il search in Australia. In addition it will force the reconsideration of ossible sources of energy for domestic needs, from the traditional black nd brown coals to the possible expansion of hydro-electricity in northern ustralia and the investigation of the vast solar energy resources of the nterior.

Despite, or perhaps rather because of, the pressure of increasing population the deliberate preservation of Australia's relict landscapes will continue o be official policy, although the pressure of the ballot box will result in nore recreation than scientific reserves, particularly with tourist visits likely o be increasing annually at over 10 per cent. Whether the vacant lands emain vacant or become some vast truly *national* resource will depend pon the strength of the conservation lobby in Canberra and the resistance f the various states, particularly Southern and Western Australia in which nost of this land lies.

The current vision of Australia appears to contain the elements of all five f the older attitudes to the landscape described in Part three and it seems kely that all will be retained, if not in the foreground at least just over the orizon in the future. To them however, will be added 'new' ideas on the nplementation of those attitudes—ideas which will probably revert in part the socialistic thinking of the late-nineteenth and early-twentieth nturies and require greater governmental controls upon individual use of e environment in place of the *laissez-faire* policies of the mid-twentieth ntury. Australia has recently been able to capitalise upon its increasing es with the United States in the sense that it has been made aware, through e American Eco-Crisis propagandists, of the dangers of environmental ollution before its own population became large enough to make an impact the magnitude of that in North America. As a result the authorities and e man-in-the-street have been made aware of the dangers and there is no oubt that future landscape modifications will be the subject of increasing concern as to their environmental impact. Already the Commonwealth an some state Governments require studies of such impacts for all ‘develop ment projects’. Indeed, Australia has been made very much aware in th early 1970s that in a crowded world it possesses some of the largest un inhabited lands yet remaining; that in a world increasingly becomin dominated by a man-made ‘built-environment’ it retains some of the larges areas of relatively untouched natural beauty; and that in a worl increasingly polluted by fossil fuels it possesses one of the largest and mos efficient collecting grounds for pollution-free solar energy. Just what made of these invaluable assets, only the future landscapes will show.

A note on the sources

Specific books and articles are cited here only in so far as they provided basic materials. Citation is generally by author and date, the full reference will be found in the Bibliography which follows.

For overviews of political, economic and social conditions and basic statistical information any study of Australia must rely heavily upon the current *Year Book of the Commonwealth of Australia*, Government Printer, Canberra, and the *Year Books* published by each of the state Governments. The *Atlas of Australian Resources* (Australia, 1955) and Devery (1968) provided continental map coverage and extracts from larger scale maps produced by the Commonwealth National Mapping Branch and the state Government Lands and Survey Departments were also sampled. Useful encyclopaedias included Jose and Carter, 1925; the ten-volume *Australian Encyclopaedia* (Australia, 1958); Barnes (1964) and the most recent, Learmonth and Learmonth, 1968. Still useful as a geography book are Taylor (1959), and Wadham, Kent Wilson and Wood (1957), while a geographer has recently taken on the traditional historian's mantle as national commentator (Spate, 1968). Limitations of space prevented full justice being done to the visual appearance of either rural or urban Australia; for the former see Learmonth and Learmonth (1971), and Serventy (1968), and for the latter see Freeland (1966).

For each part of the book, in addition to the above, the following were consulted:

Part one. For the patterns of the land – CSIRO (1960), Gentilli and Fairbridge (1951), Jennings and Mabbutt (1967), Laseron (1953), Stace (1968) and Twidale (1968); for the seasons – Foley (1957), Gentilli (1971), Gibbs and Maher (1967); for the ecosystems – Burbridge (1960), Keast and Crocker (1959), Ross Cochrane (1963). Current research is rapidly changing on information and opinion on the origins and evolution of the Indigenes, but a recent review of Australian archaeology (Anon, 1968) together with Golson and Mulvaney (1970), Lawrence (1969), McCarthy (1959), Mulvaney (1969) and Tindale's map (Tindale, 1940), now revised and shortly to be reissued, formed the basis of discussion.

Part two. For the overview – Scott (1968), Spate (1956) and personal experience; for maritime landscapes – Bird (1965), Blainey (1966), Britton (1964), Colwell (1969), Young (1967) and various volumes of *Australian*

Fisheries, Government Printer, Canberra; for pastoral landscapes – Barnard (1958 and 1962), Buxton (1967), Carter (1964), Drane and Edwards (1961), Duncan (1967), Hancock (1972), Heathcote (1965), Perry (1963) Slatyer and Perry (1969), Roberts (1968 and 1970); for agricultural landscapes – Andrews (1966), BAE (1969 and 1970), Callaghan and Millington (1956), Conacher and Murray (1973), Davidson (1966 and 1969), Donald (1967), Dunsdorfs (1956), Higginson (1973), Higginson and Emery (1972) Higman (1968), Jeans (1972), Langford-Smith and Rutherford (1966) Lovett (1973), Meinig (1962), Powell (1970), Roberts (1968), Sinden (1972), and Williams (1969); for mining landscapes – Blainey (1969) Raggatt (1968), Serle (1963); for urban origins – the architectural historians – Boyd (1960 and 1961), Herman (1970), the economic historians – Blainey (1958), Briggs (1963), Butlin (1962), Hunter (1963) and the *Australian Economic History Review* especially Volume 10, No. 2 1970, the geographers – Gale (1969), Jeans (1965), McPhail (1968), Rose (1955 and 1962), Smith (1963), Williams (1969); for urban patterns – Adelaide (1962), Bunker (1971), Christaller (1966), Daly and Brown (1964), Dick (1960), Juppenlatz (1961), Logan (1962 and 1964), Pike (1957), Rose (1967), Scott (1964), Smailes (1969), Solomon (1959) Solomon and Goodhand (1965), Tweedie (1967), Vance (1970), Williams (1966*b*), Winston (1957); for the relict landscapes – Costin and Frith (1971), Marshall (1968), Mosley (1968), Rowley (1972), Webb, Whitelock and Le Gay Brereton (1969).

Part three. A fuller documentation of the main theme will be found in Heathcote (1972); the original stimulus came from Clark (1956) and Smith (1960 and 1962), with support from Elliot (1967). Parallel ideas are in Powell (1972) and some questions for the future are raised in Rapoport (1972), Sinden (1972) and Stretton (1970).

ibliography

delaide (1962) *Report on the Metropolitan Area of Adelaide*, S.A. Government, Town Planner's Office, Adelaide.

delaide (1968) *Report on Metropolitan Adelaide Transportation Study*, De Leuw, Cather, Rankine and Hill, Voorhees and Associates, Adelaide.

IPS (1954) *Northern Australia Task for a Nation*, Australian Institute of Political Science, Angus and Robertson, Sydney.

lexander, G. and Williams, O. B. (eds.) (1973) *The Pastoral Industries of Australia: Practice and Technology of Sheep and Cattle Production*, Sydney University, Sydney.

ndrews, J. (1966) 'The emergence of the wheat belt in southeastern Australia to 1930', in Andrews, J. (ed.) *Frontiers and Men: a Volume in Memory of Griffith Taylor*, F. W. Cheshire, Melbourne, pp. 5–66.

ngas, G. F. (1847) *Savage Life and Scenes in Australia and New Zealand*, Smith Elder, London (2 vols.).

non. (1968) 'Archaeology in Australia', *Current Affairs Bulletin*, **41**, 194–207.

non. (1969*a*) 'Sydney', *Current Affairs Bulletin*, **44**, 1–16.

non. (1969*b*) 'Nature Conservation in Australia', *Current Affairs Bulletin*, **44**, 67–78.

tkinson, J. (1826) *An Account of the State of Agriculture and Grazing in New South Wales*, J. Cross, London.

ustralia (1952–60 and 1962–73) *Atlas of Australian Resources*, Department of National Development, Canberra, 1st and 2nd series.

ustralia (1958) *The Australian Encyclopaedia in Ten Volumes*, Angus and Robertson, Sydney.

A (1915) *British Association for the Advancement of Science; Report of the Eighty-Fourth Meeting, Australia: 1914*, Murray, London.

AE (1969) *The Australian Wheatgrowing Industry: an Economic Survey 1964–65 to 1966–67*, Bureau of Agricultural Economics, Canberra.

AE (1970) *The Australian Beef Cattle Industry Survey 1962–63 to 1964–65*, Bureau of Agricultural Economics, Canberra.

arnard, A. (1958) *The Australian Wool Market 1840–1900*, Melbourne University, Carlton.

arnard, A. (ed.) (1962) *The Simple Fleece: Studies in the Australian Wool Industry*, Melbourne University, Parkville.

Barnes, V. S. *et al.* (1964) *The Modern Encyclopaedia of Australia and Nev Zealand*, Horwitz-Grahame, Sydney.

Beaglehole, J. C. (ed.) (1955) *The Journals of Captain James Cook* Cambridge University Press, London (2 vols.).

Bell, J. H. (1962) 'The Aborigines of New South Wales' (Ch. 10) in Elkir A. P. (ed.) *A Goodly Heritage*, ANZAAS, Sydney.

Bird, J. (1965) 'The foundation of Australian seaport capitals', *Economi Geography*, **41**, 283–99.

Blainey, G. (1958) *Gold and Paper: a History of the National Bank o Australasia Limited*, Georgian House, Melbourne.

Blainey, G. (1962) *Mines in the Spinifex: the Story of Mount Isa Mines* Angus and Robertson, Sydney (1st – 1960).

Blainey, G. (1966) *The Tyranny of Distance*, Sun Books, Melbourne.

Blainey, G. (1967) *Peaks of Lyell*, Melbourne University, Carlton, (1st – 1954).

Blainey, G. (1969) *The Rush that Never Ended: a History of Australia Mining*, Melbourne University, Carlton (1st – 1963).

Blair, D. (1881) *Cyclopaedia of Australasia*, Ferguson and Moore Melbourne.

Boyd, R. (1961*a*) *Australia's Home: Its Origins, Builders and Occupiers* Melbourne University, Parkville (1st – 1952).

Boyd, R. (1961*b*) *The Australian Ugliness*, F. W. Cheshire, Melbourne (1s – 1960).

Bride, T. F. (ed.) (1898) *Letters from Victorian Pioneers*, Governmen Printer, Melbourne.

Briggs, A. (1963) *Victorian Cities*, Odhams, London.

Britton, J. N. H. (1964) *The Ports of Victoria: a Freight Study o Commodity Movements in the Hinterlands of Melbourne, Geelong an Portland*, Melbourne University, Carlton.

Bunker, R. (1971) 'Metropolitan form and metropolitan planning *Australian Geographer*, **11**, 619–32.

Burbridge, N. T. (1960) 'The phytogeography of the Australian region *Australian Journal Botany*, **8**, 75–211.

Butlin, N. G. (1962) *Australian Domestic Product, Investment and Foreig Borrowing 1861–1938/39*, Cambridge University Press, London.

Buxton, G. L. (1967) *The Riverina 1861–1891: an Australian Regiona Study*, Melbourne University, Carlton.

Callaghan, A. R. and Millington, A. J. (eds.) (1956) *The Wheat Industry i Australia*, Angus and Robertson, Sydney.

Carter, H. B. (1964) *His Majesty's Spanish Flock: Sir Joseph Banks and th Merinos of George III of England*, Angus and Robertson, Sydney.

Christaller, W. (1966) *Central Places in Southern Germany*, Prentice Hal Englewood Cliffs, N.J. (original German, 1933).

Clark, K. (1956) *Landscape into Art*, Penguin, Harmondsworth (1st – 1949).

Coleman, F. (1972) *Frequencies, Tracks, and Intensities of Tropica*

Cyclones in the Australian Region 1909–1969, Met. Summary, Commonwealth Bureau of Meteorology, Melbourne.

Colwell, M. (1969) *Whaling around Australia*, Rigby, Adelaide.

Conacher, A. J. and Murray, I. D. (1973) 'Implications and causes of salinity problems in the Western Australian Wheatbelt: the York Mawson area', *Australian Geographical Studies*, **11**, 40–61.

Costin, A. B. and Frith, H. J. (eds.) (1971) *Conservation*, Penguin Ringwood.

CSIRO (1960) *The Australian Environment*, Melbourne University, Parkville (1st – 1949).

Daly, M. and Brown, J. (1964) *Urban Settlement in Central Western New South Wales*, University of Sydney (Geography Research Paper 8), Sydney.

Daly, M. T. (1970) 'The development of the urban pattern of Newcastle', *Australian Economic History Review*, **10**, 190–203.

Davidson, B. R. (1966) *The Northern Myth. a Study of the Physical and Economic Limits to Agricultural and Pastoral Development in Tropical Australia*, Melbourne University, Carlton (1st – 1965).

Davidson, B. R. (1969) *Australia Wet or Dry? The Physical and Economic Limits to the Expansion of Irrigation*, Melbourne University, Carlton.

Dawson, R. (1830) *The Present State of Australia*, Smith Elder, London.

Devery, P. J. (comp.) (1968) *The Reader's Digest Complete Atlas of Australia including Papua New Guinea*, Reader's Digest Assoc., Sydney.

Dick, R. S. (1960) *Five Towns of the Brigalow Country of South-Eastern Queensland*, University of Queensland (Geography), Brisbane.

Donald, C. M. (1967) 'Innovation in Agriculture' (Ch. 3) in Williams, D. B. (ed.) *Agriculture in the Australian Economy*, Sydney University, Sydney.

Drane, N. T. and Edwards, H. R. (1961) *The Australian Dairy Industry: an Economic Study*, Cheshire, Melbourne.

Duncan, R. (1967) *The Northern Territory Pastoral Industry 1863–1910*, Melbourne University, Carlton.

Dunsdorfs, E. (1956) *The Australian Wheat Growing Industry 1788–1948*, Melbourne University, Carlton.

Elliott, B. (1967) *The Landscape of Australian Poetry*, Cheshire, Melbourne.

Farwell, G. (1965) *Ghost Towns of Australia*, Rigby, Adelaide.

Foley, J. C. (1957) *Droughts in Australia: Review of Records from Earliest Years of Settlement to 1955*, Bulletin No. 43, Commonwealth Bureau of Meteorology, Melbourne.

Freeland, J. M. (1966) *The Australian Pub*, Melbourne University, Carlton.

Froude, J. A. (1886) *Oceana or England and Her Colonies*, Longmans, Green and Co., London.

Gale, F. (1969) 'A changing aboriginal population', in Gale, F. and Lawton, G. H. (eds.) *Settlement and Encounter: Geographical Studies Presented to Sir Grenfell Price*, Oxford University Press, Melbourne.

Gentilli, J. (1969) 'Evaluation and valorization of Australian landscapes', *Proceedings Ecological Society Australia*, **4**, 101–14.

Gentilli, J. (1971) *Climates of Australia*, Reprint of Ch. 4–7, *World Survey of Climatology*, Vol. 13, Elsevier, Amsterdam.

Gentilli, J. and Fairbridge, R. W. (1951) *Physiographic Diagram of Australia* (1 : 7 500 000), Geographical Press, New York.

Gibbs, W. J. and Maher, J. V. (1967) *Rainfall Deciles as Drought Indicators*, Bulletin No. 48, Commonwealth Bureau of Meteorology, Melbourne.

Golson, J. and Mulvaney, D. J. (eds.) (1971) *Aboriginal Man and Environment in Australia*, Australian National University, Canberra.

Grenfell Price, A. (1939) *White Settlers in the Tropics*, American Geographical Society, New York.

Grenfell Price, A. (1957) 'Moving frontiers and changing landscapes in the Pacific and its continents', *Australian Journal Science*, **19**, 188–98.

Gunson, N. (1968) *The Good Country: Cranbourneshire*, Cheshire, Melbourne.

Haggett, P. (1972) *Geography: a Modern Synthesis*, Harpen Int., New York.

Hancock, W. K. (1972) *Discovering Monaro: A Study of Man's Impact on His Environment*, Cambridge University Press, London.

Harris, M. and Forbes, A. (1971) *The Land that Waited*, Lansdowne, Melbourne (1st – 1967).

Hausfeld, R. J. (1965) 'Aborigines in New South Wales', *The Australian Quarterly*, **37**(3), 69–80.

Heathcote, R. L. (1965) *Back of Bourke: a Study of Land Appraisal and Settlement in Semi-Arid Australia*, Melbourne University, Carlton.

Heathcote, R. L. (1972) 'The visions of Australia 1770–1970', in Rapoport, A. (ed.) *Australia as Human Setting: Approaches to the Designed Environment*, Angus and Robertson, Sydney, pp. 77–99.

Herman, M. (1970) *The Early Australian Architects and their Work*, Angus and Robertson, Sydney (1st – 1954).

Higginson, F. R. (1973) 'Soil erosion of land systems within the Hunter Valley', *Journal Soil Conservation Service, N.S.W.*, **29**, 103–10.

Higginson, F. R. and Emery, K. A. (1972) 'Survey of erosion and land use within the Lake Burley Griffin Catchment Area', *Journal Soil Conservation Service, N.S.W.*, **28**, 22–39.

Higman, B. W. (1968) 'Sugar plantations and yeoman farming in New South Wales', *Annals Association American Geographers*, **58**(4), 697–720.

Holmes, J. H. (1965) 'The suburbanization of the Cessnock coalfield towns 1954–1964', *Australian Geographical Studies*, 3, 105–28.

Hunter, A. (ed.) (1963) *The Economics of Australian Industry: Studies in Environment and Structure*, Melbourne University, Parkville.

Jeans, D. N. (1965) 'Town planning in New South Wales, 1829–42' *Australian Planning Institute Journal*, **3**(6), 191–6.

Jeans, D. N. (1972) *An Historical Geography of New South Wales to 1901*, Reed Education, Sydney.

Jennings, J. N. and Mabbutt, J. A. (1967) *Landform Studies from Australia and New Guinea*, Cambridge University Press, London.

Johnston, R. J. (1969) 'Zonal and sectoral patterns in Melbourne's residential structure: 1961', *Land Economics,* **45**, 463–7.

Jose, A. W. and Carter, H. J. (1925) *The Illustrated Australian Encyclopaedia*, Angus and Robertson, Sydney (2 vols.).

Juppenlatz, M. (1961) *Some Observations on the Rural–Urban Interdependence Problem in Queensland*, University of Queensland (Architecture), Brisbane.

Keast, A., Crocker, R. L. and Christian, C. S. (eds.) (1959) *Biogeography and Ecology in Australia, Monographiae Biologicae,* **8**, Junk, Den Haag.

Langford-Smith, T. and Rutherford, J. (1966) *Water and Land: Two Case Studies in Irrigation*, Australian National University, Canberra.

Laseron, C. F. (1953) *The Face of Australia: the Shaping of a Continent*, Angus and Robertson, Sydney.

Laut, P. (1968) *Agricultural Geography*, Nelson, Melbourne (2 vols.).

Lawrence, R. (1969) *Aboriginal Habitat and Economy*, Australian National University (Geography, Occasional Paper 6), Canberra.

Learmonth, A. T. A. and Learmonth, A. M. (1968) *Encyclopaedia of Australia*, Warne, London.

Learmonth, N. and Learmonth, A. (1971) *Regional Landscapes of Australia: Form, Function and Change*, Angus and Robertson, Sydney.

Linge, G. J. (1961) 'Canberra after fifty years', *Geographical Review,* **51**, 467–86.

Logan, M. I. (1962) 'Population changes in the Sydney Metropolitan Area', *Geography*, **47**, 415–18.

Logan, M. I. (1964) 'Suburban manufacturing: a case study', *Australian Geographer*, **9**, 223–34.

Lovett, J. V. (ed.) (1973) *The Environmental, Economic and Social Significance of Drought*, Angus and Robertson, Sydney.

McCarthy, F. D. (1959) 'Habitat, economy and equipment of the Australian Aborigine', *Australian Journal Science,* **19(4a)**, 88–96.

McCarty, J. W. (1970) 'Australian capital cities in the nineteenth century', *Australian Economic History Review,* **10**, 107–37.

McPhail, I. R. (1968) 'The character of the rural shire in New South Wales', *Australian Geographer*, **10**, 488–506.

Marshall, A. J. (1968) *The Great Extermination: A Guide to Anglo–Australian Cupidity, Wickedness and Waste*, Panther, London (1st – 1966).

Meinig, D. W. (1962) *On the Margins of the Good Earth: the South Australian Wheat Frontier 1869–1884*, No. 2 Monograph Series, Association American Geographers, Rand McNally, Chicago.

Mosley, J. G. (n.d. (1968)) *National Parks and Equivalent Reserves in Australia. Guide to Legislation, Administration and Areas*, Australian Conservation Foundation, Canberra.

Mulvaney, D. J. (1969) *The Prehistory of Australia*, Thames and Hudson, London.

Newman, J. C. and Condon, R. W. (1969) 'Land use and present condition', in Slatyer, R. O. and Perry, R. A. (eds.) *Arid Lands of Australia*, Australian National University, Canberra, pp. 105–33.

Perry, T. M. (1963) *Australia's First Frontier: the Spread of Settlement in New South Wales 1788–1829*, Melbourne University, Carlton.

Perry, T. M. (1966) 'Climate and settlement in Australia 1700–1930: some theoretical considerations', in Andrews, J. (ed.) *Frontiers and Men*, F. W. Cheshire, Melbourne, pp. 138–55.

Phillip, A. (1789) *The Voyage of Governor Phillip to Botany Bay*, Stockdale, London.

Pike, D. (1957) *Paradise of Dissent: South Australia 1829–1857*, Longmans Green, London.

Pike, D. (1962) *Australia, The Quiet Continent*, Cambridge University Press, London.

Powell, J. M. (1970) *The Public Lands of Australia Felix: Settlement and Land Appraisal in Victoria 1834–91 with Special Reference to the Western Plains*, Oxford University Press, Melbourne.

Powell, J. M. (1972) 'Images of Australia, 1788–1914', *Monash Publications in Geography*, **3**, 1–21.

Raggatt, H. G. (1968) *Mountains of Ore*, Lansdowne, Melbourne.

Rapoport, A. (ed.) (1972) *Australia as Human Setting: Approaches to the Designed Environment*, Angus and Robertson, Sydney.

Roberts, S. H. (1968) *History of Australian Land Settlement 1788–1920*, Macmillan, South Melbourne (1st – 1924).

Roberts, S. H. (1970) *The Squatting Age in Australia 1835–1847*, Melbourne University, Carlton (1st – 1935).

Rose, A. J. (1955) 'The border between Queensland and New South Wales: a study of political geography in a Federal Union', *Australian Geographer*, **6**, 3–19.

Rose, A. J. (1962) 'Some boundaries and building materials in south-eastern Australia', in McCaskill, M. (ed.) *Land and Livelihood: Geographical Essays in Honour of George Jobberns*, New Zealand Geographical Society, Christchurch, pp. 255–76.

Rose, A. J. (1966) 'Metropolitan primacy as the normal state', *Pacific Viewpoint*, **7**, 1–27.

Rose, A. J. (1967) *Patterns of Cities*, Nelson, Melbourne.

Ross Cochrane, G. (1963) 'The physiognomic vegetation map of Australia', *Journal Ecology*, **51**, 639–55.

Rowley, C. D. (1972*a*) *Outcasts in White Australia*, Penguin, Harmondsworth, Australian National University, Canberra (1st – 1970).

Rowley, C. D. (1972*b*) *The Destruction of Aboriginal Society*, Penguin, Harmondsworth, Australian National University, Canberra (1st – 1970).

Rowley, C. D. (1972*c*) *The Remote Aborigines*, Penguin, Harmondsworth, Australian National University, Canberra (1st – 1970).

Ryan, B. (1964) 'Kameruka Estate, New South Wales, 1864–1964', *New Zealand Geographer*, **20**, 103–21.

Scott, P. (1964) 'The hierarchy of central places in Tasmania', *Australian Geographer,* 9, 134–47.

Scott, P. (1968) 'Patterns of land use and population distribution', in *Anatomy of Australia,* Duke of Edinburgh's Third Commonwealth Study Conference, Sun Books, Melbourne, pp. 16–36.

Serle, A. G. (1963) *The Golden Age: a History of the Colony of Victoria 1851–1861,* Melbourne University, Carlton.

Serventy, V. (1968) *Landforms of Australia,* American Elsevier, New York.

Sidney, S. (1853) *The Three Colonies of Australia,* Ingram Cooke, London.

Sinden, J. A. (ed.) (1972) *The National Resources of Australia: Prosperity and Problems of Development,* Angus and Robertson, Sydney.

Slatyer, R. O. and Perry, R. A. (1969) *Arid Lands of Australia,* Australian National University, Canberra.

Smailes, P. J. (1969) 'Some aspects of the South Australian urban system', *Australian Geographer,* **11**, 29–51.

Smith, B. (1960) *European Vision and the South Pacific 1768–1850: a Study in the History of Art and Ideas,* Oxford University Press, London.

Smith, B. (1962) *Australian Painting 1788–1960,* Oxford University Press, London.

Smith, R. H. T. (1964) 'The development and function of transport routes in southern New South Wales 1860–1930', *Australian Geographical Studies,* 2, 47–65.

Smith, R. H. T. (1965) 'The functions of Australian Towns', *Tijdschrift voor Economische en Sociale Geografie,* **56**, 81–92.

Solomon, R. J. (1959) 'Broken Hill – the growth of settlement 1883–1958', *Australian Geographer,* 7, 181–92.

Solomon, R. J. and Goodhand, W. E. (1965) 'Past influences in present townscapes: some Tasmanian examples', *New Zealand Geographer,* **21**, 113–32.

Spate, O. H. K. (1956) 'Bush and city', *Australian Journal Science,* **18**, 177–83.

Spate, O. H. K. (1968) *Australia,* Praeger, New York.

Stace, H. C. T. *et al.* (1968) *Handbook of Australian Soils,* Rellim, Glenside, S.A.

Stretton, H. (1970) *Ideas for Australian Cities,* by the author, Adelaide.

Sulman, J. (1921) *An Introduction to the Study of Town Planning in Australia,* Government Printer, Sydney.

Taylor, G. (1959) *Australia: a Study of Warm Environments and Their Effect on British Settlement,* Methuen, London (1st – 1940).

Tindale, N. B. (1940) 'Distribution of Australian Aboriginal tribes: a field survey' (1 map) *Transactions Royal Society South Australia,* **64**, 140–231.

Tindale, N. B. (1959) 'Ecology of primitive aboriginal man in Australia' (Ch. 3) in Keast, A., Crocker, R. L. and Christian, C. S., *Biogeography and Ecology in Australia, Monographiae Biologicae,* **8**, Junk, Den Haag.

Trollope, A. (1874) *New South Wales and Queensland*, Chapman and Hall, London.

Tweedie, A. D. (1967) 'Water and the city', *Australian Geographical Studies*, 5, 1–15.

Twidale, C. R. (1968) *Geomorphology with Special Reference to Australia*, Nelson, Melbourne.

Vance, J. E. (1970) *The Merchant's World: the Geography of Wholesaling* Prentice Hall, Englewood Cliffs, N.J.

Wadham, S., Kent Wilson, R. and Wood, J. (1957) *Land Utilization in Australia*, Melbourne University, Carlton (1st – 1939).

Wallace, A. R. (1962) *The Geographical Distribution of Animals* (2 vols.) (Ch. 13), 'The Australian region', Hafner, New York (1st – 1876).

Walsh, G. P. (1963) 'The geography of manufacturing in Sydney, 1788–1851', *Business Archives and History*, 3, 20–52.

Ward, R. (1966) *The Australian Legend*, Oxford University Press, Melbourne.

Webb, L. J., Whitelock, D. and Le Gray Brereton, J. (1971) *The Last of Lands: Conservation in Australia*, Jacaranda, Milton (1st – 1969).

Williams, D. B. (ed.) (1967) *Agriculture in the Australian Economy*, Sydney University, Sydney.

Williams, M. (1966*a*) 'The parkland towns of Australia and New Zealand', *Geographical Review*, **56**, 67–89.

Williams, M. (1966*b*) *Adelaide*, Longmans, Croydon.

Williams, M. (1969) 'The spread of settlement in South Australia', in Gale, F. and Lawton, G. H. (eds.) *Settlement and Encounter: Geographical Studies Presented to Sir Grenfell Price*, Oxford University Press, Melbourne.

Williams, M. (1970) 'Town-farming in the Mallee lands of South Australia and Victoria', *Australian Geographical Studies*, **8**, 173–91.

Williams, R. (1961) *The Long Revolution*, Penguin, Harmondsworth.

Winston, D. (1957) *Sydney's Great Experiment: The Progress of the Cumberland County Plan*, Angus and Robertson, Sydney.

Young, J. M. R. (1967) *Australia's Pacific Frontier: Economic and Cultural Expansion into the Pacific 1795–1885*, Cassell, Melbourne.

Index

Note
Page numbers *in italic* contain illustrations (maps, photographs or tables).
State location after name indicates a settlement, thus: Abermain (N.S.W.)